The Myths of Zionism

T0373435

The Myths of Zionism

John Rose

PLUTO PRESS

First published 2004 by Pluto Press
345 Archway Road, London N6 5AA
and 839 Greene Street, Ann Arbor, MI 48106

www.plutobooks.com

British Library Cataloguing in Publication Data
A catalogue record for this book is available from the British Library

ISBN 978 0 7453 2056 4 hardback
ISBN 978 0 7453 2055 7 paperback
ISBN 978 1 8496 4195 1 PDF

Library of Congress Cataloging in Publication Data applied for

10 9 8 7 6 5 4 3 2 1

Designed and produced for Pluto Press by
Chase Publishing Services, Fortescue, Sidmouth, EX10 9QG, England
Typeset from disk by Newgen Imaging Systems (P) Ltd, India
Printed and bound by CPI Group (UK) Ltd, Croydon, CR0 4YY

In memory of Tony Cliff,
Revolutionary socialist,
Palestinian Jew

Contents

Acknowledgements

Many people have helped me with this book. First and foremost, my partner Elaheh Rostami Povey, who not only read each chapter as soon as it was written, making critical, but always encouraging, comments, but also had to put up with alternating moods of overindulged enthusiasm and doubt.

My good friend Michael Rosen also read the book chapter by chapter. A sort of unofficial editor, his email and telephone messages, always thoughtful, sometimes infuriating, usually hilarious, helped steady my nerves.

My brother Peter and my Palestinian friend Ayham Zekra, as well as other friends, Sabby Sagall, Phil Marfleet and Anne Alexander, read specific chapters. I am very grateful for all their comments.

The Jewish Studies Department at Southampton University, where I completed an MA in 2000, also helped. Some of the ideas which appear in this book were first tested in their seminars and essays (though the idea for the book came later). The Department was never short of encouragement and good humour, but also, perhaps, was a little bewildered at this ageing, Trotsky-supporting, anti-Zionist veteran from the 1968 student revolution. Needless to say, they are not responsible for any aspect of the book.

Mark Levene joined the Department after I had left. Mark is an expert on the Balfour Declaration and very kindly read my chapter on Britain's sponsorship of the Zionist colony in Palestine. I think it is fair to say that we agreed to disagree, but the chapter is certainly all the stronger for our sharp and polemical email exchanges.

Professor Antony Polonsky, Head of Eastern European Jewish history at the University of Brandeis, USA, read a draft of Chapter 3, on the Jewish economic role in medieval Europe, and I was delighted by his comments.

Sami Zubaida, Emeritus Professor of Politics and Sociology at Birbeck College, London University, and a recognised scholar of the Arab and Islamic world, read my last chapter on Arab–Jewish reconciliation. He wrote to me saying how much he enjoyed it, finding it 'well researched, lucid and absorbing'. Professor Tareq Ismael at the Department of Political Science at the University of Calgary, Alberta, and author of many books on modern Arab history, also read it. His encouraging remarks were greatly appreciated.

A discussion with Jonathan Tubb, at the Department of Ancient Near East at the British Museum, about the crisis facing Israeli archaeology and its failure to find 'biblical Israel', proved invaluable. I greatly appreciated Jonathan reading my chapter on this fascinating question.

Professor Moshé Machover, Israeli socialist and veteran anti-Zionist dissident, was always ready to respond to my email queries, however difficult or, for that matter, trivial. In addition, his forensic analysis of the final manuscript was absolutely invaluable. A particular thanks to Moshé Machover for that.

Georges Paizis, Mortaza Sahibzada and Roland Rance also helped with ideas and suggestions. Roland's many talents, including his encyclopaedic knowledge of relevant websites, proved to be an indispensable asset.

Finally, I particularly want to thank Sabby Sagall, Afif Safieh, the Palestinian Delegate-General to the UK and Professors Alex Callinicos, Moshé Machover and İlan Pappe for reading and commenting on the final manuscript.

JOHN ROSE
September 2003

THE FRONT COVER ILLUSTRATION OF THE PAPERBACK EDITION

A most fabulous archaeological discovery of late-Jewish antiquity. The mosaic floor of the ancient fourth-century (CE) synagogue near Tiberias in the Galilee – a veritable antique jewel simultaneously celebrating the imageless God and the Sun God, testimonies to Jewish–non-Jewish co-existence. The mosaic occupying the central aisle of the synagogue is divided into three panels. The front cover shows an illustration of two of these panels. The first is the representation of the Torah shrine flanked by two menorahs with burning candles. Then, remarkably, there is a circular representation of the twelve signs of the zodiac, centring on the picture of the chariot of the sun with Helios personified. See the concluding pages of Chapter 2.

Paul Foot died two months before the publication of my book. He was very much looking forward to it. I just hope it lives up to his expectations.

Introduction

The idea for this book first took root in the summer of 2002 following brazenly racist remarks by the former Israeli Labour prime minister, Ehud Barak, when he claimed that 'lying' was an intrinsic part of Arab culture (Aruri 2003: 173). This extraordinary outburst reflected very badly on Barak – perhaps suggesting something akin to the psychological process called 'projection'. Was he not projecting onto his foe a revelation about his own political ideas and beliefs buried deep in his mind-set? Certainly, the Palestinians experience Zionism as an edifice of lies.

Take a simple example. When Barak was prime minister, the number of illegal Jewish settlements on the West Bank increased, despite his supposed commitment to the 'peace process'. Zionist politicians like Barak cloak their claims to the West Bank in religious myth, invoking biblical tales about the ancient 'land of Israel'. For Palestinians, however, whose families have lived on and farmed the land of Palestine for generations, this myth is seen as a huge lie, justifying the stealing of their land.

What distinguishes a lie from a myth? According to the *Concise Oxford Dictionary* a lie is 'an intentionally false statement', a 'deliberate deception', whereas a myth is a 'widely held but false notion', without necessarily deceptive intent. But if a group of people experience injustice and oppression as a result of a myth, a falsehood, surely it hardly matters to them whether the falsehood was, or was not, deliberately deceptive in its origin.

The argument in this book is that Zionism is held together by a series of myths. A package of false notions which undermine its claims on the Jewish religion and Jewish history, its rationale as a response to Europe's anti-Semitism, and above all its justification for its aggressive and very dangerous political posturing in the land of Palestine.

The chapters that follow deal directly with the myths by responding either to specific claims made by Zionist ideologues or to widely held beliefs that have become part of Zionist folklore.

1

Zionism's greatest myth-maker, David Ben-Gurion, inadvertently helped shape the book's first and last chapters. This fixer of facts was Israel's first prime minister and Zionism's most successful leader in the twentieth century. Ben-Gurion once boasted that a myth can become a fact if people believe in it strongly enough. He deftly used this intellectual sleight-of-hand to manipulate the Bible stories to make them fit Zionism's political claims on Palestinian land.

Chapter 1 challenges Ben-Gurion's most outrageous use of religious myth, namely that the Bible gave him a 'mandate' to declare a Jewish state in Palestine. The chapter goes on to illustrate how Israeli archaeology is now undermining Zionism's claims about 'ancient Israel'.

Chapter 10 shows how Ben-Gurion destroyed any prospects of Arab–Jewish reconciliation. He sabotaged secret talks with Egypt's President Nasser, arguably the single most important Arab national leader in the twentieth century, who was seeking an honourable peace with Israel. The 'Free [Army] Officers', including Nasser, who led Egypt's national revolution in 1952, had gone to considerable lengths to build bridges to the country's Jewish community.

Ben-Gurion's behaviour here points to the book's most important conclusion that Zionism is the source of Arab–Jewish enmity. Any prospects of Arab–Jewish reconciliation depend upon its removal.

The idea of 'Arab–Jewish reconciliation' begs a vital question about an ignored earlier history. The Islamic revolution, over 1,300 years ago, heralded what several scholars have called a *symbiosis* between Arabs and Jews producing not merely a Jewish culture in Arabic, but a *Judaeo-Arabic* or even a *Judaeo-Islamic culture* (Chapters 4 and 10).

It is even possible that the highly mobile Jewish merchant class, which came to lead Jewish communities in medieval Europe and helped secure periods of prosperity and stability for Jews in the early history of Europe (Chapter 3) has its roots, at least in part, in this early Islamic Jewish period. This was certainly the view of the twentieth century's most distinguished scholar of Arab Jewish history, Professor S.D. Goitein (Chapters 4 and 10).

But what has this to do with destroying Zionist myths? There are two very different answers. First, Zionism ignores the Islamic Arab component to Jewish history; second, Zionism sees only Jewish 'suffering' during the so-called 'Exile', especially in Europe.

'Exile' is a particularly ludicrous myth that Zionism politicised as it imported it from the Bible stories. It refers to nearly 2,000 years of

Jewish history from the overthrow of the Temple at Jerusalem by the Roman army in 70 CE until the birth of Israel in 1948. Jews living outside Palestine during this period are considered to be living in 'Exile'. Now Arab–Jewish symbiosis hardly sounds like 'Exile'. In fact, Jews had been settled in Mesopotamia (a great chunk of which Britain turned into Iraq in the early twentieth century), and especially in the region around the ancient city of Babylon, centuries before the so-called 'Exile'. To this day, Iranian and Iraqi Jews speak proudly of an uninterrupted 2,500-year history. The Babylonian Talmud, which has remained the spiritual guide for all religious Jews, not least European Jews, is itself a testimony to the significance of these Jewish communities. After the Islamic revolution, Baghdad displaced Babylon as the Jewish spiritual centre for all Jewish communities, including, at that time, the much smaller European Jewish communities.

Chapters 2 and 3 challenge the 'Exile' and 'suffering' myths. In Chapter 2 we see how at the time of the fall of the Temple at Jerusalem, nearly 2,000 years ago, most Jews were living outside Palestine, scattered throughout the Roman Empire and beyond, not least in Babylon.

Chapter 3 counterposes the emergence of the Jewish merchant class in medieval Europe to the 'suffering' myth. Now there is no doubt that the Jews' economic role in medieval Europe could exacerbate as well as stimulate traditional Christian anti-Semitism. But Zionism tells only one side of the story. Christian rulers were often ready to protect their sometimes very successful, economically active Jewish subjects. In any case, Zionism steers clear of any serious discussion, let alone analysis, of the Jewish economic role in early European history.

This is sheer hypocrisy. Zionism had to confront the anachronistic image of the 'Jewish trader and financier' that survived the European Enlightenment in just the same way as did the other far more important modern Jewish movements that emerged out of the Enlightenment, the assimilationists and the socialists (Chapter 6). Shakespeare's controversial Jewish character, Shylock, has his roots in this early European Jewish history. You cannot ignore Shylock; you have to explain him. Chapter 3 attempts just such an explanation.

The Enlightenment had held out the promise of assimilation. It was a declaration of new citizen's rights and freedoms in Europe and America, for Jews alongside Christians. This included liberation from the narrow economic role that pre-modern Christian Europe had attempted to impose on the Jews. The American and French Revolutions of 1776 and 1789 began to turn the promise into practical political reality. Alas, the revolutions in the Russian Empire, where the majority of Jews lived, and which climaxed in the early twentieth century, failed that promise. Chapter 6 explores the historical background and argues that here lie the real roots of Zionism.

Chapters 5, 7 and 9 explore the deeply destructive impact of Zionism on the Arabs and their land in Palestine as it too emerged into the modern world. Chapter 5 debunks the first half of the famous double-barrelled Zionist myth, 'a land without people, for a people without land' and Chapter 6 debunks the second half. Chapter 5 tries to bring alive the thriving Arab peasant farming communities in the 'empty land' of Palestine before the Zionists arrived in the nineteenth century. In so far as the chapter succeeds, all credit must go to the brilliant, but far too little known Palestinian historian, Beshara Doumani, whose research this chapter has shamelessly plagiarised.

Chapters 7 and 9 expose the myth that Zionism's claims for Jewish national independence and liberation can be compared to the struggles of oppressed peoples in other parts of the world in the twentieth century. In fact, Zionism represented a movement in the opposite direction. After the First World War, it helped consolidate British colonial rule over the Arab world. After the Second World War, the newly created Jewish State would become nothing less than a *strategic asset* for US neo-imperialist designs for the region. In both cases Zionism has been completely dependent on the Western imperial powers.

These chapters throw some surprising light on familiar arguments. For example, Chapter 7 shows how the 1917 Balfour Declaration, which paved the way for the Jewish State, has a far seedier and more unpleasant pedigree than most people realise. Arthur Balfour, the British Conservative minister, whose name graces the Declaration, was driven in part by a quite unacceptable anti-Semitism. Not only did his anti-Semitism infect the rest of David Lloyd George's War Cabinet, Zionist leaders such as Chaim Weizmann happily acquiesced in it.

This exposes a deeply disturbing, and usually hidden, side of Zionism, which we also encounter in Chapter 6 with Theodor Herzl, Zionism's founder. This was a willingness to incorporate European anti-Semitism's views about Jews. To put it bluntly, Zionist leaders were too ready to say to reactionary European politicians, 'Too many Jews in your country? Help us dump them in Palestine.'

Chapter 7 also discusses an extraordinary claim that the main motive behind the Balfour Declaration was a belief by the British War Cabinet that 'Jewish power' in America and Russia would help consolidate the allies' position in the war with Germany.

Noam Chomsky is the main inspiration behind Chapter 9. As Palestine's greatest intellectual, Edward Said, observed, Chomsky's *Fateful Triangle* 'may be the most ambitious book ever attempted on the conflict between Zionism and the Palestinians viewed as centrally involving the United States ... [It] can be read as a protracted war between fact and a series of myths – Israeli democracy, Israeli purity of arms, the benign occupation, no racism against Arabs in Israel ...' This is an impossible act to follow, and if this chapter does nothing more than persuade people to read Chomsky, then it will have served its purpose.

However, the chapter does attempt a little originality. Under President George W. Bush the relation between the United States and Israel sometimes looked strangely reversed. Far from Israel serving US interests in the Middle East, did the US not begin to serve Israeli interests? American Jewish neo-conservatives, at the heart of the Bush Administration, are thought to have engineered this reversal of policy. Certainly some of these neo-conservatives had roots in Israel's fanatical Likud Party (the governing party at the time of writing in the summer of 2003). A complicating factor is that this nasty clique has given a new lease of life to an old anti-Semitic accusation of Zionist conspiracy. Chapter 9 attempts carefully to dissect the accusation, and considers to what extent the will of the Bush Administration was bent by the neo-conservatives.

Chapter 8 challenges the myth that the Nazi Holocaust of the Jews provides an unanswerable case in defence of Zionism. Whilst there is no doubt that the Holocaust constitutes one of the gravest crimes in human history, it cannot justify the creation of a Jewish State based upon the violent exclusion of another people from their land, which is exactly what occurred in 1948. This was a defining moment for both Zionism and the Palestinians, who remember it as *Naqba*, the Catastrophe. Far from this being a legitimate response to the Holocaust, the Holocaust properly remembered itself taints the actions, morally debasing those who use it in this way. Using writings and analyses about the Holocaust, Chapter 8 explores several ways that Zionist political action might be considered to have been thus corrupted. It argues that a blind ideological refusal to understand the political realities of the Palestinian people has itself a dangerous capacity to radicalise Zionism, tempting it to ever greater acts of violence against the Palestinian people.

And we know from its short and bloody history how that violence can turn genocidal. We have shocking historical markers from the former Palestinian village of Deir Yassin in 1948 and at the Sabra and Shatila Palestinian refugee camps in Beirut in 1982. One radical Israeli writer has coined a new term for this process: *politicide*, meaning 'to bring about the dissolution of the Palestinian people's existence' (Kimmerling 2003: 3), symbolised by the policies of the Israeli leader Ariel Sharon.

The Jewish State has an innate inability to recognise its responsibility for the *Naqba*. In truth, the shadow of the Palestinian refugee was destined to haunt it forever, physically, politically, morally, psychologically and ultimately militarily. The armed Palestinian guerrilla movement, led by Yasser Arafat and the Palestinian Liberation Organisation, had its roots deep in the refugee camps spread throughout much of the Arab world. Though it took 20 years to emerge, the PLO was the Jewish State's negative *alter ego*. It had a moral and political right to recognition on equal terms and to recognition of its equal claim on all of the land of Palestine. The suicide bomber at the beginning of the twenty-first century represents the failure of the Jewish State to understand this. The suicide bomber is sometimes literally the refugee who has not been allowed to come home.

* * *

Throughout this book I use the formulation anti-Semitism to describe hatred of the Jews. I am well aware that there is a debate about this concept (even how to spell it), but it is rather pedantic and I don't think it need concern us here.

If this book suggests the urgent need for an alternative Jewish history, both ancient and modern, to the one the Zionists thrust upon us in the twentieth century, then this is a bonus. But I make no claims to have written such a history. My main concern has been only to demolish Zionism's mythical history.

1

'The Bible is our Mandate'

When David Ben-Gurion warned the British authorities, via Lord Peel and the Royal Commission[1] in 1936, that 'the Bible is our Mandate' (Ben-Gurion 1970: 107), the twentieth century's most famous Zionist politician, who would become Israel's first prime minister, was giving modern expression to an absolutely fundamental biblical myth, which lies at the core of Zionism. According to this Old Testament story, an ancient Jewish kingdom of Israel, usually referred to as 'Ancient Israel', and sometimes called the United Monarchy of David and Solomon, is said to have existed from about 1000 to 922 BCE. The United Monarchy was allegedly the most powerful and prosperous state in the eastern Mediterranean at this time, exercising sovereignty from the Euphrates in Syria to the brook of Egypt (Wadi el-Arish) in northern Sinai.

These borders coincide with those of the promise God is said to have made to the Patriarch Abraham and recorded in Genesis, the opening chapter of the Bible.

> The Lord made a covenant with Abraham, saying, 'And I will give unto thee, and to thy seed after thee, the land wherein thou art a stranger, all the land of Canaan for an everlasting possession; and I will be their God.' (Genesis 17.8)

This is the basis for the notorious visionary geographical concept of Zionism, *Eretz Israel*, the land of Israel, the bedrock of Zionist ideology, a potent mixture of ancient Judaism and modern nationalism, which hails the promise to Abraham and claims the United Monarchy as its political expression and modern legitimating model for itself.

It is at this point that the reader needs to be alerted to a rather startling characteristic about Ben-Gurion, something he shared with many other Zionist leaders. Ben-Gurion did not particularly believe in this Bible story, or for that matter any other. What mattered, according to him, was that many Jews *did* believe it. That was enough. It did not matter whether the belief was true or not. Making sense of this strange belief system, symptomatic in general of the peculiarities inherent in Zionist ideology, will form the basis of the first half of this chapter. We will then consider something even more surprising: Zionists are great archaeologists. It is a national obsession and for over 100 years they have been excavating in Palestine in search of 'Ancient Israel'. On many occasions, false and over-excited announcements of its discovery have been proclaimed, only to collapse in the face of intense scientific scrutiny. Then, in the 1990s, the realisation began to dawn that it just might not be there ...

Some of Israel's more far-sighted archaeologists then realised that what scientists sometimes call a 'paradigm shift' was necessary. In other words, the taken-for-granted framework for understanding how to make sense of archaeological discovery was itself the problem. To put it bluntly, the Old Testament stories, far from providing guidelines for archaeological discovery, were proving to be obstacles.

The chapter concludes by looking at how archaeologists are coming to terms with what amounts to an intellectual revolution in thinking about ancient Palestine, and how they have found themselves inadvertently challenging the Zionist myth at the core of modern Israeli identity.

BEN-GURION: ZIONIST PIONEER ...

David Ben-Gurion, born in Plonsk, in Poland, in 1886, was part of a generation of young Jews in the Tsarist Russian Empire shocked by the scale and excesses of the pogroms, the anti-Semitic riots and murderous attacks on Jewish communities. (This period, including the young Ben-Gurion's political activism in Poland, is explored in detail in Chapter 6.) Some of these young Jews became Zionists and a few, including Ben-Gurion, went to live in Palestine. There were already a few established Zionist agricultural settlements in Palestine, which at that time was part of the Ottoman Empire (discussed in Chapter 5). On arrival in Palestine in 1906 Ben-Gurion went in search of the agricultural settlements which he was already describing as 'Hebrew republics' (Teveth 1987: 40). At the time there were about 55,000 Jews in Palestine out of a total of 700,000 inhabitants. Only a small minority of the Jews were working on the settlements. Ben-Gurion was soon to discover that, although these settlements were built on land which had been purchased from absentee Arab landlords, an understandably resentful peasantry which had been subsequently evicted often returned to make armed incursions. As early as 1909 we find Ben-Gurion, gun in hand, ready to defend an agricultural settlement in the Galilee (Teveth 1987: 64).

Ben-Gurion made his mark on Zionist politics in Palestine almost immediately. He was at the founding conference of the Poale Zion (the Palestine Social Democratic Hebrew Workers Party; its politics are discussed in Chapter 6), and in 1906 and he was elected to its central committee (Teveth 1987: 45). Poale Zion would go on to become *the* decisive force in Zionist politics for most of the twentieth century, and Ben-Gurion was to become its most charismatic and successful leader.

... AND MYTH-MAKER

In this chapter we are concerned with trying to understand Ben-Gurion's belief system. It provides an unparalleled insight into Zionist myth-making. Ben-Gurion explains it himself very well:

> It is not important whether the story is a true record of an event or not. What is of importance is that this is what the Jews believed as far back as the period of the First Temple. (Pearlman 1965: 227)

A writer called Yizhar, who much later became part of Ben-Gurion's inner circle, has recently tried to defend the Zionist leader from the accusation that, by mixing fact with belief-in-a-fact, he was deliberately manipulating the truth in favour of consciously shaping myths to suit the political expediency of the Zionist enterprise. In short, Yizhar tries to square the circle between myth and truth:

> Myth is no less a truth than history, but it is an additional truth, a different truth, a truth that resides alongside the truth; a non objective human truth, but a truth that makes its way to the historical truth. (Wistrich and Ohana 1995: 61)

This appears to be clever, perhaps even profound, writing, but it is deeply flawed. It is true that by persuading people to act, and if necessary to act violently, in response to myth, historical fact can be created. But this does not validate the myth by somehow injecting truth into it after the event. This, however, was Ben-Gurion's game. Intense belief in the myth made it a truth, or at least as good as a truth. This is demagogy and, in the early 1960s, it led to Ben-Gurion falling out with some of Israel's most prominent secular and religious intellectuals. The catalyst was the so-called Lavon Affair.

What concerns us here is not the Lavon Affair itself,[2] but the unexpected way it not only put Ben-Gurion's integrity in question but also exposed the fragility of the ideological character of the Israeli State. The scandal rocked Israel

> with tempestuous discord that sapped the young state's foundations, exposed Ben Gurion and Lavon to private and public travail ... and reduced the political arena to utter chaos. (Gilbert 1998: 296–7)[3]

Ben-Gurion then faced a long showdown with many of Israel's more liberal intellectuals.

BEN-GURION AND THE MESSIAH

One of Ben-Gurion's most sensational uses of myth-making, one that would eventually so antagonise his critics, was his play on the messianic theme. At first sight this may seem preposterous. After all, Ben-Gurion denied the centrality of religion as an integrating force in modern Jewish nationalism (Keren 1983: 65) and was a great believer in science and rationality. However, with Ben-Gurion, nothing was that straightforward.

He has been described as a 'crude monist', rather than an atheist.[4] This seems to mean that he believed in the enhanced spiritual powers of the human mind, 'The belief in the ability of the human mind stems from its identification with the universe it explores' (Keren 1983: 28), and allowed him a backdoor re-entry to religion when it suited him as well as the flexibility to reinterpret religion to fit in with modern political needs and their ideological justification.

In any event, his 'monism' allowed him his own 'messianic' aspirations, apparently available to human genius, with which he seems to have believed he was endowed. 'God or Nature', he wrote, 'endows the genius with sublime talents, not out of love for him, but from a desire to bestow upon the world sublime creations ... He brings into existence an intermediary ...' (Teveth 1987: 10). He saw himself as this intermediary and often employed the term 'Hazon Meshihi', 'Messianic Vision' (Wistrich and Ohana 1995: 62) in relation to the modern Jewish national movement in Palestine. He argued that there were three components to modern Jewish nationalism: the people's link to the homeland, the Hebrew language and, above all, the messianic link to redemption (Keren 1983: 65).

What was the meaning of Ben-Gurion's 'messianic vision' and its link to redemption? According to both Judaism and Christianity, God will send His representative, an intermediary, the Messiah, to earth in order to transform human society and redeem it of its sins. Redemption means 'renewal' or rebirth and is rooted in a vision of Holy Goodness for all humanity. In Judaism the Messiah has yet to arrive; in Christianity, Jesus Christ, the 'Son of God', was the Messiah and 'He' will return.

One of Ben-Gurion's harshest critics, the writer Avraham Avi-hai, has argued that Ben-Gurion stripped the concept of Messiah of its personification, a concept common to Judaism and Christianity. Ben-Gurion instead substitutes Zionism as a Messianic movement for the Messiah-as-Person. Hence the redemption of mankind is to be preceded by the redemption of the Jewish people, restored to their own land (Keren 1983: 65).

Ben-Gurion talked about the establishment of a model society which will become 'a light unto nations' (lifting the theme from the Old Testament prophet Isaiah), 'Through it will come universal redemption, the reign of righteousness and human brotherhood and the elimination of wickedness' (Keren 1983: 65). Ben-Gurion's statement here reads as though he is actually quoting Isaiah, but in fact what he is doing is using biblical language himself to justify the creation of the state of Israel, a device commonly employed by Zionists who describe themselves as non-believers.

Ben-Gurion often interlaced remarks like this with references to the Jews performing the noble task of settling the 'ancient home-land' as a necessary condition of universal redemption for all on account of the fact that they were, or at least could become, the 'chosen people' (according to the Bible, the Jews are God's 'chosen people'). One cannot but admire the sheer gall of the man. Ben-Gurion had usurped Christianity as well as Judaism. The Jewish people resettled in the ancient land, after 2,000 years, will be a sort of national collective Christ, providing a light unto all other nations of the world.

Yet a satirical edge quickly vanishes when it is realised how easily Ben-Gurion could slide his political messianism into place in support of Israel's political and military adventures. The messianic people could pursue aggressive and nationalist expansionist aims in Palestine and beyond, legitimately, because they alone were entitled to respond to an Old Testament script.

Thus he remembered Moses during the Suez Crisis of 1956, the blatantly imperialist military adventure when Israel joined Britain and France in trying to topple Egypt's leader, Colonel Nasser, who had nationalised the Suez Canal. According to Ben-Gurion, the thousands of Israeli soldiers involved in the battle of the Sinai desert between Egypt and Israel were likely to have been inspired by memories of how their Jewish ancestors had been led to Mount Sinai by Moses who had received the Ten Commandments from God:

> this was no mere battle. The halo of Sinai and all the deep and mystical experiences associated with that name for thousands of years glowed over our soldiers' heads as if their parents were present at the Mount Sinai event. (Keren 1983: 69)

Biblical quotations peppered all of Ben-Gurion's speeches. Prophetic statements were incorporated into the political language, and his biblical heroes, even when they disagreed with God, pointed ominously to his contemporary attitudes. On one occasion Ben-Gurion praised Jeroboam II, a king of biblical Israel, who 'did evil in the eyes of the Lord', but who nevertheless enlarged his kingdom by capturing Damascus (Wistrich and Ohana 1995: 69).

BLASPHEMY! THE JEWISH RELIGION HELD 'MISTRESS OF SECULAR GOVERNMENT'

Two very accomplished Jewish religious philosophers, Martin Buber and Yeshayahu Leibowitz, who called themselves Zionists, were nevertheless appalled at the way they saw Ben-Gurion manipulating the Jewish religion for narrow political ends.

Ben-Gurion had hijacked the spiritual concept of Zion, Buber argued, which should have no place in nationalist power politics:

> Zion implies a memory, a demand, a mission. Zion is the foundation stone, the bedrock and basis of the Messianic edifice of humanity ...
> Zion in its modern form was 'Quasi-Zionism' not 'True Zionism' ...
> Quasi-Zionism is nothing more than one of the vulgar forms of nationalism in our day, one which recognizes no authority other than an imaginary national interest. (Keren 1983: 77)

Buber here is arguing that Ben-Gurion's nation-state had displaced the authority of God. At one point Buber explicitly accused Ben-Gurion of blasphemy. He argued that Ben-Gurion's secularisation 'keeps men from hearing the voice of the living God' (Keren 1983: 78).

Ben-Gurion could not dismiss Buber as a religious obscurantist. First, Buber was highly respected by believers and non-believers alike; second, Buber was keenly aware of the dilemmas facing Jewish politics in modern Palestine. By insisting that a Jewish State of the type that Ben-Gurion was defending was unacceptable to the teachings of a true Judaism, Buber was also making a statement about his humanistic brand of Judaic ethics. This was a humanist ethics incompatible with the oppression of another people. As Edward Said, Palestine's most prominent intellectual, has noted, this meant that Buber had to take a stand on what kind of modern political state should emerge in Palestine. Buber and several other Jewish humanists argued for a bi-national state (Said 2000: 314), where the Arab and Jewish communities would share power within a single constitution. For Buber it had the particular merit of unambiguously separating state politics from religion. This actually made Buber a more modern political thinker than Ben-Gurion, who deliberately cultivated the ambiguous mixing of Judaism and state politics.

Buber was a more modern political thinker and he certainly had a much more universalist vision. This became clear when the two men fell out over the trial of Adolf Eichmann, the Nazi and member of the SS, deeply implicated in the Holocaust and captured in Argentina by Israeli agents in 1960, and tried in Israel in 1961. Buber had wanted Eichmann tried at an international tribunal because his crimes were crimes against the human race as a whole. Ben-Gurion insisted that the trial should be held in Israel as a way, as Hannah Arendt observed (1963), of bolstering the legitimacy of the Jewish State.

Yeshayahu Leibowitz, another religious philosopher and scientist, was also incensed by Ben-Gurion's use of political messianism. He was particularly outraged by Ben-Gurion's biblical justification of what Leibowitz described as 'an over-zealous reprisal' (Keren 1983: 82) when an Israeli army unit, led by Ariel Sharon, killed 50 Palestinian Arab civilians at the village of Kibya. Leibowitz was not afraid to use strong language. He denounced justifications of acts of statehood on grounds of religious ethics as 'a prostitution of the Jewish religion in the interest of national cannibalism and lust for power' (Keren 1983: 83). He accused Ben-Gurion of keeping religion 'a mistress of the secular government', and defined the State of Israel under Ben-Gurion as 'a secular brat known in public as religious' (Keren 1983: 84).

Leibowitz specifically challenged Ben-Gurion on the 'sacredness' of the land, the religious idea of the 'sacred' being used in a way 'for which it was not destined, with all the danger implied by this distorted use' (Keren 1983: 83).

BEN-GURION CALLED ARABS 'DESTROYERS' OF THE SACRED LAND

Ben-Gurion not only claimed that the 'land of Israel' was sacred, but he also believed that the Arabs had somehow contaminated it. For Ben-Gurion it is 'the land in which all the cultures will come together and from it will emerge mankind's ultimate genius, to spread its rule over the entire world', but under one condition – that the land be managed by 'its children'. For if once again the children of Israel cease to inhabit the land, it will become 'bereft of life' and be transformed into a heap of ruins. This is because of the Arabs, who, according to Ben-Gurion, in the history of the land of Israel, had behaved as 'destroyers' (Wistrich and Ohana 1995: 75).

An 'evil spirit of Israeli chauvinism' was how Isaac Deutscher, one of the twentieth century's greatest Jewish socialist writers, would describe Ben-Gurion (Deutscher 1968: 142).

Ben-Gurion even ludicrously claimed sometimes that until the arrival of new Hebrew, the land had been 'barren' for 2,000 years (Wistrich and Ohana 1995: 75). This idea had been conveniently rooted in Zionist mythology from the time of the earliest settlements in the late nineteenth century. In one of his early letters from Israel in 1906, Ben-Gurion wrote of 'foul miasma which rises from the fallow earth when it is ploughed for the first time in 2000 years' (Wistrich and Ohana 1995: 76). The early Zionists apparently believed that between the time of the destruction of the second Jewish Temple in Jerusalem by the Roman army in 70 CE and the new Zionist settlement, the land had become a crust under which noxious gases accumulated!

This is the type of rhetoric that accompanies the deeply entrenched double-barrelled Zionist myth that Palestine was a 'land without people for a people without land'. These myths are the subjects of chapters of this book. In Chapter 5 the reader will discover a thriving Arab peasant agriculture on the Palestinian land that the early Zionists chose to settle in the late nineteenth century. Ben-Gurion's dishonesty here is particularly brazen. As we noted at the beginning of this chapter, he had firsthand experience of those early Zionist settlements, which had been purchased from absentee Arab landlords. He even had to arm himself to defend one settlement from the furious, evicted and hence ruined Arab peasantry, who had been working the land for generations.

DEMAGOGY: BEN-GURION REWRITES THE BIBLE

On 12 May 1960 Ben-Gurion called a press conference in Tel Aviv. Local and foreign journalists, military and civilian officials, writers, artists, members of his family and other dignitaries arrived carrying pocket Bibles in their hands. The *Jerusalem Post* reported the event under the headline: 'Ben-Gurion Gives His Version of the Tale of Exodus from Egypt.' It described how the prime minister had challenged the biblical view of the Exodus by claiming that only a small minority of Hebrews had made the journey from Egypt and that the great majority of the children of Israel never went to Egypt. Serious Bible critics had been making this point for years, but Ben-Gurion claimed that the source of inspiration for this insight was the 1948 War of Independence and the settlement patterns of modern Israel (Keren 1983: 102). It is tempting to conclude that he was cynically catching up with what would slowly emerge as the scholarly consensus. But for Ben-Gurion it was the 'revolutionary occurrences' after 1948 that were providing new insights into ancient history.

Of course, a great debate ensued, which always suited Ben-Gurion because such debates reinforced the Bible's authority as the reference point for directing the country.

Biblical scholars were unimpressed. His most effective critic turned out to be a right-wing Bible scholar, Israel Eldad. Eldad accused Ben-Gurion of media sensationalism and misuse of political power. Eldad compared the publicity surrounding the archaeological discovery of the Dead Sea Scrolls with the way Ben-Gurion had used the media to promote his biblical 'discovery' about Exodus. His argument was that the archaeological excavations revealed material findings while Ben-Gurion's news conference involved mere hypotheses. Hypotheses ought to be thoroughly investigated rather than be presented to the public. That Ben-Gurion was the country's prime minister made this obvious caution even more vital.

As Eldad, and many others, pointed out, there was an important difference between the statesman and the scholar. To the statesman engaged in symbolic politics, the medium might be as important as the message. To the scholar, any but the most important forum to express the message might lead to distortion. The scholar works alone, nourished by peer review, and is confined to a relatively small audience. The statesman speaks to large crowds, unable to listen with the necessary scepticism and who take his authority for granted. This was obviously detrimental to any evaluation of knowledge (Keren 1983: 117).

Eldad distinguished three approaches to the subject. First, there is the believer who accepts the story, by definition, because it is in God's book. Second, there is the scientist, who has exactly the opposite approach. Nothing in the Bible should be beyond doubt, whether supernatural events or 'natural' ones. Third, there is the interpreter who studies the Bible not for its own sake but as a means of deriving contemporary, or universal, lessons. All three approaches are legitimate provided they are kept distinct, Eldad's complaint was that Ben-Gurion had conflated them (Keren 1983: 114).

Eldad had touched Zionism's raw nerve. In the end science and religion were incompatible. Within Zionism, the tension between the two becomes unbearable when Jewish history is subjected to the rules of evidence-based argument and scholarship; that is, when there is proper adherence to the standards of scientific inquiry.[5]

IN SEARCH OF 'ANCIENT ISRAEL'

We need now to disentangle three factors: the Zionist misuse of the Bible stories, the Bible stories themselves and the historical period that the Bible is claiming to describe. This will take us to the argument literally at the 'cutting edge' of Israeli archaeology. But first let us try to set out the background using as our focus 'Ancient Israel'. We have an immediate difficulty because there are several 'Ancient Israels' in the Bible. We will concentrate on the so-called 'United Monarchy of David and Solomon' from about 1000 to 922 BCE, because this is the 'Ancient Israel' upon which Zionism makes its most outrageous claim.

Readers with any familiarity with the Bible may recall that the land of the time had another name, Canaan. One of the astonishing features that always crops up when serious historical and archaeological research engages with the biblical stories is that the artifacts which have been discovered are clearly Canaanite rather than

'Israelite'. In fact 'Israelite' artifacts have *never* been discovered from this period. But perhaps that doesn't matter. After all, the Bible stories carry images so powerful that even the most sceptical assume there must be at least grains of historical authenticity.

After all, which schoolchild does not know that David (who would become the Israelite king of the 'United Monarchy'), in his warrior days, toppled the Philistine Goliath with a slingshot? Is this not one of the greatest, and certainly one of the most famous, single acts of courage that has been passed down to us from the ancient world? It's an invitation from the Bible that we can hardly refuse, to take for granted the Israelite David's moral and spiritual superiority over the Philistine, Goliath. It is a fable etched deeply into the imagination of Western civilisation, and brilliantly captured in the European High Renaissance by Michelangelo's sculpture of 'David', and by the painter Rembrandt in his stunning *David Presenting the Head of Goliath to King Saul.*

Nevertheless, modern Zionism has shown increasing difficulty defending the biblical David as a credible historical personality and, at the same time, absorbing the implications of serious biblical analysis and archaeological research.

In the 1980s a prominent Israeli politician, Abba Eban, with a reputation as an outstanding Bible scholar, presented a television documentary, *Heritage, Civilisation and the Jews.* The series, which was accompanied by a best-selling, beautifully illustrated coffee-table book, purported to show the history of the Jews from biblical times to the present day. What was interesting about the series were the concessions that Eban repeatedly had to make to serious critical Bible scholarship and archaeological discoveries, which undermined his Zionist beliefs about the Bible. This was starkly revealed when he came to the David and Goliath fable. As he pointed out, 'Biblical antagonism towards the Philistines survives in the term's modern meaning: a *philistine* is a person ignorant of, or smugly hostile to, culture' (Eban 1984: 45). And he admitted in the very next sentence 'The fact is however that outside the fields of theology and ethics, the cultural accomplishments of the Philistines were markedly superior to those of the Israelites.' A really wonderful colour photograph drives home the point. It is of an exquisitely decorated vessel with the unambiguous caption: 'the Philistines were not barbarians but skilled craftsmen' (Eban 1984: 40).

How did he know, at least in theology and ethics, that the Israelites were superior to the Philistines? The answer is that he does not. This is what Bible critics call an example of *redaction.* The Bible stories were written much later, so any claims about the respective merits of the belief systems of the Philistines and the Israelites at this time are impossible to sustain. To use a concept much favoured by Bible critics, the stories may well be *apocryphal*; in other words, inventions. In any case, as Eban was compelled to make clear, the Bible itself raises many difficulties about the religious and historical life of David and Solomon.

BIBLICAL CONFUSION AND MELTDOWN OVER DAVID AND SOLOMON

On the one hand, there is the enormous impact of David: the 'messianic' tradition starts with him. Later Hebrew prophets were so impressed with what seemed to be God's special blessing on David that they envisaged a future monarch, an anointed one, or *maschiach*, the Hebrew word for Messiah (Eban 1984: 47). Nearly 1,000 years later, Psalm XXIII captured the monotheistic and messianic tradition, for both Judaism and Christianity:

> The Lord is my shepherd, I shall not want ...
> though I walk through the valley of the shadow of death,
> I will fear no evil: for thou *art* with me ...
> ... thou annointest my head with oil; my cup runneth over.
> Surely, goodness and mercy shall follow me all the days of
> my life: and I will dwell in the house of the Lord for ever.

> (cited Eban 1984: 48)

On the other hand, David indulged in one of the great biblical scandals, expressing contempt for any system of theology and ethics in his dealings with local tribal chieftains, whether friend or foe. He impregnated Bathsheba whilst her husband, Uriah the Hittite, was away fighting the Ammonites on David's behalf. Uriah was then sent to the 'hottest battle' where his comrades were to leave him, on David's orders, to die at the hands of the enemy (II Samuel 11: 15; Eban 1984: 49).

According to the highly respected contemporary Bible scholar, Karen Armstrong, David's conduct would have offended even contemporary standards of 'pagan' justice, let alone later standards of Jewish justice (Armstrong 1996: 40).[6]

Like Abba Eban, the writer Paul Johnson, in his very popular *History of the Jews*, is desperately keen to stand by the Bible stories, yet even his reading of the Bible has cast doubt on David's Israelite origins: 'He was originally a shepherd descended from the humble and enchanting Ruth the Moabitess ...' (Johnson 1993: 55).

The problem is even greater with Solomon. Like David, his pedigree is suspect, for he was, after all, David's second son by Bathsheba. Solomon developed the most spectacular empire, specialising in pagan marriages of convenience. As Eban tells us:

> His ships built and manned in large part by the Phoenicians, sailed to Arabia, East Africa, and India ... bringing back gold and ivory, sandalwood and precious stones, even peacocks and monkeys for the Royal Court ... the Queen of Sheba came overland from southern Arabia with camels that bore spices and very much gold (I Kings 10: 2) ... And ... Dynastic marriages – with Ammonite, Edomite, Hittite, Moabite, and Phoenician princesses, as well as with Pharaoh's daughter were signed to add both to the glory of the court and to the stability of the kingdom. (Eban 1984: 50–1)

And it was Solomon, of course, who built the first Temple at Jerusalem. Eban ties himself up in knots as he tries to reconcile the biblical claim with the pagan temple-building programme which typified the period.

Eban begins by noting that local pagan monarchs, like the Phoenician Hiram of Tyre, supplied the skilled craftsmen and masons and the building materials, the famed 'cedars of Lebanon'.

Eban asks to what extent these architectural borrowings should be taken as evidence of a deeper bond between the religions of the Canaanites and Phoenicians and the religion of Israel.

His answer is very important because, although he does not say so, it reflects the struggle between science and religion within Israeli archaeology, which was developing at the time he was writing his book and which has since reached crisis proportions:

> The differences in religious belief should be plain enough ... and there were also significant divergences in religious practice. Israel was ... forbidden to worship its deity in the form of an image, and human sacrifice, cult prostitution, and orgiastic fertility rites were likewise excluded. *But we should not blind ourselves to the ways in which ancient*

Israelite worship more closely resembles Canaanite practice than it does the Jewish religion since Roman times. [emphasis added]

The most obvious borrowing – and the most striking divergence from later Jewish practice – is the sacrificial rite, highly developed at least since Sumerian times. The Temple sacrifice was the centre of state religion in the age of Solomon and remained so as long as the Temple remained in Jerusalem. (Eban 1984: 50)

By recognising the break between ancient forms of worship and the religion called Judaism, Eban is undermining Zionist insistence on a continuous line from the early Bible stories and the present day.

But we must now turn to a much bigger problem, which goes to the very heart of Zionist interpretation of the Bible.

ANCIENT ISRAEL: WHERE WAS THE WORD?

The Jewish religion celebrates the power of words, the most famous of which are the Ten Commandments which Moses is supposed to have received from God on Mount Sinai, over 3,000 years ago, as he led the former Hebrew slaves out of bondage in Egypt, towards the 'Promised Land' which would become (Ancient) Israel. The Old Testament is full of holy words which provide spiritual guidance for the Jewish people as a religious people. These are, of course, *written* words, with hugely sophisticated meaning, providing a profound system of theology and ethics, which continue to inspire millions of people in the modern world. Yet we have still to uncover any trace of written words from the period of the United Monarchy of David and Solomon, Ancient Israel, just under 3,000 years ago. And that is the problem. The written word marks a society's advance in terms of its civilisation. Ancient Israel is portrayed as an advanced form of civilisation, but where are its words?

According to Finkelstein and Silberman, authors of the path-breaking book, *The Bible Unearthed: Archaeology's New Vision of Ancient Israel and the Origin of its Sacred Texts*, not a single trace of tenth-century BCE Israelite literary activity has ever been discovered (Finkelstein and Silberman 2002: 235–8). As Israel Finkelstein is one of modern Israel's leading archaeologists, the implications are far-reaching. They reflect nothing less than the implosion of Israeli archaeology.

Literacy in the ancient world, record-keeping, administrative correspondence, royal chronicles and the compiling of religious scripture *'especially one as proud and as sophisticated as the Bible are linked to a particular stage of social development, namely state formation with a centralized religious cult and monarchy'* (Finkelstein and Silberman 2002: 22; emphasis added). The implication is that the failure to discover literary activity at this time suggests that there was no state formation, centralised cult or monarchy. Yet Solomon's Temple was the crowning glory of a building programme that rivalled those of the Pharaohs.

After decades of excavation, using details from the Bible to search for the remains of these buildings, a scholarly consensus is slowly and very reluctantly emerging amongst the archaeologists of modern Israel, that the buildings never existed, or rather there are the remains of buildings but they cannot be dated to the period of Solomon:

> Jerusalem has been excavated time and again … fieldwork … failed to provide significant evidence for tenth century occupation (the period of David and Solomon). Not only was any sign of monumental architecture missing, but so were even simple pottery sherds … The most optimistic assessment of this negative evidence is that tenth century Jerusalem was rather limited in extent, perhaps not more than a typical hill country village. (Finkelstein and Silberman 2002: 33)

A temple certainly was built in Jerusalem, several centuries later, probably in the tiny city-state of Judah. Indeed, this is Finkelstein's argument for the period when the Bible itself began to take written form. But the fact of the matter is that the David and Solomon stories are the figment of some of the ancient world's most creative imaginations (Finkelstein and Silberman 2002: 123–45).

'GOD'S BIBLE? LOOK AT IT – IT WAS MADE AS A LIE BY THE FALSE PEN OF SCRIBES' (JEREMIAH VIII. 8)

In the 1980s the journalist John McCarthy was one of a number of Europeans and Americans taken hostage by Islamic militants in Beirut. His endurance made him and fellow captives famous. McCarthy read the Bible twice during his captivity, not least because it was the only book his militant Islamic prison guards would allow the hostages.

He became intrigued by 'Ancient Israel' and when he was released went in search of it, only to stumble across teams of Israeli archaeologists, like the one led by Finkelstein, who had also been looking for it in vain. McCarthy became so fascinated that he decided to make a television documentary about it: *It Ain't Necessarily So*. Now his producers must have panicked at its radical content because the six half-hour transmissions were given a midnight slot with minimum publicity and hardly anyone watched them.[7]

A flavour of the devastating impact of the documentary is given by the translation from the prophet Jeremiah, which opens the narrative of each half-hour programme:

> God's Bible? Look at it – it was made as a lie by the false pen of scribes. (Jeremiah VIII. 8; Sturgis 2001: 186)

Rather like the Philistines, Jeremiah has had a very poor press over the last two millennia and dismissed as the prophet of doom – another example of the way the Bible and its prejudices haunt the modern imagination.

Actually, it is possible that Jeremiah may have been a very honest witness in the tiny city-state of Judah (about which more in a moment), at the time when some books of the Bible were possibly taking written form.

McCarthy based his series on the work of Israeli archaeologists like Finkelstein and his colleague, Professor Ze'ev Herzog. In October 1999, Herzog summarised their discoveries in a sensational article in the magazine of the Israeli newspaper *Ha'aretz* ('Deconstructing the Walls of Jericho', *Ha'aretz Magazine*, 29 October 1999: 6–8). In the article, Herzog described how what he calls the 'crisis stage' in Israeli archaeology has matured in recent years. He described it as nothing less than a scientific revolution. It is a process well known to all research scientists familiar with the dynamic of scientific breakthrough:

> A crisis stage is reached when the theories within the framework of the general thesis are unable to solve an increasingly large number of anomalies. The explanations become ponderous and inelegant, and the pieces do not lock together ...
>
> This is what archaeologists have learned from their excavations in the Land of Israel: the Israelites were never in Egypt, did not wander the desert, did not conquer the land in a military campaign and did not pass it on to the 12 tribes of Israel. Perhaps even harder to swallow is

the fact that the united monarchy of David & Solomon which is described by the Bible as a regional power, was at most a small tribal kingdom ... (*Ha'aretz*, 29 October, 1999)

In other words, no Abraham, no Moses, no Joshua; David and Solomon at best pagan tribal chieftains. He goes on: 'And it will come as an unpleasant shock to many that the God of Israel, Jehovah, had a female consort ...'. Her name is Asherah and she has her own programme in John McCarthy's series. As Matthew Sturgis, who wrote the book accompanying McCarthy's series, explains:

> Asherah is identified as another Canaanite deity. She was a fertility goddess and the recognized consort of the chief god El (and later of Baal). Many small figurines representing her have been found at early Canaanite sites. The statuettes, with their large breasts and well-defined sexual organs, are closely related to those found at the slightly later Israelite sites. It is a relationship that has led scholars to suggest that Israelite fertility figurines may represent Asherah too. (Sturgis 2001: 186)

Notice how archaeology is now compelled to shake off significant distinctions between Canaanite and Israelite sites. At some point *after* the biblical fiction known as the United Monarchy of David and Solomon, perhaps about two centuries later, very roughly 800–700 BCE, a historical entity called Israel did emerge, though in its first incarnation it was distinctively pagan, with a pagan god, Jehovah, and goddess, Asherah. Furthermore, Jerusalem was not its spiritual centre.

In the late 1960s, the archaeologist Bill Dever discovered Asherah, in inscription form, written in ancient Hebrew, when he was carrying out excavations at Khirbet el-Kom near Hebron. On the wall of a late Iron Age tomb, dating from the mid- to late eighth century BCE, he discovered a bold drawing of what appeared to be a hand together with an inscription that ran: 'Blessed ... by Yahweh [Jehovah] ... and his Asherah.' Dever recalls:

> When I first discovered it, I didn't really want to publish it, as a young scholar. It was too controversial. But then in the 1970s a second site was found by Israeli archaeologists – also in the eighth century in Sinai. And you have the same expression: 'may X be blessed by Yahweh and his Asherah'. (Sturgis 2001: 173)

This discovery was made at Kuntillet Ajrud, in northeastern Sinai. The inscription, written in ink on an old storage jar, was accompanied by a drawing of two curious figures, one apparently male, the other female, and both crowned. As Dever remarks, 'It seems that Yahweh did have a consort, like all the other gods of the ancient Near East – at least in the minds of many Israelites.'

Like all the other gods of the ancient Near East ...

As Herzog has argued, the discovery of inscriptions in ancient Hebrew that mention pairs of gods, Jehovah and Asherah, much later than the United Monarchy period, throws wide open the question of exactly when monotheism was adopted. And it seems likely that the small tribal kingdoms of David and Solomon, if they existed at all, worshipped polytheistic pagan gods.

Now, archaeologists like Herzog and Finkelstein are not particularly politically minded, but they are very conscious of the implications of their research for modern Israel's ideological claims to the biblical past.

Herzog reports that the Israeli public are trying to ignore the findings despite the fact that they have been known for decades. He goes on:

> Any attempt to question the reliability of the biblical descriptions is perceived as an attempt to undermine 'our historic right to the land' and as shattering the myth of the nation that is renewing the ancient Kingdom of Israel. These symbolic elements constitute such a critical component of the construction of Israeli identity that any attempt to call their veracity into question encounters hostility or silence ... The blow to the mythical foundations of the Israeli identity is apparently too threatening, and it is more convenient to turn a blind eye. (Ha'aretz, 29 October 1999)

How progressive Israeli archaeologists like Herzog and Finkelstein are now beginning to explain the origins of the Bible is beyond the scope of this book.[8] But one intriguing irony deserves further comment. They argue that the 'real' Ancient Israel was a pagan state, with Samaria its 'capital' or spiritual centre. Readers will be familiar with the modern Zionist claim on Judaea and Samaria on Palestine's West Bank. Less well known is the explosively bitter religious feud between Judaea and Samaria, or rather to use their biblical names, Judah and Israel.

Herzog and Finkelstein argue that it is this feud that partly lays the foundation for the Bible stories and for the real birth of Judaism. It is a feud in which Judah, or Judaea, its Roman name, became the ultimate victor. Samaria (the real 'Ancient Israel') became an outcast. By the first century CE, Samaria, with its own temple far away from Jerusalem and home to the 'Good Samaritan' of Gospel fame, was considered not properly Jewish at all by the priestly authorities at the Temple at Jerusalem in Judaea. In other words, 2,000 years ago, the century of the great Jewish revolt against Rome, the 'real' Ancient Israel was not considered Jewish.

In the next chapter we will explore the damaging implications of this for modern Zionist claims on Palestine when we look at the Jewish Diaspora in the Roman Empire. But we should not leave this chapter before we have paid our unqualified respects to the great Jewish Bible writers of ancient times. The Bible is most certainly not a mandate for modern Jewish chauvinist claims on the land of Palestine, but, with Finkelstein and Silberman, we can most certainly agree that it is a

> sacred scripture of unparalleled literary and spiritual genius ... an epic saga woven together from an astonishingly rich collection of historical writings, memories, legends, folk tales, anecdotes, royal propaganda,[9] prophecy and ancient poetry ... the literary masterpiece would undergo further editing and elaboration (so that it would) become a spiritual anchor ... for communities all over the world. (Finkelstein and Silberman 2002: 1–2)

2

'The Distinguishing Characteristic of the Jews has been their Exile'

This is the opening sentence of David Vital's *The Origins of Zionism* (1975: 3), a highly recommended scholarly introduction to Zionism which, according to *The Times Literary Supplement*, sets 'new standards for historians of Zionism to emulate'. Now Vital is indeed a very serious and readable historian. That as a reputable scholar he is ready to promote 'Exile' as apparently the most important, and it seems unquestionable, 'historical fact' about the Jews reflects the successful metamorphosis of this old religious myth. It has been turned into nothing less than a secular ideological weapon, part of the battle-cry of twentieth-century Jewish nationalism's historical claim on Palestine. The myth of 'Exile' is, however, a profound intellectual embarrassment to Israel's new generation of radical historians who are struggling to shake off Zionism's stranglehold on Jewish history.

According to one recent and highly authoritative critical Israeli scholar, Yael Zerubavel, 'Exile' is the second half of what she calls 'The Zionist Periodisation of Jewish History' (1995: 15–17).[1] This is a crude two-stage model, 'Antiquity' and 'Exile'. In the beginning ('Antiquity') we have the retelling of the Bible story as a story of national Jewish liberation but ending in a series of failed national revolts. Then, with the 'Exile', we have the Jews driven from their land, dispersed amongst hostile peoples, in what is described as the Jewish Diaspora, only to rediscover their true national identity 2,000 years later.

There are many objections to this approach.

First, 'Exile' is dated from 70 CE, the date Rome put down the Jewish Revolt in Judaea, a Jewish province of the Roman Empire, and destroyed the Temple at Jerusalem. The existence of flourishing Jewish communities at this time, an ancient Jewish Diaspora, throughout the Mediterranean and beyond, not least in Rome itself, is simply ignored, written out of history.

Second, it matters a great deal what the majority of those Jews, living in the ancient Diaspora, thought about their relations to

Judaea and the Temple at Jerusalem. Did they believe that they were already in Exile?

Third, was there actually a Jewish 'Exile' after 70 CE?

Finally, there is the assumption that the very modern idea of 'nationalism', in this case 'Jewish nationalism', can be imposed on events 2,000 years ago.

This chapter will attempt to develop these objections, but first we need to understand something about the historical background to Jewish history 2,000 years ago. Jewish history for this period has its very own historian, Josephus, and any discussion about 'Exile' has to consider his historical writing. All modern historians are dependent on him, even though he is notoriously unreliable, but providing Josephus is interpreted with considerable caution, he can provide unique and illuminating insight into the period.[2]

Josephus is more accurately described as a *Roman* Jewish historian. He was fluent in Greek, the language of the Roman educated classes. He respected the wider culture and politics of the Roman Empire. He was certainly proud of his Jewish heritage, but he saw it coexisting with the Roman Empire. Josephus was part of the Jewish landowning aristocracy in Jerusalem who had been heavily cultivated by the leaders of the Roman Empire. Rome ruled Judaea through this Jerusalem Jewish leadership. Though concentrated in Judaea, and in particular at the Temple site in Jerusalem, the Jewish religion was well known throughout the Roman Empire, because so many Jews lived in different parts of it. In fact, a tremendous tradition of pilgrimage had developed, as Jews from all over the Mediterranean and beyond travelled to the Temple at Jerusalem to pay their respects. The great religious Jewish festivals were especially popular, and vast crowds from faraway places would gather there (Goodman 1987: 52).

Judaism had evolved in Judaea (or Judah, see Chapter 1) and Babylonia more than 2,500 years ago. How this occurred is certainly beyond the scope of this book.[3] But Josephus has a gloriously poetic homily about what happened after Alexander the Great had defeated the Persian Empire and made his first acquaintance with the Jews of Jerusalem, just over 2,300 years ago:

> For when Alexander while still far off saw the multitude in white garments, the priests at their head clothed in linen, and the high priest in a robe of hyacinth-blue and gold, wearing on his head the mitre with the golden plate on it which was inscribed the name of God, he approached alone and prostrated himself before the Name and first

greeted the high priest. Then all the Jews together greeted Alexander
with one voice and surrounded him. (Josephus, *Jewish Antiquities*, 11;
cited Modrzejewski 1995: 52)

2,000 YEARS AGO AND 70 YEARS BEFORE EXILE
'A MAJORITY OF JEWS LIVED
OUTSIDE JUDAEA'

Professor Modrzejewski, Professor of Ancient History at the Sorbonne,
advises us not to take too seriously this description of the celebra-
tory first meeting between Alexander and the Jews in Jerusalem.
Nevertheless, 'the victorious campaigns of Alexander the Great
(336–323 BCE) marked a turning point ... A new era in the history of
the Mediterranean region began when Greek rationalism encountered Jewish spirituality ... Alexander's conquests laid down the
boundaries of a universal empire ... it was to serve as a model for the
Romans' (Modrzejewski 1995: 47).

Modrzejewski claims that Josephus is recording an event of
immense significance, even if only symbolically. A Jewish Diaspora
began throughout the Mediterranean in the wake of Alexander's
conquests. According to John Barclay, who has made an exhaustive
study of Jews in the ancient Mediterranean Diaspora in this period,
this was particularly true in Egypt when it became part of the
Alexandrian Greek Empire. Jews were recruited in considerable
numbers as soldiers and government officials. Many also came as
slaves or as economic migrants (Barclay 1996: 20–2). In return,
Alexander and his successors in Egypt, known as Ptolemaic, agreed
to respect and protect Jewish law (Modrzejewski 1995: 55). There is
some evidence that Alexander was following a precedent already
established by the Persian Empire, where there was also a (smaller)
Jewish Diaspora. This was to tolerate Jewish religious independence
based on the Temple at Jerusalem in return for Jewish services.
There are intriguing documents from a much earlier Judaean colony
in Elephantine in Egypt, servicing the Persian Empire, dating from
the period of Persian control (Modrzejewski 1995: 21–44).

These precedents seem to have fixed a familiar pattern for relationships between the Jews and the rulers of ancient empires, even
stretching forward to the medieval states, 1,000 years later.

In Alexandria, the city built to commemorate its founder on
Egypt's Mediterranean coast and which became the political and
commercial heart of the Empire, the Jewish community grew at an

extraordinary rate to number no less than a third of the total population of 500,000 (Modrzejewski 1995: 73). When Rome took control of the disintegrating Ptolemaic Greek Empire, and certainly by the first century of the common era, *the majority of Jews were living outside Judaea* (Barclay 1996: 4n.1).

THE JEWS OF EGYPT 2,000 YEARS AGO

One of the Jewish Diaspora's most illustrious families in the Roman Empire was headed by Philo of Alexandria. No doubt there were many illustrious families. But our sources are very limited and dependent for their survival after 2,000 years upon accidents of history, like the dry sands of the Egyptian desert which sometimes stored papyri documents, or in this case Christian fascination with this Greek Jewish philosopher. 'Early Christians were familiar with a Greek saying, *Either Plato philonises or Philo platonises*, according to the Christian monk, Jerome' (Barclay 1996: 165).

Philo 'stood at the peak of the Jewish community in Alexandria ... at the climax of a Jewish philosophical tradition ... deeply engaged with Hellenistic [i.e. Greek] culture' (Barclay 1996: 158). He was a platonic philosopher but, in Philo's words, 'in the school of Moses' (Barclay 1996: 163).

Philo's brother was Alexander the 'Alabarch', Chief Inspector of Customs Duties, collected on the eastern side of the Nile. He was one of the richest men in the city, giving a gift to the Temple at Jerusalem of massive gold and silver plate for its nine gates. Josephus claims he was also an 'overseer', possibly an adviser, though its meaning is uncertain, to the mother of Claudius, the Roman Emperor (Barclay 1996: 158–60).

Tiberius Julius Alexander was a nephew of Philo. Appointed by the Emperor Claudius as procurator of Judaea, he later helped put down the Jewish revolt in Jerusalem. Josephus tells us that Tiberius had abandoned the customs of his forefathers (Modrzejewski 1995: 186–8).

It would be foolish to draw general conclusions from a single family, perhaps, especially this one. But one characteristic does stand out. Though a highly assimilated family, two of its leading members remained firmly committed to Judaism. The third made a clean break with the religion. But even here there is not necessarily an indication of attitude towards the wider 'pagan' Roman Empire.

Josephus, who was a commander of the Jewish revolt against the armies of the Roman Empire in the Galilee, infamously changed sides. Yet even with Roman patronage, he swore his continuing commitment to his Jewish faith.

There were high levels of assimilation across Jewish society in Egypt. Jews had served in all ranks of the Alexandrian Greek army, in the infantry and cavalry, 'from humble footmen to officers and paymasters' (Barclay 1996: 115). In most cases they served in military units of mixed ethnicity.

Many Jews had been involved in the *cleruch* system, the mechanism for imposing Roman rule in the countryside. Along with migrant mercenary soldiers from other parts of the Empire, they were given plots of land and hence evolved into small landowners tied by gratitude and obligation to the imperial bureaucracy (Tcherikover and Fuks 1957: 11–17).[4] This inevitably led to polarisation and resentment between the immigrant *cleruchs* and the native peasantry (Modrzejewski 1975: 84).

Was assimilation, then, only with imperial Greek, and later Roman, society rather than with native Egyptians? It is true that 'Egyptian Jews abandoned Hebrew and Aramaic and produced a luxuriant literature in Greek' (Modrzejewski 1995: xi, xii). Yet we should be wary of dogmatic generalisations. There was, in addition, a poor Jewish peasantry in Egypt. We hear of a shepherd, Pasos the Jew, who worked on the estate of a non-Jew. Pasos 'was at least recognised of Judaean descent' (Barclay 1996: 115), as was 'Seos the Jew', who owed wool to a non-Jewish wool trader. We find another Jew tending the flock for an Egyptian temple of Pan (Barclay 1996: 115). We also have artisans, builders, weavers, donkey owners, boatmen, sometimes working for non-Jews (Barclay 1996: 116).

Some sense of assimilation with native Egyptian society is reflected in the writings of one Jewish author, Artapanus, albeit in Greek, sympathetic to Egyptian religious cults (Barclay 1996: 127–32) (though most Jewish religious writing was very offensive to Egyptian cults (Barclay 1996: 46)). But we can only guess at attitudes to assimilation. However Philo leaves us in no doubt about where, in his view, Jews should call their homeland.

PHILO: THE ANCIENT 'DIASPORA' *IS* THE HOMELAND

Whilst Philo considered Palestine, or at least parts of it, the *Holy Land*, this was not at all the same thing as *homeland*. Sarah Pearce has argued that Philo's

> discussions about the journey towards wisdom stress that the wise person, exemplified by Abraham … should abandon the homeland, often explicitly identified with ignorance or false religion, in favour of the true homeland, that is the realm of God, or virtue … Detachment from a particular homeland also forms a part in Philo's presentation of the wise as 'world citizens' who transcend attachment to particular places … (Pearce 1998: 100)[5]

What is so fascinating about Philo's perspective is how it anticipates the modern internationalism that grew out of the medieval European Jewish Diaspora and which became such a magnificent part of the Enlightenment Jewish tradition. There is a darker side to this, of course. This is the tradition that always helped fuel the modern anti-Semitic attack on the Jewish 'rootless cosmopolitan', which the Zionists would sometimes mimic.[6] Jewish cosmopolitanism, it seems, is nearly 2,000 years older than Zionism!

Philo recognises the inevitable importance that people attach to their homeland: 'Patriotic devotion … is amongst the highest goods and demanded by divine commandment in the Law of Moses' (Pearce 1998: 100–1). But the 'homeland', '*patris*', is 'above all, one's place of birth and education'. Indeed, the 'Holy Land' is not the 'homeland' but a 'strange land':

> Philo assumes a common sense of emotional attachment to local homelands when he portrays pilgrimage to the Jerusalem Temple as constituting the 'severest test', which requires temporary abandonment of patris and family for life in a strange land.
>
>   There is no doubt that devotion to the Temple and its laws is central to Philo's Jewish identity. This does not mean, however, that his expression of that commitment should be read in terms which marginalize his local allegiances … (Pearce 1998: 101)

Here we have confirmation that there is no necessary link between the religious focus on pilgrimage and Temple with a patriotic devotion to the 'Promised Land'.

How does Philo's perspective fit with the rest of the Jewish Diaspora in the ancient world? Our sources are far more limited. Nevertheless here is Barclay's conclusion to his assessment of the sources for the Jews in Rome, 2,000 years ago:

> Our survey of the history of the Jews of Rome has been conducted
> largely on the basis of 'snapshots' ... Yet these have provided ... a
> remarkably coherent picture. As one among many immigrant minori-
> ties in Rome, Jews were subject to the cultural and social snobbery of
> the Roman elite, even though exceptional Jewish individuals were
> known in the imperial court. However, the durability of the Jews'
> ancestral customs, and their particular attractiveness to Romans of
> many social classes, were special features of the Jewish profile, suffi-
> ciently important to attract hostile attention from Tiberius, Claudius
> and Domitian ... At no point were the Roman Jews so numerous or so
> threatening to the Roman plebs or the governing classes as to occa-
> sion the sort of violence we have witnessed in Syrian, Egyptian and
> Cyrenaean cities. With their hands clean of the wars in Judaea and the
> Diaspora Revolt of 116–117 c.e., the Jewish community in Rome could
> sustain an unbroken history, which has lasted to the present day.
> (Barclay 1996: 318–19)

JEWS AND NON-JEWS IN THE ANCIENT DIASPORA

It seems reasonable to infer that the Jews of Rome regarded Rome as
their 'homeland'. Yet Barclay writes of violence elsewhere in the
Diaspora. It is impossible to judge its levels of intensity or its impact
on local Jewish rootedness. It was sometimes connected to the way
imperial rulers played off the different religious cults and ethnic
groups against the other. The 'Alexandrian pogrom' in 38 CE (sometimes misleadingly called the first anti-Semitic pogrom) was incited
partly by the way Rome was manipulating relations between Greeks,
Jews and Egyptians in the city (Barclay 1996: 48). Undoubtedly, Jews
were subjected to particular animosity if they were seen to be
enforcing unpopular imperial policies (like the *cleruch* system in
Egypt). And in general terms, Jews, known for their self-conscious
religious differences, their one invisible god, circumcision, dietary
laws and Sabbath worship, could easily attract hostility. 'Loyal to
each other', they 'hate all others', according to the Roman historian
Tacitus (Goodman 1987: 98).

Josephus often refers to the Syrians' deep-seated hatred of the Jews
(Barclay 1996: 248). He is usually our only source and we should be
cautious, because he has also left us a very tantalising alternative picture. In the very period when tensions between Jews and non-Jews

were rising rapidly, just before the Jewish revolt against Rome, Josephus provides evidence of non-Jews being attracted to the Jews. He writes that every city had its 'Judaizers', Jewish proselytisers seeking converts, and a 'mixed' element neither clearly Jewish nor non-Jewish (Barclay 1996: 248). In Damascus he claims that 'all but a few wives' of Damascenes' had 'submitted to the Jewish religion'. And in Antioch, an ancient city in the same region, Judaism was attracting the many ethnic Greeks (Barclay 1996: 254).

New Testament sources make the same claims; in Caesarea, Judaism was spreading even amongst the military, according to Cornelius (Acts 10: 1–2) (Barclay 1996: 254). Josephus was quite confident that Judaism was ultimately irresistible:

> The masses have for a long time shown great eagerness for our piety ... there is not one city, Greek or barbarian ... which the custom of the 7th day, which we keep free of work, has not infiltrated, and where the fasts, and burning of lamps, and where many of our prohibitions with respect to meats are not observed ...
> ... without the alluring bait of sensual pleasure, but only because of its intrinsic merit, the Law has proven so effective. (Josephus 1996: 282)

Perhaps, as most modern scholars insist, Josephus is exaggerating. But, at the very least, he is surely reflecting the self-confidence of a community immensely proud of its religiosity. It is hardly a description of a cowed and isolated community living in 'Exile'. (Indeed it is at just this intersection between Jew and Gentile that the Jewish Christian cult begins by cutting away some of Judaism's more restrictive prohibitions. That most famous 'Diaspora Jew', Paul of Tarsus, would tour the Diaspora communities, preaching in their synagogues, uniting Jew and Gentile sympathisers. The rest, as they say, is history, a hostile history to the Jews, certainly, but still a testimony to the dynamism and creativity of the Diaspora Jewish community in the first century CE.[7])

2,000 YEARS AGO: JEWS LIVING IN A PART OF THE 'LAND OF ISRAEL' – SAMARIA, GALILEE AND JUDAEA

What about the Jews living in the so-called 'land of Israel'? First, we must recall from Chapter 1 that the 'land of Israel' is itself a religious myth. Two thousand years ago there were three very distinctive geographical and political component parts to that area of the 'land of

Israel', on which modern Zionism makes its claim: Samaria, Galilee and Judaea. Each needs to be considered separately.

Samaria exposes one of the deepest fault-lines for Zionism. To this day, there is a unique Samaritarian Jewish identity, with no affiliation to modern Israel or to modern Judaism as it is understood in the West. One historian, Coggins, has rightly pondered the significance of the three Samaritan candidates who took part in the elections to the inaugural Palestinian legislative council on the Palestinian West Bank in 1996. As he writes, the 'distinctiveness of the Samaritans, as neither Arab nor Israeli, was thereby acknowledged' (Coggins 1998: 66).

The Samaritans insisted they were Jewish but in the first century they were at daggers drawn with Judaea. The hatred was fuelled by the Samaritans' refusal to recognise the Temple at Jerusalem. Instead, they worshipped on their own mountain, Mt. Gerizim. The difficulty here is that there are no surviving documentary references from Samaria. Most of the documentation is Jewish, in the Jerusalem Temple sense, and is very hostile. Millar has summarised what little we know about the Samaritans:

> How they saw themselves is expressed most vividly by two Greek inscriptions from [the Greek island of] Delos [which indicate the existence of a Samaritan diaspora].
>   'the Israelites[8] ... who pay their tithes to sacred [holy] Argarizein [Mt. Gerizim]'. The real history, size and settlement patterns of the Samaritan community in Samaria itself are all extraordinarily little known. In evidence from this period we encounter them only from the outside, for instance in the description in St. John's Gospel of how Jesus talked with a Samaritan woman at the Well of Jacob: 'Our fathers worshipped on this mountain; but you say that in Jerusalem is the place where one should worship'. Not long after this ... dramatic date, Pontius Pilate was to send a detachment of troops to massacre a crowd of Samaritans who had gathered at a village near Mt. Gerizim, in the hope of being shown sacred vessels deposited there by Moses, (according to Josephus). Three decades later, in the early stages of the Jewish revolt, a large number of Samaritans again gathered on their holy mountain, and in the summer of 67 C.E. over eleven thousand were slaughtered by forces sent by [the Roman Emperor] Vespasian ... (Millar 1993: 341)

There is no evidence that Judaean Jews and Samaritan Jews were ever able to find common cause in the struggle with Rome despite the ferociousness of their common enemy. This makes a very telling point. Two thousand years ago ancient Judaea could not assert its authority over Samaria and Samaria refused to recognise Jerusalem's religious authority. The question of recognising its national authority has no meaning outside this religious framework.

Galilee poses perhaps even more serious problems.

The Dead Sea Scrolls scholar, Geza Vermes, has described Galilee in his remarkable book *Jesus the Jew*, which examines the Jewish roots and context of the Jesus story. His forensic capacity to extract real history from such deeply propagandist and flawed sources as the Gospels, rabbinic Jewish religious writings like the Talmud and Josephus has produced astonishing results. He reveals a rough-and-ready peasant Judaism, in the first century CE, as much at odds with Jerusalem as with Rome. At first Galilee was ruled separately from Judaea, 'a fact that cannot have failed to have reinforced Galilian self-awareness' (Vermes 1983: 45). This local and regional awareness also reflected the economic geography. Galilee was extraordinarily fertile, its olive oil, for example, was exported all over the Mediterranean. Its economic self-sufficiency 'is likely to have nourished the pride and independence of its inhabitants' (Vermes 1983: 46).

Temple leaders in Jerusalem detested the Galileans. They were '*am ha-arez*', 'peasants', but the word also carried the stigma of a religiously uneducated person. The following Talmudic quotation reflects the sentiments between the 'orthodox' Jews of the Temple and the *am ha-arez*:

> No man may marry the daughter of the 'am ha-arez', for they are like unclean animals, and their wives like reptiles, and it is concerning their daughters that Scripture says: 'Cursed be he who lies with any kind of beast'. (Vermes 1983: 54–5)

A quote from the Talmud also suggests that hatred between Jewish Jerusalem and the Jewish Galilean countryside was more intense than between Jew and Gentile:

> Greater is the hatred of the 'am ha-arez' for the learned than the hatred of the Gentiles for Israel, but the hatred of their wives is even greater. (Vermes 1983: 55)

Vermes finds a remark in one of the Gospels echoing a similar sentiment: 'Surely the Messiah is not from the Galilee' (Vermes 1983: 55).

As with the Samaritans, there is no evidence that Galilee joined with Judaea in a common struggle against Rome. Indeed, Rajak, in her biography of Josephus, called her chapter on Galilee, 'The Civil War in Galilee', highlighting the fact that the fighting within the region was more about fighting each other than Rome. She claims the situation was close to total anarchy (Rajak 1983: 165). Josephus was Jerusalem's chief commander for the Galilee at the start of the Jewish revolt. Rajak is very revealing about Galilean loyalties to their Jerusalem commander:

> Josephus tells us ... about brigands that he could not disarm, and whom he therefore bound to himself as mercenaries ... finds himself the aspirant leader of something like a band of wild men, swollen with homeless peasants and angry villagers ... (Rajak 1983: 145)

Nevertheless, some Galileans came to Judaea, or rather Jerusalem, to fight. What they and the Judaeans were fighting for is the question we must now try to answer.

THE JEWISH REVOLT AGAINST ROME 66–70 CE

The Jewish revolt against Rome (66–70 CE) symbolises a major turning point in Ancient Jewish history. That it was a war for Jewish liberation is not in doubt; whether it serves as a legitimate model for a modern Jewish nationalist movement like Zionism most certainly does raise doubts.

Let us begin with the extraordinary revolutionary family dynasty of Judas of Galilee. Born at the beginning of the first century CE, Judas led opposition to co-operation with the Roman census, which was a means of avoiding paying taxation. Forty years later two of his sons, Jacob and Simon, were crucified for revolutionary agitation. A surviving son, Menahem, later became one of the revolutionary leaders in Jerusalem. A nephew of Menahem, Eleazar, was the legendary captain at Masada, where a few hundred Jews, after holding out against the Romans following the fall of Jerusalem, finally committed mass suicide.

It may be objected that our only source concerning this family dynasty is Josephus and hence the history is unreliable. But the Zionists are more than happy to use Josephus when it suits them. Masada has become one of modern Israel's greatest tourist attractions, used brazenly as a means of making Zionist propaganda.

According to Yigael Yadin, Israel's most famous archaeologist who excavated the site, it is 'through visits to Masada we can teach our brethren [in the Diaspora] what we today call Zionism' (Zerubavel 1995: 67). Tourist brochures often include excerpts from Eleazar's famous 'freedom' speech on the eve of the mass suicide (Zerubavel 1995: 134). The speech is an extract from a Josephus history and is generally believed to have been fabricated by him, exposing the supremely unattractive side of Josephus' character.[9]

Recourse to Josephus requires great care. The dispassionate scholar, Martin Goodman, has written what is arguably the most brilliant recent account of the Jewish Revolt, *The Ruling Class of Judaea, The Origins of the Jewish Revolt against Rome 66–70*, by skilfully disentangling Josephus the propagandist from Josephus the real historian.

The Jewish revolt against Rome was a peasant war against the very wealthy Jewish ruling class in Jerusalem, as well as being a war against the rule of Rome. Indeed, it is Goodman's main contention that Rome turned on the Jewish ruling class because of its inability to control the peasantry.

Goodman's analysis of the earlier rebel peasant movement led by Judas the Galilean deserves our special attention, because it introduces us to the mind-set of the peasant revolutionary activists. Goodman's use of Josephus' evidence about Judas suggests that Judas was leading a messianic movement, which respected neither national boundaries nor national leaders. Goodman writes:

> What Judas is said to have proposed was not just that subjection to Rome was evil but that acceptance of any human master was wrong since Jews should be ruled by God alone ... The effect of this ideology was anarchy and revolution.
>
> The most compelling motive for any Jew to join in violent struggle was a belief that the messianic age was not just a future hope ... but a present actuality. Once the messiah had arrived and the last battles, so graphically imagined in the Qumran War Scroll,[10] were ready to commence ... [you] had no choice but to participate. (1987: 93–4, 91–2)

We have here a 'messianic anarchism', a form of Jewish liberation which recognises no state structure, nationalist or otherwise.

The Josephus expert, Rajak, whilst considering the messianic emphasis overstated (1983: 40–1), reinforces this neo-anarchist interpretation with secular concepts, 'banditry' and 'brigandage', as political explanations:

> Brigandage was, of course, the enemy of the settled and propertied
> throughout the ancient world; even Rome could not always keep it at
> bay in the empire ... Bandits are an extreme case. What ... Josephus
> scarcely recognizes ... is that most of the rebels had grievances of a dif-
> ferent order from those of his own class, and some of them at least
> were driven by a vision – perhaps indistinct, and occasionally
> Messianic, but for all that not devoid of practical content – a better
> society ... .
> ... the revolutionaries ... must have had clear social and political
> objectives, even if these were vague and ill-defined ... vagueness ...
> was compounded by the general lack of conscious revolutionary ide-
> ology in the ancient world ... we may assume [the aims] ... standard in
> the Greek world – [to be] demands for the abolition of debt (recall the
> destruction of the money lenders' bonds in the Jerusalem Temple
> archives) and for the redistribution of land [on which Josephus does
> not comment]. (1983: 85, 139)

Rajak cites Eric Hobsbawm's books *Primitive Rebels* and *Bandits*.
Peasant banditry and brigandage, as forms of primitive social and
political protest against injustice and inequality, have a long and
honourable history throughout the ancient and medieval worlds.

The Zealots were the most important, organised revolutionary
group in the revolt, briefly taking power in Jerusalem. There seems
some historical continuity with Judas of Galilee, at least according
to Vermes. They recruited bandits to strengthen their power base in
Jerusalem (Goodman 1987: 225). When they seized the Temple they
selected the new high priest by lottery, thereby avoiding candidates
from the traditional ruling-class families. The high priest chosen
was a village stonemason, probably the first high priest from such
lowly origins. This seems to have a ring of truth, if only because
Josephus is so furious about it, dismissing him as a boor and igno-
ramous (Rajak 1983: 133).

The Zealots 'minted the best coins of the revolt' (Goodman 1987:
201n.3). Coins are invaluable because they are the best evidence
available, separately from Josephus, about the general aims of the
revolt. 'The slogans emphasised liberty and the holiness of the city
of Jerusalem ... The counting of the years from the declaration of
independence demonstrated the arrival of the new era' (Goodman
1987: 178). They suggest a struggle for a free and independent

Judaism and the armed defence of its spiritual centre, the Temple at Jerusalem, perhaps in anticipation of the arrival of the Messiah. But here also Rajak urges caution in treating the slogans as exclusively religiously inspired:

> The one slogan ... is the single word 'freedom', from the coinage, as well Josephus. Theologically minded commentators on Josephus, and they are the majority, have read this eschatologically, as referring to the conditions that will arise at the End of Days. Yet even ... such circles ... allow that the kind of freedom of which they dreamt ... must have had a prominent component of practical liberation of the oppressed. (1983: 139)

Goodman argues that it was the failure of the Jewish ruling class in Jerusalem to control the anarchic elements of grass-roots independence in the revolt that so incensed Rome. This was inflamed by the tradition of developing independent interpreters of the Torah (God's law) amongst the peasantry, who were also ready to provide religious justification for independent peasant ownership of the land.

'The peasant will have known', writes Goodman, 'that the divinely ordained ideal in the Torah required each man to own his own land as a free and equal citizen' (1987: 67). He goes on:

> There were many priests and experts in Torah interpretation who, despite being excluded from the ruling class, could command much prestige among the population, but they made no attempt to seize power on their own behalf because, like the poor in general, they lacked the institutions ... The danger to society lay not in revolution but, more insidiously, in anarchy ... (1987: 137)

We cannot take the argument any further; it is inconclusive. We can see the outline of a bitter revolutionary struggle, but it is shrouded in the mists of time. We can though extract important insights from the scraps of evidence. We can engage enthusiastically with the ingenious interpretations of Josephus, but we should also be aware of the observation from the outstanding Classics scholar G.E.M. de Ste Croix: 'if the Greeks did not have a word for something ... it may be a salutary warning that the phenomena we are looking for may not have existed ...' (de Ste Croix 1983: 35).

Nationalism is a modern idea. It requires the mass participation by a people conscious of themselves as citizens-to-be in a state structure within a nationally defined territory (Hobsbawm 1990: 19). We simply have no evidence from the Jewish Revolt to see it as a struggle for the national liberation of Judaea, let alone the national liberation of the 'Land of Israel'.

EXILE TO GALILEE?

Did the destruction of the Temple at Jerusalem, following the defeat of the Jewish rebels at the hands of the Romans, lead to 'Exile', at least for the Jews of Jerusalem and Judaea?

Certainly it seems likely that the Jerusalem area, and following further revolts in the Diaspora[11] itself, and in the Judaean countryside led by Bar Kokhba,[12] the rest of Judaea was forcibly cleared of Jews. No doubt there was migration into the Jewish Diaspora, but there was also concentrated migration into Galilee, where the Jewish religion, in a revised rabbinic form, would flourish with Roman approval. Goodman has traced the arrival of exiled Judaean rabbis into Galilee at this time, using their own religious sources. The story he tells is the tale of two Judaisms in the immediate aftermath of the Jewish revolt. There is the 'already existing' peasant Judaism of the prosperous villages of Galilee, described earlier by Vermes, and there is the attempt by the artisan[13] immigrant rabbis to introduce a stricter adherence to Jewish law. Rome displayed a spectacular lack of interest in this process (Goodman 1983: 154), at least in its early stages, and was concerned only with the collection of taxes (Goodman 1983: 146).

As we record just a few of the highlights of the struggle between these two forms of Judaism – in the shadow of the defeat of the Jewish revolts and the destruction of the Temple – what impresses is Jewish *continuity* as well as relaxed relations with the non-Jews of Galilee. Here we have a glimpse of the give-and-take with non-Jewish neighbours in the countryside.[14]

The Zionist view that now began the pain and the anguish of the long night of 'Exile' in a world dominated by hatred of the Jews has no place in Galilee. Goodman writes that we learn of Jews

> eating together with gentiles, though not necessarily their food ... A gentile might help water his neighbour's animal on the Sabbath ... Jews should travel with gentiles rather than risk the roads alone ... should

demonstrate sympathy in times when gentiles mourned, comforting them and burying their dead. The reason given 'for the ways of peace' suggests that such relationships actually existed *and compelled the rabbis to be lenient against their will* ...

Friendly contact would ripen into closer relationships. A Jewish woman might lend her blouse to a gentile friend, a man might lend his ass, and there are plenty of comments about financial loans in both directions. Co-operation could extend to joint ownership of vineyards and farms ... From such activities might grow a considerable trust, so that a Jew might entrust his goods or family to a gentile guardian to look after, after his death ... A Jew might also be appointed guardian by a gentile ... (1983: 44; emphasis added)

The rabbis' writings 'permitted pictures of possible pagan divine figures to appear on everyday things such as boilers, kettles, pans, basins, but not on precious objects such as jewelry' (Goodman 1983: 69). Again, 'Greek conventions often provided subject matter for decoration – the lion's head, wreaths, eagles and cherubs of synagogue reliefs ...' (Goodman 1983: 71).

Is Galilee 'Exile', the 'Diaspora', the 'land of Israel' or a Jewish province of the Roman Empire? Galilee is the setting for the production of the Palestinian Talmud, which, alongside the Babylonian Talmud,[15] was destined to become a spiritual guide for Judaism until the Enlightenment, 1,300 years later.

Yet here is the ultimate paradox. Galilee is also the setting, on the mosaic floor of an ancient synagogue, for the most fabulous archaeological discovery of late Jewish antiquity: a veritable antique jewel simultaneously celebrating the imageless God and the Sun God, testimonies to Jewish/non-Jewish coexistence.

THE FOURTH-CENTURY CE, SYNAGOGUE NEAR TIBERIAS, WITH THE SUN GOD FLOOR

Perhaps no other product of the period more fully exhibits the confident expression of Jewish tradition and identity within a multilingual context, or combines that with so many elements of Graeco-Roman artistic decoration. The mosaic occupying the central aisle of the synagogue is divided into three panels. The first is the representation of the Torah shrine flanked by two menorahs with burning candles. Then, remarkably, there is a circular representation of the twelve signs of the zodiac, centring on the picture of the chariot of the sun with Helios personified: each sign is named in Hebrew, for instance 'RYH, the lion, or DGYM ('fishes') for Pisces. They are grouped into four seasons, for which the Hebrew term TQWPH is used, and they are represented as young women, also identified in Hebrew by using the Hebrew names of four months: Nisan, Tammuz, Tishri, Teveth.

The third panel contains, between representation of two lions, a series of brief inscriptions in Greek giving the name of benefactors ... The name of a further benefactor ... can be restored from another, parallel Greek inscription, this time accompanied by a blessing in Aramaic: 'Let there be peace ... on anyone who has carried out a commandment in this holy place ...' (Millar 1993: 384)

3
'... Eighteen Centuries of Jewish Suffering'

In the Zionist view of history, Jewish communities, which expanded far beyond the Middle East, into Asia, Europe and finally into America, in the many centuries following the fall of the Second Temple in Jerusalem in 70 CE, were powerless, downtrodden and subjected to unrelieved persecution. Theoreticians of Zionism like Theodor Herzl argued that only the transfer of Jews to 'our ever memorable historic home' in Palestine could end 'eighteen centuries of suffering' (Vital 1975: 266). The reality is far more complex. Indeed, this Zionist myth is a crass insult to the dynamism, mobility and immense creativity of the Jews faced with the task of steering within and between the changing fortunes, shapes and sizes of the burgeoning and mutually hostile Christian and Islamic empires which grew to dominate the long historical period. Salo Baron, one of the most accomplished and certainly the most productive Jewish historians in the early twentieth century (his *Social and Religious History of the Jews* ran to 18 volumes), dismissed the Zionist approach as 'lachrymose'.

Two extraordinary facts are worth considering at the outset. Why is it that by the year 1000 a Jewish peasantry had virtually disappeared, making the Jewish people, by definition much reduced in numbers, almost exclusively an urban people (Johnson 1993: 171)? And why is it that by the beginning of the nineteenth century more than half of the world's Jews were living in Poland-Lithuania (Hundert 1992: xi)?

These questions beg another. For nearly 2,000 years the Jews not only survived, but often achieved sustained periods of prosperity, yet, increasingly over the centuries, they rarely farmed the land. This was particularly true in Christian Europe, which forbade Jewish landownership during the period which economic historians call feudalism, and where prosperity depended, above all, upon agricultural production.

Here we come to one of the most difficult and least understood facts of them all. For it was in this period that the Jews developed an international trading network that would help to service the two religious empires; that would sustain and develop the internationally scattered Jewish communities; and, that would make their own distinctive religion seem inseparable from this economic role.

Karl Marx theorised that Jewish survival from Roman times until the nineteenth century actually depended upon this economic role. This has infuriated some modern scholars, who dismiss Marx's view, because he was an 'apostate'![1] Yet it was Edward Gans, one of Marx's Jewish tutors, when he was a student at the University of Berlin in the 1830s, who argued that Jewish unity across the ages had indeed depended upon the Jews becoming, or at least being led by, a social class of merchants (Mendes-Flohr and Reinharz 1995: 216). Gans cannot so easily be ignored. He was founder of one of nineteenth-century Germany's most enlightened and respected Jewish intellectual pressure groups, *Verein*, the Society for Culture and Science of the Jews.

Modern Jewish Studies have finally begun to come to grips with this argument. Scholars of Jewish economic history, like Baron, Kahan and others, have contributed the astonishing insight that not only was there a Jewish merchant class in late antiquity, but that it may itself have been a trigger for conversions *to* Judaism, at the same time as the Jewish peasantry was assimilating into a 'pagan', then increasingly Christian and later Islamic countryside. It seems that large numbers of Phoenicians and Carthaginians became Jewish, 'bringing their commercial skills' into the communities (Baron et al. 1975: 21). In fact, Abram Leon, leader of a tiny revolutionary socialist group in Nazi-occupied Belgium, and who was to perish in Auschwitz, wrote the first pioneering study in this field, even though it remains unrecognised by modern scholarship.[2]

Hostility to Jews in the medieval world, but also their success, over the centuries, cannot be understood without taking into account their economic role. Religious harassment almost always became intertwined with it. Of course, for both Christianity and Islam, Judaism was an inferior creed. Yet both religions were always ready to search their holy books to find reasons to pardon and protect the Jews. Jewish usefulness to their societies usually outweighed Jewish blasphemy against Jesus or Mohammed. Their international economic role, cultivated over many generations, embedded unparalleled energy and resourcefulness in Jewish families. It not only made multilinguists of some Jews, with all the additional skills that this implied, not least detailed knowledge of far-flung and exotic parts of the world, it often put them at the forefront of scientific advance. In medieval Islamic countries Jews were often known as merchants and as medical experts. Some Jews also played a key diplomatic role.

> Jewish traders served as important mediators in a world divided by Islam and Christianity ... By the 9th century Hebrew had become a leading international language. (Baron et al. 1975: 28–9)

In truth, rulers very much needed their Jewish communities. They were more than just 'tolerated'; they had a recognised place in medieval society, and this meant that they often achieved long periods of stability and a degree of political and legal independence. Of course, when things went wrong – disease, plague, crop failure, exposure of gross courtly corruption or a ruler's need to over-tax the peasantry for an unpopular foreign adventure, which could in turn lead to popular unrest – the Jews could become scapegoats. But this was not a permanent condition, even if it was an ever-present possibility.

The old Jewish medieval trading network finally began to break up as Western Europe slowly emerged as the economic power house which would lay the foundations for global empire-building and industrial capitalism. The new nation-states of Western Europe created massive new markets which produced their own merchants. At first, this was a period of intense anti-Semitism as Jews were ejected from the emerging nations and their markets. Here begins the long Jewish trek to Eastern Europe, and Poland-Lithuania in particular, where Jews were able to continue their important economic role. But then there was also a spectacular Jewish revival, which plunged the Jewish minority in Western Europe headlong into the forefront of modernity. This period is misunderstood and yet it is essential to understanding both the rejection and the final accommodation of Jews in the modern world. The critical moment is the beginning of the seventeenth century. It is the moment when medieval superstition and religion begin to give way to modern science. It is the moment when Christianity in Western Europe, already fractured by the Reformation, begins its long retreat. It is the dawn of the Enlightenment. It is also the moment of the High Renaissance when two of its greatest artists, the poet and playwright Shakespeare in

London and the painter Rembrandt in Amsterdam, make their own contributions to what is sometimes called the 'Jewish Question'. To help our understanding of this moment I shall conclude this chapter by calling two vital witnesses, Shakespeare's infamous, fictitious Jew, Shylock, and Rembrandt's little known but just as important, factual real Jew, who was called Menasseh ben Israel.

Shakespeare and Rembrandt illuminate the contradictions Jewish communities faced in a rapidly changing world, as the newly emerging capitalism began to shake the old order to its very foundations. Zionism sees a static, unchanging and hostile world where Jews can find no peace – except by retreating into their own private, exclusive place, which, of course, also provides no peace. Yet modernity and modern thinking have shown history to be dynamic, where our social and political attitudes, hostile or otherwise, and the circumstances which create them, are always subject to challenge and change. As Marx and Engels famously put it, in *The Communist Manifesto* of 1848, with a little borrowing from Shakespeare:

> all that is solid melts into air, all that is holy is profaned, and man is at last compelled to face with sober senses, his real conditions of life, and his relations with his kind.

In medieval times, the economic Jew sometimes buttressed the religious Jew and sometimes undermined him. Modernity promised to abolish the first distinction and allow individual conscience the flexibility to determine the meaning, if any, of the second. On this basis, Jews and non-Jews would discover a 'common humanity'. Even if the promise has only been partly fulfilled, we have to go on struggling for it.

THE MEDIEVAL JEWISH ECONOMIC ROLE

But first let us look more closely at that earlier Jewish economic role. One of its characteristics, brazenly ignored by both the Zionists and Western European historiography, was that its dynamism was often driven by the immense success of the Islamic Arabian empires from the eighth to the thirteenth centuries. Here is the carrier of civilisation, science, art, technological development, west of, though often interacting with, the civilisations of India and China, from the break-up of the Roman Empire to the Renaissance in Western

Europe. Indeed, seen through the eyes of Jews from the Islamic empire, who travelled into the European heartlands, much of the continent presented a sorry spectacle of shocking backwardness.

Ibrahim-Ibn-Jakub was sent by the Caliph (the Islamic Arab leader) of Cordoba to investigate trade and diplomatic prospects in Central Europe in the mid-tenth century.

> They have no bath houses as such, but ... they build a stone stove on which, when it is heated, they pour water. They hold a bunch of grass in their hands and waft the steam around. Then their pores open, and all excess matter escapes from their bodies.

As Norman Davies notes in his *History of Europe*, this Jewish diplomat from Muslim Spain is looking on the European interior with all the curiosity of a modern anthropologist surveying the tribes of Papua (1996: 325).

Two centuries later, another Jew, Benjamin of Tudela, would write his *Book of Travels* describing his observations across Europe and the Middle East. It became renowned as the best travel book of the Middle Ages, eventually translated into nearly all European languages to become a primary source book for scholars in the sixteenth century.

Constantinople, at this time the largest city in the world, particularly fascinated him. There were about 2,500 Jews living there. He found craftsmen in silk and merchants of all kinds. Many were rich but none was allowed to ride a horse except Rabbi Solomon the Egyptian, who was the king's doctor. Jewish courts of law were independent. Anti-Semitic acts were forbidden. Synagogues were legally protected, but no new ones were allowed. The Jewish festival of the Passover had to shift its date so that it always took place after Easter. There was popular hostility towards some of the Jews, but Benjamin was probably surprised by its cause: 'They are tanners and pour their dirty water outside their houses.' As well as the tanners of Constantinople, he found highly skilled Jewish craftsmen everywhere – glassworkers in Aleppo, silkweavers in Thebes, dyers in Brindisi (Johnson 1993: 169–70).

The testimony of Ibn-Hurdadbih, head of the Caliph of Baghad's postal and intelligence service in the middle of the ninth century, is widely regarded as the best evidence we have for the group of international Jewish merchants known as the 'Radanite' Jews. They traded over vast distances from the 'Frankish' lands (roughly today's

France) to the Caspian Sea (on the northern coast of today's Iran).
They spoke Arabic, Persian, Greek, 'Frankish', Spanish and the 'Slav'
languages. Scattered throughout this well-travelled trading zone
were Jewish colonies which organised the exchange of forest prod-
ucts, horses and hides, swords, and slaves of both sexes from the
West for luxury goods from the East, as well as impressive quantities
of Arabian money, mainly in silver. Jewish trade and craftsmanship
in silver was renowned across the continent. The Hungarian Queen
Gisela authorised two Jewish minters to make her silver coins. A
hundred years later Jews ran the mint in embryonic Poland producing bracteates (thin silver plates) with the Polish sovereign's
name in Hebrew letters, together with the names of the minters
(Abramsky et al. 1986: 15–18).

Jewish prosperity and political influence at this time impacted on
the empire of the Khazars, which had developed along the Caspian
coast. Trapped between the Islamic and Byzantine empires, the
pagan Khazari elite converted to Judaism late in the ninth century
as a means to maintain its political independence and integrate
itself into the Jewish trading network (Abramsky et al. 1986: 16).[3]

JEWISH AUTONOMY AND RIGHTS IN
MEDIEVAL SOCIETY

The American Jewish theology scholar David Biale has comprehensively challenged the view that Jewish communities were powerless
in medieval society. He argues that the principle enunciated in late
antiquity by the third-century Babylonian rabbi Samuel, close to
the Persian court, that in return for recognition of the authority of
the gentile political authorities the Jews would receive internal legal
and political autonomy, established an enduring and far-reaching
precedent (1986: 54–6). It meant that Jews, far from becoming a
'pariah people on the outer margins of society, in both the Christian
and Moslem worlds, inhabited an uneasy region close to the centres
of power ...' (Biale 1986: 59).

Biale argues that the legal status of Jews in Spain, France, Germany
and Poland was considerably better than that of serfs and in many
cases approached that of the nobility and the burgher class. The *servi
camerae* concept, a definition of Jews as 'serfs of the royal chamber'
(Biale 1986: 66) captures the ambiguity. The Jews paid taxes to the
king only and in return he conferred certain privileges on them. On
the other hand they were dependent upon him and his whims.

The *Sachsenspiegel*, the thirteenth-century German law code, regarded the Jews as a free people. This conferred specific rights in feudal society: freedom of worship and, specifically, freedom of movement. This was a legal recognition of the contribution made by Jewish commerce for which freedom of movement was a necessity. This explicitly distinguished the Jews from those bound to the land and made the status of Jews closer to that of knights, who had the right to live wherever they wished.

Nevertheless political protection of the Jews in the Middle Ages lacked consistency, especially at times of popular unrest when the authorities themselves were under attack or when they lost control of their own policies. It also failed abysmally to protect them from the onslaught of the first crusade in 1096, although the warning issued to his followers by Saint Bernard of Clairvaux, the spiritual leader of the second crusade in the 1140s, against repeating this, was heeded (Chazan unpublished: ch. 6, p. 11). In any case, whilst the threat of violence against Jews was always a possibility, Jews were not simply hapless victims.

> The prevailing image of the medieval Jew is that of the martyr dying without resistance. This is an erroneous view ... Jews were not merely passive objects ... In widely scattered times and places, they took up arms in self defence ... . (Biale 1986: 72)

In Western and Central Europe the *Waffenrecht* (arms law) allowed the Jews to bear weapons; they were even allowed to issue duel challenges. This extraordinary and little known freedom posed an intriguing dilemma for the Jewish religious authorities. Should Jews carry their weapons on the Sabbath? Biale reports several heroic examples of Jewish armed resistance during the crusades. In addition, he notes that Jews not only also served in the medieval armies of the Carolingian kings of France, in some cases became experts in the manufacture of military hardware. Some of the Jews expelled from Spain and Portugal in the sixteenth century, brought skills to Turkey to help the Turks make 'artillery, arquebuses, gunpowder, cannonballs and other weapons' (Biale 1986: 73–6).

Whilst it would be foolish to tilt the historical balance too much and claim that Jews were not vulnerable in this period, Biale has provided evidence which demands a much more nuanced perspective.

The crusades marked a turning point. Leon called them the 'expression of the will of the [Christian] merchant to carve a road to the Orient' (Leon 1970: 137). Certainly, the struggle between Christian Europe and Islam intensified at this time, reaching a climax with the final defeat of Islam in Spain in the fifteenth century. It also marked the beginning of the expulsion of the Jews from the embryonic nation-states of Western Europe.

THE EXPULSION OF THE JEWS FROM WESTERN EUROPE

In England, waves of anti-Semitic incidents formed the background to the expulsions in 1290: the allegations of kidnapping by Jews of Christian children for ritual killings; the massacres of the Jews at York. Variations on the theme of the Jews as killers of Christ fed into the mass hysteria – that bread for the Jewish festival of Passover needed a substitute for the blood of Christ was one of the most sordid medieval superstitions. Nevertheless, 'the slanders must be seen against a background of Jewish moneylending' (Johnson 1993: 210–11).

The Jews were a moneylending and banking community. At the highest level, the Jews were official bankers to the king. There was an Exchequer of the Jews, a department of the Great Exchequer of the Realm, graced with an impressive Latin motif, *Scaccarium Judaeorum* (Roth 1949: 30).

The Jewish royal bankers were just one of the countless resentments the feudal landowning barons held against the king. At the beginning of the thirteenth century the struggle between the barons and the king reached a climax with what would come to be seen as one of the great foundation documents of English democracy, the Magna Carta of 1215.

Famous for its clause that no free man could be imprisoned or exiled 'except by the lawful judgment of his peers', the Magna Carta was in essence an attempt to impose constitutional and embryonic *national* order on the relations between the king and the barons (Holt 1992: 188–9).

The Magna Carta contained two 'Jewish' clauses, dealing with debt relief. Put very simply, the clauses reduced the amount of money owed by a debtor's family, if the debtor died, by cancelling interest on the debt. This struck at both the Jews and the king, because if the Jewish creditor died the debt accrued to the king. At the same time, of course, the clauses brought some relief to impoverished debtors.

As Roth notes:

> These clauses, with their burning sense of grievance which underlies them, give some idea of the animosity with which the royal [Jewish] satellites were now regarded. (1949: 36–7)

Salo Baron observed the significance of the new national framework within which the religious-economic grievances against the Jews were surfacing:

> Pre-occupation with the Jewish problem deeply affected English national thinking ... Edward [I] is rightly considered the monarch under whose regime the Franco-Norman and Anglo-Saxon ethnic strains were finally fused into the new English nation creating a fairly cohesive national state. (Cited Shapiro 1996: 245n.40)

At the same time, the 'first real Christian bankers', such as the Knights Templar, were taking over the major Jewish financial roles (Johnson 1993: 213).

Outstanding research and analysis of the European Jewish economy for this period has been compiled by Jonathan Israel. He points to underlying economic factors that preceded the waves of expulsion of Jews across Western Europe:

> Jews ... were being squeezed out economically by the general development of Christian trade, industry and banking. Christian merchants and craftsmen wanted no Jewish competitors, as and when they became sufficiently powerful, the aim of their guilds was to eradicate Jewry from crafts and trade. (Israel 1985: 27)

The Spanish Inquisition, at the end of the fifteenth century, is Western Europe's most notorious and bloodiest symbol of the Jewish expulsion. Again we see the mixture of new national identities, economics and religious ferocity – the new Spain, which would conquer parts of America with its Christian merchants attempting to dominate the new and flourishing Atlantic trade routes, defines itself by rejecting both its Islamic and Jewish heritage.

A general pattern of terror drove most Jews eastwards. At first, the momentum came from the new towns and was led by the lower clergy. In Italy, new Christian civic institutions, *monti di pietà*, replaced the Jewish loan banks (Israel 1985: 7, 9). Then, as the Reformation erupted, Martin Luther, its principal inspiration, at first sympathetic to the Jews, turned against them in blind fury, as he realised they were impervious to his arguments.

From now on the unfolding dynamic of the Reformation fuelled religious and economic anti-Semitic hatred across the continent.

The traditional Jewish economic role became more and more of a provocation. In 1614–15, Jewish traders in Frankfurt undercut the Lutheran clothmaking guilds by importing cheaper Dutch and English cloth. Lutheran rhetoric whipped up popular fury, scapegoating the Jews for the city's economic misfortunes and leading to the worst riots in the city's history (Israel 1985: 68).

Everywhere Jewish economic activities were being curtailed, leaving only restricted moneylending to the poor (Israel 1985: 23).

The Counter-Reformation would prove just as ferocious in its anti-Semitism. The Reformation had opened a fundamental debate about the meaning of both the Old and New Testaments. At first, especially in Italy, the spirit of the Renaissance infused the debate with an openness and allowed the participation of Jewish scholars. Even popes and cardinals began to take an interest in Hebrew literature. But mainly it was taken for granted that the Jews would lose the argument and that conversion would follow. Panic erupted when a Franciscan friar began agreeing with the Jews, denying Christ and espousing Jewish arguments (Israel 1985: 18). He was burned at the stake in Rome. Word of his martyrdom spread through all the Jewish communities in Europe. Immediately afterwards, in 1553, the pope banned the Talmud, the basis of post-biblical Jewish tradition and law. The general burning of Jewish books was ordered. A policy of ghettoisation was imposed, followed by expulsion. 'Marranos', Portuguese Jews who had been forced to convert to Christianity and who had subsequently reverted to Judaism, were rounded up, tortured and burned alive (Israel 1985: 18–19).

In the same way that the emerging nations seemed to be defining themselves by their exclusion of the Jews, the deep rooted theological insecurities exposed by the Reformation made both sides of the divide in Christianity entrench anti-Jewish sentiment. However devastating this was for Western Europe's Jewish communities – and the mass exodus eastwards was the only feasible response – this phase proved to be remarkably short-lived. An astonishing Jewish religious and economic revival was pending, as the crisis of the Reformation found no satisfactory conclusion as the meaning of modernity in Western Europe began to take clearer shape. But before exploring this, we need to look at the new Jewish refuge in Poland.

THE JEWS OF POLAND

In 1500 there were roughly 30,000 Jews living in Poland. By 1575 the figure had multiplied four or fives times to between 100,000 and 150,000, probably slightly more than Spanish Jewry on the eve of its expulsion. The Jews gravitated to the east of the country, which was much less developed and where the landed magnates wielded undisputed control. The ability to manage estates and tolls and handle long-distance trade was especially in demand. The region was beginning to benefit from Western Europe's appetite for cheap Polish grain, well served by eastern Poland's river network. Most of the new Jewish migrants began to settle in the numerous small towns and villages belonging to these great landlords, creating thousands of small Jewish communities (Israel 1985: 27–9) and giving rise to what became known as the Arenda system.

Essentially this system described arrangements whereby the Polish nobles leased their estates to Jewish management. This extraordinary development meant that Jews literally ran estates, mills and distilleries:

> Jews were thus the main agents ... of a vast traffic encompassing the whole of Europe ... for just as they sold the produce of the land for shipment to Holland and beyond, it was they who distributed the western cloth, salt, wine and luxuries, such as spices and jewellery ...
> ... there was also widespread Jewish involvement in crafts such as soap making, tanning, glazery and fur-processing. (Israel 1985: 30)

This distinctive economic role led to a unique political Jewish development, echoing an earlier phase of Jewish political life in Europe. An annually convened assembly, known as the Council of the Four Lands, was allowed to supervise the entire network of Jewish communities throughout Poland. It dealt with education and religious matters, collected taxes, dealt with poor relief, and administered relations with Polish town councils and the Catholic Church. At first there was a tremendous sense of Jewish emancipation. Nowhere else in Europe was there anything to compare with what amounted to internal Jewish political autonomy or self-rule. Indeed, such was the prestige of the Council of the Four Lands that it sometimes intervened in the affairs of Jewish communities outside Poland (Israel 1985: 185–8).

However, there was an ominous side to this development. There is a curious pattern in Jewish relations with the rulers of the lands on which they settled and it is one that would have to be broken to achieve the final emancipation of the Jews. It is a pattern which traces its origins to the time of Alexander the Great, and continues to this day with the Zionist settlement in Palestine. Jews sell their highly valued skills and services to a ruler in return for a degree of autonomy – traditionally, protection of their religion. However, the services provided sometimes involved oppressive means of exploiting the poor.

There are intriguing parallels between the *cleruch* system in Ptolemaic Egypt (see Chapter 2) and the Arenda system of medieval Poland. Indeed, there is also a parallel with the Zionist system which protects US economic and political interests in the Middle East in return for support for the independence of the Jewish State, which in turn is rooted in the Zionist colonisation of Palestinian land. We will return to this argument in later chapters, but meanwhile we should note that Jewish freedom has always been compromised by the institutionalised 'Jewish middleman role'.

Polish Jewish historiography is surely right when it describes the Arenda system as 'heaven for the Jews, paradise for the nobles, hell for the serfs' (Abramsky et al. 1986: 3). As one of seventeenth-century Poland's leading rabbis, Joel Sirkes, put it: 'The danger was vast from the shouting of the Gentiles in a majority of places, who complain that the Jews reign and rule over them and hold them as do kings and princes' (Levine 1991: 67).

In 1648 the Ukraine exploded. Over half the landed estates there were managed by the Jewish Arenda on behalf of absentee Polish landlords (Levine 1991: 61). Led by Chmielnicki, a minor noble, the Ukrainian peasantry, backed by Cossacks and Crimean Tartars, rose up against Polish rule and its Jewish agents. The targets were the Polish nobility, the Catholic clergy and the Jews who, as they were more numerous than the others, bore the brunt of the losses. Thousands of Jews were killed, and though estimates vary, there is a consensus that nearly 20 per cent of the Jews lost their lives (Abramsky et al. 1986: 5).

The Arenda system everywhere began to stagnate and Polish feudalism sank into an atrophy that would pave the way for the partition of Poland between Russia, Prussia and Austria at the end of the eighteenth century.

Endemic poverty and despair, both economic and spiritual, began to stalk the Jews living in the small towns and villages, nearly as much as the Polish peasants. Many of the pages of *Polin*[4] capture the mood of these times. In Chapter 6 we will see how this history helped shape the emergence of the politics of modernity in Jewish life in Eastern Europe in the nineteenth century.

In the immediate aftermath of the Ukraine massacres, messianic Jewish movements, like that of Shabtai Zvi,[5] erupted. The Hassidic Jewish revivalist movement also has its origins in this period (Abramsky et al. 1986: 5). A new, though limited, migration westwards also began, especially as the Jewish trading economy seemed to be reviving.

JEWISH EMANCIPATION IN WESTERN EUROPE

Gridlock in the Reformation had expressed itself in religious wars within and between countries across the continent. The anti-Semitic fury on both sides abated and independent initiatives for the readmission of the Jews began to surface. In Bohemia by 1577, and especially in Prague, Jews were readmitted and the Jewish community sustained growth. This partly reflected the long 'bohemian' tradition, sceptical of the inner certainties of both Protestantism and Catholicism (Israel 1985: 40), but it also reflected Prague's role in the changing international trading system and the importance of Jewish crafts in jewellery, silver and gold. Within four decades Prague became the largest urban Jewish centre in Christian Europe, outside Rome.

Attitudes towards the Jews were in a state of utter confusion. Venice epitomises this. On the one hand, there was the Venice ghetto, which was surrounded by high walls. The gates were closed from sunset to dawn, so that the Church and State could make sure there was no contact between Jews and Christians in the evening or at night! A Jew discovered outside the ghetto at night without a special permit, would be arrested. On the other hand, in the 1570s, the Venice Board of Trade insisted that the Jews were indispensable to the regional economy, and there was absolutely no question of expulsion (Israel 1985: 57). By the end of the seventeenth century there was considerable Jewish involvement in the city's cloth, grain, salt and olive oil trade – despite a formal ban on Jewish shopkeeping and retailing (Israel 1985: 174–5).

Elsewhere in Italy, the Duke of Savoy recognised the Jews in 1652 'as inventors and introducers of new crafts'. These included tobacco spinning and blending, the manufacture of soap and candles, and even polishing red coral obtained off the Naples and Tunisian coasts (Israel 1985: 180).

This was also a time when the Prussian Crown Prince Frederick could thoroughly enjoy himself at the wedding of the daughter of his 'Court Jew' Kossman Gomperz (Israel 1985: 144).

Lack of space prevents a proper consideration of the extraordinary phenomenon of the 'Court Jew'. Jonathan Israel writes that the age of the Court Jew, 1650–1713, marked the 'zenith of Jewish influence in early modern Europe' (1985: 123). One of their chief functions was extensive involvement in supplying the army during the Thirty Years' War. Their banking skills were also essential to the absolutist German princes, at least for the period when there was Jewish dominance of the gold, silver and other metal trade markets in Central Europe (Israel 1985: 132). Efforts began to integrate at least the Jewish financial elite into the emerging commercial middle classes of the early Western European capitalist economies. As today, aristocratic 'gongs' would help the process. The case of Solomon de Medina is instructive, a Dutch Jew involved in the English diamond and bullion markets, as well as a regular supplier of bread and wagons to the English forces abroad. In 1700, Medina became the first professing Jew to be knighted in England (Israel 1985: 130).

The Jewish trading role had revived because the Western world in general was experiencing unprecedented trading opportunities. But the new capitalist economies were becoming increasingly centred on manufacture rather than trade:

> European states now adopted comprehensively protectionist policies, concentrating on the promotion of manufacturing activities rather than long distance trade. (Israel 1985: 248)

This proved fatal for the Jewish trading communities, which fell into long-term decline. The question now was, could the Jewish communities be integrated into the wider societies.

Still largely scorned by the outside world, and trapped in a web of legal restrictions, these communities, and their economic and religious structures, increasingly came under the spotlight of Jewish reformers. These were men from wealthy families, who began campaigning on behalf of their communities for what today we call human or civil rights. Reform was double-edged. It meant civic, legal, political and full economic emancipation – not least so that all occupations could be open to Jews. But it also meant internal reform within the community. The old trading structure, rather like the medieval rabbinical structure of countless daily instructions concerning personal behaviour, was both an embarrassment and an anachronism. In its heyday, with a small Jewish wealthy elite at its apex and at its base an increasing number of beggars, the trading structure

> resembled a pyramid, the middle strata which consisted of metal deal-ers of Frankfurt, Hamburg and Prague, and the base of which was composed of thousands of poor Jewish peddlers who scoured the towns and the villages of central Europe, buying up old metal and coin, which they fed into the major ghettoes. (Israel 1985: 132)

The leading eighteenth-century Jewish reformer, Moses Mendelssohn, hated it:

> Mendelssohn realized that the gentile community had formed its image of the Jews ... at trade fairs. There the poorer Jews hawked their wares, drove hard bargains, and repelled the Christians by their strange manners and customs ... [He] was prepared to admit that insatiable avarice existed among the 'common rabble' (though he suggested that the Christians were probably responsible). (Meyer 1967: 27)

Mendelssohn was a product of the Enlightenment. His perspective anticipated the demands of the French Revolution. He was an assimilationist, that is to say, he demanded respect for a reformed Judaism in Western European societies where Jews should be accorded full citizens' rights. All the Jewish reform movements, the assimilationists led by Mendelssohn, and later the socialists and the Zionists, agreed that the role of the classic Jewish petty trader, mem-orably described by one writer as the 'walking price list' (Kahan 1986: 24), had to be transformed. In Chapter 6 we will see the tug-of-war between the assimilationists, the socialists and the Zionists about how this should be achieved. But all would agree on the importance of *educating Shylock*.

SHAKESPEARE'S JEW

It was a recent Jewish writer on Jewish economics, Derek Penslar, who posed the question in this way, no doubt as lighthearted irony.

But if there was ever a troubling legacy from one of the greatest writers in world art and literature to our understanding of the 'Jewish
Question' then it is surely Shakespeare's Shylock.

Shylock is the historic and cultural emblem for anti-Semites,
buried deep in popular consciousness: the symbol of the Jew as the
manipulator of other people's money. As Isaac Deutscher reminds
us, the Nazis seized on it, 'magnified it to colossal dimensions, and
constantly held it before the eyes of the masses ... [too many] gleefully watched Shylock led to the gas chamber' (Deutscher 1968:
150–1). Yet the immense power of Shakespeare's play resides in
something far more profound than the lingering stereotype of the
moneylender who demands his 'pound of flesh' from Antonio, the
Merchant of Venice, who defaults on his debt. At a critical moment,
Shakespeare has Shylock make an impassioned defence of his
Jewishness, a challenge to Christianity's humiliations, which turns
into a plea for a common humanity:

> he [Antonio] hath disgrac'd me ... laugh'd at my losses, mock'd at my
> gains, scorned my nation, thwarted my bargains, cooled my friends,
> heated mine enemies, – and what's his reason? I am a Jew. Hath not a
> Jew eyes? Hath not a Jew hands/organs, dimensions, senses, affections,
> passions? ... [are we not] warmed and cooled by the same summer
> and winter as a Christian is? If you prick us do we not bleed? ... (The
> Merchant of Venice, III-i, The Arden Shakespeare 1955: 73)

The introduction to my Arden edition of the play, a highly recommended schools edition, worries that the speech has sometimes
made such an impression on theatre audiences that they forget that
it is a villain speaking! (1955: xi). Of course, the play is overwhelmingly on the side of Antonio, the apparently honourable and
wronged hero. Nevertheless, Shakespeare has sown a seed of doubt
about Shylock's villainy. And is it such a large step away from the
play to see Antonio as representative of a Christianity that had
plunged a thousand knives into Jewish flesh? No wonder the Jew
fights back.

The power of the play is the power of paradox. And paradox
is everywhere. We might despise the moneylender and hail the
merchant, but Jews had also been merchants in Venice before the
city imposed restrictions on them, reducing them to usury. Then, as
we have seen, the city changed its mind. Every city in Europe put
its Jews on the same rollercoaster.

Deutscher captures this paradox beautifully. Shakespeare's England would eventually readmit the Jewish merchant: 'The bourgeois Christian took another look at Shylock and welcomed him as a brother' (Deutscher 1968: 39).

REMBRANDT'S JEW

The transformation of Jewish life in Europe was accelerated by the 'golden age' of the Dutch Republic in the seventeenth century. This corner of north-west Europe had emerged from the bloody religious wars of the continent as both the most advanced economy in the world and as the most tolerant civil society.

The Jews made a major contribution to the booming colonial trades and processing and manufacturing industries; diamonds, tobacco, chocolate and, to a lesser extent, sugar refining (Israel 1985: 179). We also see the emergence of a very modern phenomenon, the Jewish 'proletarian' or worker, in the Dutch tobacco workshops and diamond processing. And something else strange began to happen. In some quarters at least, Jews became popular.

In London's National Gallery, facing Trafalgar Square and, as we shall see, appropriately enough, just twenty minutes' walk from the statue of Oliver Cromwell in Parliament Square, there hangs an Old Testament painting by the Dutch artist Rembrandt, titled *Belshazzar's Feast*.

> The monumental canvas depicts a drunken scene from the [Old Testament] book of Daniel. A mysterious hand inscribes a cryptic message in Hebrew letters. Belshazzar, the last of the Babylonian kings, and his debauched guests, are terrified. Daniel is summoned to decipher the code. Daniel tells Belshazzar, son of Nebuchadnezzar who had sacked the temple at Jerusalem, that it is the hand of God, appalled at the oppression of the Jews, and who will divide up Belshazzar's kingdom between the Medes and the Persians. (Zell 2002: 59–60)

Art historians are now satisfied that Menasseh ben Israel, the Dutch Republic's leading rabbi, helped Rembrandt construct the message in Hebrew letters. Close co-operation between the two men is well known and was typical of a wider movement of dialogue and reconciliation between Christians and Jews, which we now call Philosemitism.

Philosemitism is not the opposite of anti-Semitism. But it certainly implies approval of the Jews, although it holds out hope for Jewish conversion. It also reflected the lasting damage the Reformation had done to Christianity. As Israel has put it: 'To those filled with doubt concerning the claims and official theology of the major churches, the Jews were precious as a lifeline, a thread leading back to the essence of divine revelation ...' (Israel 1985: 228). Philosemitism, as he points out, represented 'a transitional phase preceding the Enlightenment' (Israel 1985: 224).

For much of his life, Rembrandt lived in the heart of Amsterdam's Jewish quarter, just behind the synagogue of Rabbi Menasseh ben Israel. Of his 200 male portraits, nearly a fifth are identified as Jews, a remarkably high percentage as Jews represented little more than one per cent of the city's population. Even in his representations of Christ, he was keen to emphasise Jesus' Jewish features. Rembrandt's art captures a 'solidarity in paint' from 'inside' the mind and body of his subjects (Molyneux 2001: 73–5). Even if deeply veiled in religious mysticism, Rembrandt seems to have put his art at the disposal for breaking down the barrier between Christian and Jew.

It was Rabbi Menasseh ben Israel who led the negotiations with Cromwell to seek the readmission of the Jews to England. The financial benefits to the economy were emphasised, alongside the mystical religious implications. The English Civil War had created a fertile environment for millenarian enthusiasm, and many Protestant groups, including the Puritans, were keenly interested in the special role the Jews would play in the realisation of Messianic expectations (Zell 2002: 92).

Two centuries later, Victorian England would produce a famous prime minister who would be the very embodiment, albeit strictly down to earth and of this earth, of all these earlier efforts at Christian–Jewish reconciliation. Although Benjamin Disraeli had been baptised a Protestant, he remained fascinated by his Jewish heritage. Describing Christianity as 'completed Judaism', he delighted in describing himself as the 'missing page' between the Old and New Testaments (Johnson 1993: 324).

The Dutch Republic also signalled a very different Jewish route to the modern world. A certain Jewish merchant of Amsterdam would turn his back on both the religion and a life of commerce. He was called Baruch Spinoza and he wrote a philosophy that would sound the retreat of both Judaism and Christianity at the dawn of the modern world. Spinoza was one of the greatest Enlightenment thinkers. The modern demand for the separation of religion from state, politics and economics might be said to begin with him. He was also the first of what Deutscher would call 'non-Jewish Jews', Jewish heretics who

> transcend Jewry but who belong to a Jewish tradition, who ... were exceptional in that as Jews they dwelt on the borders of various civilizations ... Their minds matured where the most diverse cultural influences crossed and fertilised each other ... It was this that enabled them to rise above their ... times ... and strike out mentally into wide new horizons and far into the future. (Deutscher 1968: 26–7)

Karl Marx, another famous non-Jewish Jew, was one of the greatest leaders in the struggle for democracy in nineteenth-century Europe (Nimtz 2000: vii), spurred on by the slogans of the French Revolution of 1789. Lobbied by Gabriel Riesser, the leader of the Jewish Emancipation movement in Germany, Marx threw his weight behind Riesser's demands:

> Herr Riesser correctly emphasizes the meaning of the Jews' desire for their free humanity when he demanded, among other things, the freedom of movement, sojourn, travel, earning ones living etc. These manifestations of 'free humanity' are explicitly recognized as such in the French Declaration of the Rights of Man ... (Draper 1977: 127)

The emergence of democracy in Western Europe and North America has guaranteed these rights to Jews in modern times.

'The West', especially America, which today hosts the largest Jewish population in the world, proved to be a magnet for millions of Jews who migrated, at the turn of the nineteenth century, often from conditions of extreme poverty in Eastern Europe. These Jews have proved themselves to be the most successful of ethnic minorities in terms of any measure of equal opportunities and social mobility. A majority of Jews might today reasonably describe themselves as belonging to the professional middle classes and be rightly proud of their many outstanding contributions to the arts, sciences, education, medicine, journalism, politics and, not least, commerce. This success story has proved possible not only because of the resilience needed to protect their religious independence, but also because of the 'commercial and artisan character of Judaism, heritage of a long historical past' (Leon 1970: 236) that developed in the urban context of the civilisations of the Middle East and Europe. Yes, there was suffering, but this tells us only part of the story about the extraordinary economic and intellectual ingenuity, developed over the many centuries. Hopefully, this chapter has done a little to redress the balance.

Finally, an undeniable objection might be lodged that where democracy has broken down, as in Nazi Germany, anti-Semitism has returned with an unimagined and terrible vengeance. We will consider the Nazi period later but we will also turn to how intense anti-Jewish feeling is also fuelled when Jews deny democracy to others in the land they claim exclusively belongs to them.

4
'Us' Jews, 'Them' Arabs I:
A Message from a
Cairo Synagogue, a Thousand
Years Ago

Zionism has forced Arabs and Jews apart in a way that runs against the grain of the long history of Islamic Arab civilisation. This is such an important and misunderstood aspect of the argument against Zionism that it will be taken up again in Chapter 10. This chapter will examine Arab–Jewish relations at the height of Islamic civilisation, approximately between the tenth and thirteenth centuries. The final chapter will examine these relations in the modern period, as the backcloth to understanding how Arab–Jewish reconciliation might be achieved. Both chapters challenge the fundamentalist Zionist myth that Arabs and Jews are so different (which usually implies that Arabs are inferior) that they cannot live together.

The majority of Jews lived in Arab countries until 500 years ago. In Israel today, over a million of its Jewish citizens originate from the Muslim countries of the Middle East and North Africa. A small but significant number of these Jews, some of whom describe themselves as Arab Jews, are determined to set the record straight. Here is part of a particularly eloquent testimony:

My personal narrative questions the Eurocentric opposition of Arab and Jew, particularly the denial of Arab Jewish (Sephardic) voices. I am an Arab Jew. Or, more specifically, an Iraqi Israeli woman living, writing and teaching in the U.S. Most members of my family were born and raised in Baghdad. When my grandmother first encountered Israeli society in the '50s, she was convinced that the people who looked, spoke and ate so differently – the European Jews – were actually European Christians. For her generation was inextricably associated with Middle Easterness. My grandmother, who still lives in Israel and still communicates largely in Arabic, had to be taught to speak of 'us' as Jews and 'them' as Arabs. For Middle Easterners, the operating distinction had always been 'Muslim', 'Jew' and 'Christian', not Arab versus Jew. The assumption was that 'Arabness' referred to a common shared culture and language, albeit with religious differences. If you go to our synagogues, even in New York, Montreal, Paris or London, you'll be amazed to hear the winding quarter tones of our music which the uninitiated might imagine to be coming from a mosque. For our families, who have lived in Mesopotamia since at least the Babylonian exile, who have been Arabized for millennia, and who were abruptly dislodged to Israel 45 years ago, to be suddenly forced to assume a homogeneous European Jewish identity based on experiences in Russia, Poland and Germany, was an exercise in self-devastation. This binarism has led many Oriental Jews (our name in Israel referring to our common Asian and African countries of origin is Mizrahi or Mizrachi) to a profound and visceral schizophrenia. As Iraqi Jews, while retaining a communal identity, we were generally well integrated and indigenous to the country, forming an inseparable part of its social and cultural life. Thoroughly Arabized, we used Arabic even in hymns and religious ceremonies. The liberal and secular trends of the twentieth century engendered an even stronger association of Iraqi Jews and Arab culture, which brought Jews into an extremely active arena in public and cultural life ...

Even our physiognomies betray us, leading to internalized colonialism or physical misperception. Sephardic Oriental women often dye their dark hair blond, while the men have more than once been arrested or beaten when mistaken for Palestinians. What for Ashkenazi immigrants from Russia and Poland was a social *aliya* (literally 'ascent') was for Oriental Sephardic Jews a *yerida* ('descent'). (Ella Habiba Shohat, Professor of Cultural Studies and Women's Studies, City University of New York)

Professor Shohat is a member of the Mizrahi Artists and Writers International. Their web-site is full of similar testimonies. It also includes a 'Sephardi Survival List', a recommended reading list which amounts to a full-frontal challenge to the Zionist conception of Jewish identity. Its most highly recommended book is the five-volume masterpiece, *A Mediterranean Society: The Jewish Communities of the Arab World as Portrayed in the Documents of the Cairo Geniza* by Shelomo D. Goitein.

As magisterial as scholarship gets, Goitein reconstructs the world of the Arab Jewish communities of the Levant with painstaking accuracy and erudite brilliance. Their world has never been, and will never be, as fully illuminated: one of the greatest feats of scholarship in this, or any other century. (http://www.ivri-nasawi.org)

INTRODUCING THE *GENIZA*

The rest of this chapter will be devoted to Professor Goitein's studies:[1] but first some introductory remarks and an outline of the historical context.

The Cairo *Geniza* was a room or storage space, full of documents, in an eleventh-century Cairo synagogue. *Geniza* is a Hebrew word, similar to the Arabic *janaza* ('burial'), and both derive from the Persian *ganj*, meaning a storehouse or treasure. For hundreds of years, the documents were forgotten, left in a room, sealed from view, until their discovery in the late nineteenth century.

Goitein describes them as a 'repository of discarded writings', deposited by Jewish merchants, scholars, craftsmen and others. However serious, however trivial, they wrote God's name on them. This meant that in the minds of the people, 'after having served their purpose, they should not be destroyed' (Goitein 1999 I: 1). Thus the *Geniza* preserved a unique historical record:

> Alongside carefully worded and magnificently executed deeds, one finds hastily written notes, accounts or letters, jotted down in nearly illegible script and in sloppy or faulty language. The very shortcomings of the *Geniza*, however, constitute it uniqueness and its glory. It is a true mirror of life, often cracked and blotchy, but very wide in scope and reflecting each and every aspect of the society that originated it. (Goitein 1999 I: 9)

Jewish communities in this period were an integral part of an Islamic culture in an empire which achieved extraordinary prosperity and influence. As the modern Arab historian Albert Hourani has noted, it extended

> across the two great sea basins of the civilised world, the Mediterranean and the Indian Ocean. The movement of armies, merchants, scholars, pilgrims between them became easier, and also that of their ideas, styles and techniques ... strong governments, large cities, international

trade and a flourishing countryside maintaining the conditions for each other's existence. (Hourani 1991: 43)

Bernard Lewis, a modern writer on Islam, and an intellectual sometimes criticised for viewing Islam through the distorted prism of Western culture,[2] has provided powerful confirmation of what he calls the 'symbiosis' of Arabs and Jews at this period in Islamic history. He describes a highly successful *Islamic* Jewish tradition, 'a shared cultural frame of reference, that made possible a degree ... of co-operation that is comparatively rare in the history of the Jewish diaspora' (Lewis 1984: 78). (Lewis cites a possible explanation from Goitein for the decline in Islamic tolerance: a rolling backwards from embryonic bourgeois society to a form of military feudalism; Lewis 1984: 57.)

A wonderful introduction – part-subversive history, part-travel writing, part-detective story – to the *Geniza*, is provided by the Indian writer Amitav Ghosh. In *In an Antique Land*, Ghosh goes in search of an Indian slave of a Tunisian Jewish merchant, Ben Abraham Ben Yiju, who lived in Mangalore, a port on the southwestern coast of India, nearly 1,000 years ago. The *Geniza* letter, which fired Ghosh's investigative imagination, was written by a Muslim merchant friend of Ben Yiju, Khalaf ibn Ishaq, who was based in Aden, 'that port which sits like a fly on a funnel, on the precise point where the narrow spout of the Red Sea opens into the Indian Ocean' (Ghosh 1992: 13).

Ghosh's book faithfully reflects the spirit of the *Geniza* in that nothing is quite as it first appears. Ben Yiju is not just a merchant, he is also a distinguished calligrapher, scholar and poet (Ghosh 1992: 19) and, according to another letter from Khalaf, Ben Yiju's Indian slave, whom Ghosh calls Bomma, turns out to be Ben Yiju's 'business agent and a respected member of his household' (Ghosh 1992: 18). This is a strange combination to our modern eyes, made stranger by the probability that Bomma converted to Judaism and that Bomma, Ben Yiju and perhaps Khalaf too shared a common fascination with the Sufi traditions of Islam. Ghosh's exploration of these themes (1992: 259–63), is beyond the scope of this chapter, although, as we will see, the *Geniza* throws a surprising light on the impact of Sufism on medieval Judaism in Cairo.

There is clearly a very special history about this period still to be uncovered. Meanwhile the *Geniza* has begun to inspire the novelist's imagination, with both Salman Rushdie and Tariq Ali, among others, soaking up its atmosphere.

THE *GENIZA*, ISLAM AND THE MERCHANT'S ECONOMY

Goitein's penetrating study of the *Geniza* turned him inadvertently into an authority on the wider Islamic Arab economy. Janet Abu-Lughod, in her award-winning book, *Before European Hegemony (The World System AD 1250–1350)*, quotes his observations about a potentially highly sensitive area, the modalities connecting Islam itself to the booming merchant's economy at the heart of empire.

Islam had raised the status of the merchants of Arabia, morally endorsing their contribution to society. 'The income of the honest merchant', wrote Goitein, 'is regarded in Muslim religious literature as a typical example of *halal*, as earnings free of religious objections. In addition, the merchant was particularly able to fulfil all the duties incumbent on a Muslim (prayer, study of religious books)' (Abu-Lughod 1989: 217).

From its very inception, the pilgrimage to Mecca was associated with the great transcontinental trade and remained so throughout the Middle Ages. The standing wish for a Muslim pilgrim was: 'May your *hajj* be accepted, your sin be forgiven and your merchandise not remain unsold' (Goitein 1999 I: 55).

This is also the period when Shariah law developed as a progressive approach to justice and rules governing business and personal conduct. As Harman has noted, it is almost impossible to recognise this now, given the abuse heaped on the Shariah today in the West. But the Shariah system was well in advance of the value systems of the Christian agrarian feudal empires which competed with it. Harman quotes one scholarly study of Islam which recognises its 'egalitarian expectations of relative mobility ... which maintained its autonomy as against the agrarian empires' (Harman 1999: 130).

The Middle East and Far East trading economy required and developed a highly sophisticated warehousing, banking and credit system characterised by all kinds of business partnerships (Abu-Lughod 1989: 222–30), as confirmed by documentation lodged in the *Geniza*. It required transcontinental, that is, universally agreed, values and rules for its operation. To take just one of many examples cited by Abu-Lughod, European bankers did not develop a proper 'bill of exchange' until the fourteenth century. Yet its Persian precursor, the *suftaja*, had been in use for several centuries in the Middle East. 'As a rule', writes Goitein, '*suftajas* were issued and drawn up by well-known bankers or representatives of merchants, a fee was charged for their issue, and after presentation a daily penalty had to be paid for any delay in payment' (Abu-Lughod 1989: 223–4).

A fascinating question, which forms the basis of Abu-Lughod's book, is why this mercantile system did not develop into a fully fledged capitalist system, and thus pre-empt Western Europe. Tempting though it is, we cannot travel down that road here, though let us at least endorse her thesis that its influence on Western Europe's economic development has been conspicuously understated and under-researched. In fact, although large-scale investment was rare, there was nevertheless an impressive array of 'manufactured' goods in Egypt, produced not in large factories but small workshops (Abu-Lughod 1989: 230–1). Here workers owned their own tools and often combined the activities of manufacture and sales, which incidentally could blur the distinction between artisan and merchant. Among the industries of Cairo Goitein lists are workshops for metallurgy and metal objects, including military hardware, glass and pottery, leather tanning and the fabrication of leather objects, parchment, paper, bookbinding, construction, stone-cutting, furniture manufacture, and food preparation and processing. In addition, there were large plants, *mataabakhs* (literally kitchens), in which sugar was refined or paper made. These were usually owned by the sultans and employed relatively large numbers of workers. Textile manufacture and distribution was the dominant 'industry'.

Little wonder that Al-Muqaddasi, the first ruler of the Fatimid dynasty in the tenth century, who built Al-Qahirah (later Europeanised to 'Cairo') could proclaim the city as

> the glory of Islam and the centre of world commerce … it has effaced Baghdad … the fruits of Syria and al-Maghrib [North Africa], reach it in all seasons, and travellers are ever coming to it … from the eastern countries, and the ships of the peninsular and of the countries of Rum [Byzantium/Europe] … (Abu-Lughod 1989: 225)

Little wonder too that the invading European crusader armies should eye it so enviously.

SALADIN AND THE CRUSADES

The period of the *Geniza* is divided roughly between two dynasties, the Fatimids (founded 969) and Saladin's Ayyubids (concluded roughly 1250). A critical date is 1168, when Saladin helped rescue Cairo from the crusaders. Goitein describes Saladin, the epoch's greatest leader, as a genius. The Jews at the time famously hailed him as their saviour, the new Cyrus (Armstrong 1996: 298). When the crusaders captured Jerusalem, they slaughtered all the Jews and the Muslims in the city. Saladin drove the crusaders out, liberated Jerusalem and invited Jews to return there.

The symbolism of this momentous event echoes down the centuries to us and requires no further comment. It is a fitting complement to the 'spirit' of the *Geniza* unearthed by Goitein.

Let us turn now to a more detailed examination of Jews in the Islamic Arab world as reflected in the *Geniza*.

'GLOBALISATION'

An early indication of the tolerance of the Fatimids, and indeed the spirit of the times, is reflected in the biography of Ibn Killis. Ya'quib Ibn Killis was a Jewish merchant from Iraq who lived for a while in Ramle in Palestine, before moving to Egypt. He became a representative of the merchants in Cairo and caught the attention of the Fatimid rulers. They were keen to employ his talents in government service and appoint him as vizier, or chief government representative. Ibn Killis had to convert to Islam in order to be accepted, but made it clear that religion should not be an obstacle to government appointments. As vizier he earned a reputation for employing both his former co-religionists and Christians 'to the highest positions' (Goitein 1999 I: 34).

Reading Goitein, a very modern word inescapably lodges itself in the mind. He was probably not familiar with the word, as he died in the 1980s, though he would immediately recognise the idea it describes: globalisation. Of course it's not really global. But the internationalisation of the peoples and the goods they made and traded has uncanny similarities with today.

Consider two typical *Geniza* Jews, a Tunisian trader and a Persian upholsterer in Cairo.

In a letter written in 1085, and deposited in the Cairo *Geniza*, the Tunisian reports a sale to a European in a Palestinian seaport of brazilwood, one of the most popular commodities traded at the time. (The name of the wood refers to a brazier; it is a wood of flaming colour, grown in the East Indies, from which a valuable red dye was made.) Several traders, including this one, report excellent profits to be made from dealing with Europeans, who apparently lacked the trading skills of their Mediterranean partners! (1999 I: 45–6).

Upholstery from Tabaristan, which Goitein describes as the beautiful Persian province south of the Caspian sea, was famous throughout the empire, so much so that the province gave its name to this particular type of upholstery. It was so widely reproduced in Egypt that insistence on genuine Tabaristans was expressly stipulated in marriage contracts discovered in the *Geniza*! But there is an interesting copyright ambiguity here that might equally exercise a twenty-first-century legal mind. When was a Tabaristan not a Tabaristan? It seems that some Persian Jewish and Muslim upholsterers, having acquired their skill in Tabaristan, then migrated westwards. This is corroborated by the fact that many people in Egypt and Tunisia had Persian names (Goitein 1999 I: 50).

Often, an almost throwaway line from Goitein throws extraordinary light on the highly sophisticated international economic relations between Europe and the Middle East, Christians, Muslims and Jews, rich and poor. We want to know more, but there is no more. We have a single, documented fact, a passing reference in a letter or business document. Thus, we learn that nearly 1,000 years ago Jewish and Muslim traders imported cheese from Europe, which was the protein staple of the Egyptian poor (1999 I: 46).

We also learn that the Islamic world took for granted a principle that is claimed today as a modern liberal principle although it is never practised – that free trade should always be accompanied by the free movement of peoples, whatever their creed or colour. Modern politicians should pay close attention to Islamic attitudes to immigration, which appear far more civilised than our own.

As the crusades gathered pace, there was an increasing Jewish migration from Christian Europe, especially France, to the Islamic world, which imposed no restrictions on them:

> Nowhere has a hint been found that the Egyptian government impeded this flow of people from a country whose rulers, as the events of 1219 and 1249 showed, were intent on the conquest of Egypt itself. (1999 I: 67).

Indeed, it was a topsy-turvy world 1,000 years ago. This was also the case in the Jewish community itself. The Jewish European poor migrant needed financial help from the Jewish community in Cairo, according to the *Geniza* records. By contrast, the Yemenite Jewish merchants, craftsmen and scholars in the city are listed as contributors to the public purse (1999 I: 57). Unfortunately, the ironies that captivate the attention of the modern critical Jewish reader cannot be explored here.

The taken-for-granted freedom of travel cut across the three religions: 'Reading the *Geniza* letters, one forgets political boundaries existed at all' (1999 I: 60). And economically-driven travellers were by no means the only ones. Goitein describes the phenomenon of the 'wandering scholar' and a freedom of inquiry at least within religion's limitations. Thus we hear of a Jewish judge from Sicily who travelled in Egypt, Palestine and finally to Baghdad, where, he studied the psalms with the Jewish community's most respected scholar. One psalm puzzled both of them, so they approach the head of the Nestorian Church. Goitein remarks how unexpected it was to discover 'such co-operation ... in Baghdad nine hundred and fifty years ago' (1999 I: 52).

It seems books, ideas, erudition and tastes travelled widely too.

> In Mayence, the ancient Roman town on the banks of the Rhine, it was possible, in the tenth century, to find not only all the more important spices of India and the Far East, but also a man able to translate a book of instructions for bible cantillation from Arabic into Hebrew – and this fact is by no means stated as something extraordinary. (1999 I: 64)

Such an exchange of ideas can also incite fear and intolerance. Thus we read that French Jews burned books written by the Islamic world's most famous Jewish philosopher, Maimonides (1999 I: 64).

Jewish religious scholars travelled widely to take up appointments, whether in renowned centres of learning at Cairo, Jerusalem or Baghdad, or as teachers, judges and religious leaders in towns and villages throughout the empire. 'Not a single instance has been found of government ... interference' (1999 I: 66).

Of course calamities, war, especially the crusades, and upheavals created by Muslim dynasties, which harassed Muslims from different tendencies as well as non-Muslims (and we will return to this matter later), also drove the movements of peoples.

In general, such mobility was taken for granted, a way of resolving problems: 'a change in domicile brings good luck'. We read in the *Geniza* of the blind singer who preferred begging en route to somewhere rather than staying at home. Finally, there was always another reason to leave home, albeit one that carries the risk of an accusation of sexism. But I hope that Goitein's humour here will be accepted as a reason not to censor this rather unusual example of symbiosis between Muslim and Jewish men:

> Indelicate as it might sound, it must be conceded that running away as far as possible from one's wife was practised as vigorously by the people represented in the *Geniza*, as by the husbands in the stories of the *Arabian Nights*. (1999 I: 58)

However, despite all these examples of what Goitein describes as 'cosmopolitanism', he is at pains to insist that what he calls 'local patriotism' (1999 I: 64) was just as important to the people of the *Geniza*.

'HOMELAND'

Here we come to the one of the most fascinating issues of all in the *Geniza* documents. It is clear, beyond a shadow of doubt, that the Jewish people of the Islamic Arab civilisation, as represented in the *Geniza*, the Jewish majority at the time, the people, let us remember, who carried the Jewish religious tradition from biblical times to the present day, had their own, very definite conception of 'homeland', which contrasts sharply with the debates of modern times.

One senses that Goitein is aware of the controversy. Although he does not bring a modern political critique to the surface, he is pre-occupied with the relationship between the Jewish communities in Islamic Arab lands and 'homeland'. He returns to the issue on three occasions in the five volumes. He describes the 'extremely delicate' (1999 IV: 40) character of the evidence. He engages sophisticated arguments and marshals evidence to persuade the reader to start thinking about concepts like 'homeland' and 'nation' in an entirely different way. He is basically asking us to jettison contemporary versions and think it through as if in the mind of the *Geniza* Jew. He doesn't say so, but it seems that the modern versions are not to be considered as more 'progressive'. On the contrary, it could reasonably be argued that the medieval Islamic Arab and Jewish concepts of 'nation' and 'homeland' are more progressive than our own.

Let us join Goitein as he introduces these ideas. Whilst it is the case that Islam considers Christianity and Judaism incapable of grasping complete religious truth, and this meant that religious discrimination was always a possibility, at least in the period we are discussing, this was rarely an important issue. True, non-Muslims had to pay a special poll tax, but this was accepted as an inevitable burden. It created much less tension than the modern mind might expect. It was an argument with the tax-collecting authorities, but you would not blame your Muslim neighbour, fellow Muslim craftsman or Muslim business partner. Here we come to the distinction between nation, *umma*,[3] and homeland, *watan*. The Muslim, Christian and Jewish communities each formed a separate nation, *umma*. It supervised most aspects of daily conduct, in the personal, religious and legal sense: 'At the root of all this was the concept that law was personal and not territorial. An individual was judged according to the law of his religious community, or even religious school or sect, rather than that of the territory in which he happened to be' (1999 I: 66). Goitein goes so far as to say that with the exception of some local statutes, the states as such 'did not possess any law': 'For the Jews of Spain or France to seek "High Court decisions" in Jerusalem or Baghdad, or later, with Maimonides and his successor in Cairo, was the normal and natural thing to do.'

But the different religious communities shared a homeland, a dwelling place, *watan*. 'Whilst it was natural to be treated differently as a member of a different religion, it was revolting to be discriminated against as a permanent resident of the same country' (1999 II: 274). Goitein explains this by giving what he calls a 'beautiful' illustration in a passage from a letter written by a Jewish judge from Barqa, in eastern Libya, living in Alexandria, to a friend in Cairo. He had intended to join his friend and make a pilgrimage to Jerusalem, but the route was unsafe, the winter was cold 'and our judge was clearly homesick'. He was tempted to go home to Barqa instead. In his letter he describes how he has already paid the fare for himself and his goods, on the caravan setting off that very day. He would be the only Jew. In the letter, he describes how the other travellers, mostly fellow Barqis, 'have promised me to be considerate with regard to the watering places and the keeping of the Sabbath and similar matters'. Goitein comments that apart from his trust in God, it was the fact of travelling in the company of *compatriots* that gave this lonely Jew the sense that he would be safe (1999 II: 274).

A little later in the same section, Goitein observes how the inevitable tendency to exclusivity in any religion, because of its claim to have found the only path to God, is undermined 'when people of different religious allegiance mix closely'. They discover 'that the *invisible republic* of decent men [and women] stretches beyond the barriers of religion, party and race ...' This *invisible republic* should not be seen as homespun, indulgent philosophising on Goitein's part. On the contrary, his very next sentence makes it clear that he is generalising from decades of studying the *Geniza* documents. He had come across, and quotes, only two critical letters, one of a Muslim and a Christian respectively:

> The astonishing fact about the *Geniza* is that quotations like the two given are so rare. As a matter of fact, thus far I have not come across any others of the same type, and nowhere else are Christians and Muslims as a group cursed or even spoken of detractively. (1999 II: 276)

In his earlier volume, Goitein had quoted an Arab proverb making the same point. In fact his whole paragraph is worth reproducing:

> in this period Jews mingled freely with their neighbours and, therefore, cannot have been much different from them. For, as the Arab proverb has it, *people are more akin to their contemporaries than they are to their own forefathers.* It stands to reason that a twelfth-century Jewish doctor, who worked in a government hospital in Cairo or Aleppo, was in most respects representative of the medical profession of his time in general, while a Jewish glassmaker or silk-weaver, or metal founder would use the same techniques and occupy the same social position as his Christian or Muslim fellow workers. Mutual help, as expressed in small, but not too small, loans, is attested in the *Geniza* as prevailing as between members of different faiths but of similar professions. (1999 I: 71)

Muslims, Christians and Jews lived 'in close proximity to one another, to a far higher degree than one would have assumed on the basis of our literary sources' (1999 II: 289). Jewish 'quarters' are rarely mentioned in the *Geniza*. The close inter-faith relations, particularly in old Cairo, are evidenced by the fact that houses and shops were held in partnership by members of different religious communities (1999 II: 292). In Jerusalem too we read about a house or compound (in about 1040) where some rooms belonged to a Muslim and others to a Jew. Of course, doubts and difficulties could easily arise. Can you share the same well? Muslim women were secluded in a way that Jewish women were not. Special privacy arrangements had to be put in place. No doubt, countless informal arrangements were made. But when in doubt, you could appeal to the appropriate religious authorities.

Maimonides legally approved the following query concerning Muslim/Jewish partnerships in workshops, in one case a goldsmiths, the other glassmakers. 'What does our master say. They have agreed amongst themselves, that gains made on a Friday should go to the Jews and those on a Saturday to the Muslims' (1999 II: 296). Indeed, the Jewish authorities threatened a Jewish carpenter with a flogging when he tried to make a profit from his Muslim workmen making doors on a Saturday (1999 II: 297).

Returning to the idea of *watan* in a later volume, Goitein describes it as meaning 'home town' or city as much as 'homeland'. This seems a better translation. He offers the following interesting distinction. Homeland implied a country and 'countries were political complexes often changing their borders and characters, cities were *units of life*' (1999 IV: 42). Clearly nationalism, including Jewish nationalism, had yet to be conceived. What Goitein is describing is the emotional attachment to one's birthplace and/or a place where you have lived for many years and/or immediate and extended family and/or networks of friends/neighbours/working colleagues of whatever faith.

But this has religious implications which cut across the *umma/watan* dichotomy. These are religious people and they needed God's blessing in all the areas of their lives. There is a biblical phrase 'May the Most High establish her forever' to be used exclusively for the Holy City of Jerusalem. But Goitein came across a *Geniza* letter where the writer had applied the same blessing to Cairo.

That other biblical phrase, *the inheritance of my fathers*, one might imagine was reserved for the Holy City of Jerusalem. On the contrary, Goitein came across letter-writing Jewish pilgrims, temporarily resident in Jerusalem, yet pining for that inheritance in an unexpected way: 'May the Creator of the World presently let us meet together in joy, when I return under his guidance to my homeland and the inheritance of my fathers,' writes a pilgrim in Jerusalem to a friend or relative in his native Morocco (1999 I: 63).

Goitein describes other blessings attached to towns and cities. He then develops the argument that in later centuries it became common practice for Jewish letter-writers to attach blessings to the congregation rather than the city. The change 'reflected [a] deterioration of relations between the various religious communities' (1999 IV: 42). The implication is clear and is something that can stir the emotions in even the most modern and secular minds. In the period of the *Geniza* many Jews were ready to ask God to bless their Muslim and Christian neighbours.

Goitein describes how 'yearning after one's home', *al-hanin ila 'l-watan*, was a great topic too in ancient Arabic poetry. It was embedded in the culture, irrespective of religion. The *Geniza* letter-writers use the Arabic word *baladiyya* to describe their feelings and concern for the inhabitants of one's town. A Jewish dignitary from the Maghreb, writing to the Egyptian Jewish authorities about a Muslim merchant neighbour who was murdered on his way to the Yemen, comments, 'He was my *baladina* and I am particularly concerned about him' (1999 IV: 45).

Goitein concludes this section with great flourish and symbolism. He shows similarities between remarks about city life in the Talmud, the vital source-book of Jewish biblical commentary, and the writings of Al-Sha'rani, a great Muslim mystic, who thanks God for his 'exodus', by the Prophet's blessing, from the countryside to Cairo. '*Geniza* man was an eminently social being', who would sign up to the 'ancient Near Eastern maxim: *Good company or death*' (1999 IV: 47).

RELIGIOUS TENSIONS

Did anti-Jewish sentiment exist at all in this period? Yes it did, and the *Geniza* has a special word for it: *sin'uth*, 'hatred'. However the 'phenomenon is nowhere referred to as general; it is mentioned throughout in connection with certain groups, towns or persons' (1999 II: 278). It was much in evidence in Alexandria, but nowhere in Cairo. The most conspicuous illustration of religious difference was supposed to be the enforced wearing by non-Muslims of a badge of a different colour, belt or headgear. Countless references are found in Arabic literary sources. However, Goitein was unable to find a single reference to it in the *Geniza*, despite a constant preoccupation with clothing. He came to the conclusion that the ruling had been dropped or at least was ignored (1999 II: 286).

The one area where Islam would clash bitterly with the other religions was over conversion. The poll tax could be seen as an instrument to encourage conversion. Goitein emphasises the worry that the poll tax gave the people of the *Geniza*:

> Whereas, in high circles, the prospects of appointments to leading government posts acted as an inducement for embracing Islam, mass conversions in the lower classes might well have been caused in part by the intolerable burden of the poll tax. (1999 II: 392–3)

Goitein found no evidence of mass conversion for this particular period, but 'a very considerable section of the non-Muslim population must have been unable to pay it [the poll tax] and often suffered humiliation and privation on its account'. In the later period, religious harassment, no doubt combined with these economic pressures, did indeed result in mass conversions.

Conversion was a very serious matter. A Muslim converting to Judaism faced the death sentence. Nevertheless, Maimonides openly favoured proselytising and the *Geniza* contains two letters from him to new converts from Islam, who had to emigrate to avoid putting their lives at risk. Intriguingly, most of the converts to Judaism mentioned in the *Geniza* are European Christians (1999 II: 304).

Whilst it would be foolish and misleading to ignore this bleaker and more problematic side of Jewish life in medieval Islamic society, the balance of the *Geniza* is overwhelmingly positive.

SCIENCE AND THE SPIRIT OF THE AGE

A unique measure not just of Jewish success, but of a very special contribution to Islamic Arab civilisation at this time, is provided by the really impressive participation of Jews in the medical profession.

Private correspondence preserved in the *Geniza* 'abounds in references to medical advice sought and often paid for with one's last penny'. In the *Geniza* papers, 'we find a Jewish doctor, and often more than one, in many a little town or large village and occasionally Christian and Muslim colleagues are mentioned as well' (1999 II: 241).

Thirteenth-century police records complain that many towns had only Christian or Jewish physicians. And the Christian and Jewish contributions to Arabic medical texts were out of all proportion to their numbers. The first Fatimid caliph to rule Egypt and the neighbouring countries had a Jewish physician, Moses b. Elazar. Moses, an Italian Jew who had been seized by Muslim raiders and taken to

Tunisia, had developed 'marvellous concoctions which had wrought wonders' in Tunisia (1999 II: 243). He was so successful that he was able to develop a family dynasty of physicians; two of his sons, one grandson and a great grandson all served the caliphs. Goitein describes how the Jewish communities themselves invariably had physicians as their leaders.

The most famous Jewish physician leader of his community was Moses Maimonides, who was also a physician to Saladin. Goitein is in awe of his son, Abraham, also physician to the caliph (a note in the *Geniza* from a fellow Muslim physician praises his excellent medical skills) and pays tribute to him with a detailed biographical sketch.

Abraham was an immensely complex figure. Goitein writes that he stood for 'everything regarded as praiseworthy' in *Geniza* society. On the one hand, he was deeply steeped in every aspect of Judaism, 'a paradigm of learned orthodoxy' (1999 V: 475). On the other, he 'deeply admired the Muslim mystics, the Sufis, and went as far as to say that some of them were worthier disciples of the Prophets of Israel than many of the Jews of his day' (1999 V: 478). He was also 'devoted to science with a fervour bordering on faith' (1999 V: 475).

Whilst Abraham's fascination with Sufism, and his willingness to make such an outrageous declaration, intrigues, it was his profound belief in science, and the principle it upheld, that ultimately matters more to us:

> The medieval doctors of the Mediterranean were the torchbearers of secular erudition, the professional expounders of philosophy and the sciences. While the lawyers studied and applied the sacred laws of their religions, and therefore were limited in outlook by their very profession, the physicians were the disciples of the Greeks, and as heirs to a universal tradition formed a spiritual brotherhood that transcended the barriers of religion, language and countries.
>
> Their noble calling as exponents of the sciences would perhaps not have sufficed to bestow upon the medical profession the halo of social prestige it enjoyed in the period studied in this book. For the main concern of man in those days was religion, and consequently it was excellence in this field that was honoured most. [Yet] the physician had another feather in his cap. Almost any doctor of distinction was also a member of the entourage of a caliph, a sultan, a vizier, a general or a governor. He shared the glory of the great of his world without being involved in their crimes and their hateful ways of oppression.

Why did medieval rulers, many of whom were soldiers with only scant education, care to attract so many physicians to their courts? The answer is that even those rough soldiers could not escape the spirit of their age. In those times the immense belief in books, in ancient books in particular, prevailed, and it was the doctors who knew the books. The more doctors around, the more knowledge was available, and the better the prospects for its successful use. (1999 II: 241)

'Even those rough soldiers could not escape the spirit of their age ...'

It is worth reminding ourselves, as we conclude this chapter, that the spirit of the age was rooted in the Islamic revolution that had taken place several centuries earlier. One is struck by the similarities of Goitein's remarks, based, at least in part, upon his absorption in the *Geniza* and his implicit pride in medieval Judaism's contribution, with those of Arab historian, Albert Hourani, whose *History of the Arab Peoples* is also high up on the Arab Jewish, Mizrahi Artists and Writers' International 'Sephardi Survival (reading) List'.

Discussing the translation of Greek philosophy in Arabic, and commenting on the impact of Iranian and Indian influences, Hourani writes:

The motives ... may have been partly practical; medical skill was in demand, and control over natural forces could bring power and success. There was also, however, a wider intellectual curiosity, such as is expressed in the words of al-Kindi (801–66), the thinker with whom the history of Islamic philosophy virtually begins:

'We should not be ashamed to acknowledge truth from whatever source it comes to us, even if it is brought to us from former generations and foreign peoples. For him who seeks truth there is nothing of higher value than truth itself.'

(Hourani 1991: 76–7)

5

'A Land without People ...'

According to a powerful Zionist myth, Palestine was 'a land without people', and hence was particularly suitable 'for a people without land', especially when they could claim it as the 'land of their forefathers'. Whether the Jews were really a 'people without land' will be addressed in the next chapter.

This chapter is about Palestinian peasants who, for centuries, had lived in that empty land. How can that be? Were the Zionists simply lying? Somehow people were there and not there at the same time. Here is Israel's Labour prime minister, Shimon Peres, in 1986:

> The land to which they [the Jewish settlers] came, while indeed the Holy Land, was desolate and uninviting; a land that had been laid waste, thirsty for water, filled with swamps and malaria, lacking in natural resources. And in the land itself there lived another people; a people who neglected the land, but who lived on it. Indeed the return to Zion was accompanied by ceaseless violent clashes with the small Arab population ... (Said 1988: 5)

Well, yes, there were people there, though a people without a name; a 'small' number, who had in any case 'neglected' the land.

The second Zionist Congress, held in 1898 in Basle, had heard a rather different story, that there were 650,000 Arabs living on the 'most fertile parts of "our" land' (Gilbert 1998: 17).

In fact, in recent years there have been some rather more honest accounts from a small number of mainstream Zionists. One of the most interesting is the former deputy mayor of Jerusalem, Meron Benvenisti, whose book, *Sacred Landscape: The Buried History of the Holy Land since 1948* (2000), exposes the ruthless ideological manipulation of the Zionist map-makers and their role in concealing Palestinian peasant villages. His father was one of them and, as a boy, Benvenisti accompanied him on his map-making expeditions. The experience continues to haunt him and is well captured in his book:

> I recall the first time I felt the tragedy of the Palestinians penetrate my Zionist shield. Five years after the [1948] war ... measuring underground water levels, I went to inspect the village well of Rana, near Beit Jibrin. I remembered the place from a trip with my father, and the desolation – the empty houses still standing, the ghost of a village once bustling with life – stunned me. I sat with my back against an old water trough and wondered where the villagers were and what they were feeling.

Benvenisti was to find out 15 years later after the Israeli occupation of Jerusalem in the 1967 war. He visited a refugee camp near the city and met a survivor from Rana:

> Suddenly I saw before my eyes the geography of my childhood ... I could not share their sense of loss, but I could and did share deep nostalgia mixed with pain for the lost landscape and a nagging feeling of guilt, for my triumph had been their catastrophe.

He asked himself the ultimate question that every Zionist has to ask: 'Have we transformed a struggle for survival into an ethnic cleansing operation, sending people to exile because we wanted to plunder their land?' (Benvenisti 2000: 3)

LOOKING IN VAIN FOR THE PALESTINIAN PEASANT

Peres had substituted the word 'neglect' for 'emptiness'. It's not quite the same, but morally it served the same purpose of justification for Zionist behaviour. It was as though the land was empty because the 'small' number of people there had 'neglected' it. Zionism would redeem the Jewish people as it redeemed the land. Ben-Gurion had played on identical themes. The land had been 'barren' for 2,000 years and the Arabs were 'destroyers' (see Chapter 1). But in any case, 'neglect' is a trigger-word for a wider argument. It leads us to Europe's conception (and Zionism's conception as part of a European ideology) of the Middle East at the turn of the twentieth century, brilliantly summed up in both a word and a book: Edward Said's *Orientalism* – Europe's fascination with, and its desire to control, the 'Orient', the Middle East, the Far East, made especially exciting because it was always spiced with danger.

The 'essence of Orientalism is the ineradicable distinction between Western superiority and Orientalist inferiority' (Said 1995: 42).

One of *Orientalism*'s most potent claims is that 'Oriental' societies, even though they are a reservoir of a wonderful cultural heritage (upon which, of course, the 'West' feels it has a claim), became stagnant over the centuries, *neglected*, and especially unable to cope with the impulses of Western modernisation.

Most of the Middle East, including Palestine, from the early sixteenth century until the beginning of the twentieth century, was part of the political, economic and religious structure known as the Ottoman Empire, controlled from its capital, Istanbul.

Ottoman is almost a synonym for Orientalism. After all, it brought Islam into the Central European heartlands: 'dangerous' certainly, a 'threat to Christian civilization' without doubt, but always 'fascinating'. The theatre in Renaissance England was enthralled with tales from the battlefields of Europe between Ottoman Islam and Christianity (Said 1995: 61). Several centuries later, Europe could delight in the very obvious 'decay' of the Ottomans (Said 1995: 207), and come to the rescue, knights on white chargers, literally sometimes, of its 'subject peoples'. Thus did the early twentieth century give us the epic romantic tales of the British military intelligence agent, Lawrence of Arabia, 'leading' the Arabs in their struggle against Ottoman oppression, an Orientalist classic if ever there was one. And of course it was the Brits, not the Zionists, who 'liberated' Palestine, the 'Holy Land', from the Ottomans.

Arab nationalist resistance to British (and French) control of their lands quickly discovered the appropriate political noun for the European Orientalists: *Imperialism*. Nevertheless, Arab nationalists had something in common with their new oppressors, a desire to modernise. Of course, the difference was that the emerging Arab political leadership, understandably enough, wanted to wrest control of the processes of modernisation and shape their own destiny.

However, when it came to understanding their own history, not an unimportant precondition for building a popular resistance movement, Arab nationalists sometimes inadvertently bought into the Orientalist conception of their own past. Their understandable hostility to centuries of Ottoman rule sometimes persuaded them to acknowledge the Orientalist's picture of neglect and stagnation, and to see themselves, or rather the generations who had preceded them, as passive victims trapped in Ottoman decay (Pappe 1999: 18).[1] This could give unwitting credibility to the Zionist 'neglect-of-the-land' thesis, which can seem similar to the 'decay-under-the-Ottomans' thesis.

Certainly, despite a century of Palestinian peasant resistance to Zionism, we still know far too little of the history of the Palestinian peasant as a strong, indeed impressive, actor in his or her own interests in the region before the Zionists arrived. We still know far too little of just how successfully the peasants farmed the land and just how ready they were to engage with the pressures of modernisation. However, in recent years, all of this has begun to change. A new generation of Palestinian historians has finally begun to get to grips with the problem. There is one particularly outstanding contribution, Beshara Doumani's *Rediscovering Palestine* (1995), which forms the core of this chapter. This remarkable Palestinian historian has found a voice for nineteenth-century Palestinian peasants and allowed them to emerge after a century of insults which has blotted them out of history.[2]

REDISCOVERING PALESTINE'S PEASANTS

Doumani's book is subtitled *Merchants and Peasants in Jabal Nablus, 1700–1900*. As a single unit, the old city of Nablus and its hinterland constituted a discrete unit known for centuries as Jabal Nablus. It formed a powerful infrastructure in what would become known as modern Palestine. Doumani convincingly argues that tracing historical Palestine in the period prior to the Zionist settlements through Jabal Nablus is far more effective than trying to see it through the eyes of Jerusalem, though we will need to consider Jerusalem later in the chapter.

> During the eighteenth and most of the nineteenth centuries, the city of Nablus was Palestine's principal trade and manufacturing centre. It also anchored dozens of villages located in the middle of the hill regions which stretched north-south from the Galilee to Hebron and were home to the largest and most stable peasant settlements since ancient times. (Doumani 1995: 1)

In a looser sense, by the middle of the nineteenth century, up to 300 villages, a considerable area, were oriented on Nablus. These villages stretched along the coastal plains from Haifa to Jaffa in the west, to the Ajlun and Balqa regions beyond the River Jordan in the east, as well as the north–south axis from Galilee to the hills of Ramallah and al-Bireh (Doumani 1995: 30). This included *Marj Ibn Amir* (known in Israel as the valley of Yizrael),

> the most fertile plain in all of Palestine, in the hinterland of Jenin, famous for its plentiful grain harvests, as well as the quality of its tobacco, watermelons and cotton. This wide plain also had a strategic importance: it constituted the broadest expanse connecting the coast with the interior, and astride it ran one of the main trade routes to Damascus. On its soil numerous famous battles were fought, from the time of the pharaohs to … Salah al-Din (Saladin) [and] … his decisive blow to the crusader armies. (Doumani 1995: 31)

In the eighteenth century the plain, and its ancient market town of Nazareth, became the focus of armed conflict between the ruling clans of Jabal Nablus and Galilee (Doumani 1995: 31, 41–2). In the nineteenth century, it became concentrated in the hands of large landowners who produced vast quantities of grain for the world market. The pressures on small landholding Palestinian peasant farmers to allow this process to occur will be closely scrutinised in this chapter. One particularly large land purchase on the plain, by a Lebanese Greek Christian merchant family, the Sourouks, proved to be an unmitigated disaster for all social classes of Palestinians, for later, the land was resold to Zionist settlers (Doumani 1995: 270n.54).

The idea of the city 'anchoring' villages, the 'Jabal' in Jabal Nablus, helps us understand a tough, enduring, regionally-based merchant–peasant society nurturing the productive capacity of the land. It also turned out to be a remarkably successful launch-pad to lead the response to the challenges to the market for peasant agricultural produce posed by Western European intervention.

The signing of the 1838 free trade Anglo-Turkish Commercial Convention, followed by the *Tanzimat*, the political, administrative and fiscal reform programme of the Ottoman Empire, accelerated the impact of Western European pressures (Doumani 1995: 106). But the Palestinian peasants were to prove that they had nothing to fear from free trade:

> *In the third quarter of the nineteenth century, large agricultural surpluses were generated as Palestinian wheat, barley, sesame, olive oil, soap,*

cotton were sold on the world market. At this stage, exports exceeded the imports of European machine-manufactured goods. (Doumani 1995: 4; emphasis added)

The productive capacity of Jabal Nablus, as well as its stunning beauty, have captured the imaginations of visitors to the area from Muslim travellers in the Middle Ages to young Englishmen in search of adventure in the nineteenth century:

Embedded between two steep mountains in a narrow but lush valley and surrounded by a wide belt of olive groves, vineyards, fruit orchards, and a sprinkle of palm trees, the ancient city of Nablus has long been described as resembling, in the words of Shams al-Din al-Ansari in the fourteenth century, 'a palace in a garden'.

The secret was water – the primary reason why Nablus was able to support a large population and a wide range of manufacturing establishments. Its twenty-two gushing springs were channelled into the city's public fountains, mosque courtyards, gardens, tanneries, and dye and pottery establishments, as well as the private homes of the rich. Water was also carried down the 1220-metre long valley that widened westward via aqueducts that fed irrigation channels and powered the large, round stones of grain mills. In the summer heat, evaporated water formed a thin blue mist that enveloped the city and accentuated its charms.

'Its beauty can hardly be exaggerated ... Clusters of white-roofed houses nestling in the bosom of a mass of trees, olive, palm, orange, apricot, and many another varying the carpet with every shade of green ... Everything fresh, green, soft, and picturesque, with verdure, shade, and water everywhere ... a rich blue haze from the many springs and steamlets, which mellows every hard outline' wrote H.B. Tristram [London 1881–2].

The phrase 'Little Damascus', which its inhabitants constantly use to describe Nablus, sums up the look, feel and essence of the city. (Doumani 1995: 22)

The Reverend John Mills agreed with these glowing sentiments: 'The inhabitants are most proud of it, and think there is no place in the world equal to it' (Doumani 1995: 21). In 1864, Mills was on a special mission to Nablus. He had come to investigate the tiny community of the Samaritans, virtually the only survivors of the people claiming ancestry with the biblical Samaritans. One of the steep mountains overlooking Nablus, whose biblical name was Shechem (Benvenisti 2000: 13), is Mt. Gerizim, the spiritual centre of the Samaritans. It seems that the Samaritans had remained part of the community of Nablus for over 2,000 years. In the nineteenth century, they had their own quarter there. A few worked as scribes or accountants to the governors, one or two were rich merchants, but mostly they were relatively poor retailers or artisans (Doumani 1995: 23).

There was also a small Christian community, and there had also been a small Jewish community in the past as evidenced by the small stairway near the middle of the central marketplace referred to as 'the Jews' stairs' (*daraj al yahud*) (Doumani 1995: 267n.22).

Is not a little, albeit 'reverse', Orientalist indulgence justified here? For there is surely an irony in that the heart of late medieval and early modern Palestine lay in Nablus, in the shadow of the great Samaritan mountain, 2,000 years ago the spiritual centre of dissident 'Israelites', excommunicated by the Jerusalem priests (see Chapters 1 and 2). There is at least poetic, if not historical, symmetry here. And how appropriate that modern Samaritans in Nablus should consider themselves Palestinians and not Israelis.[3]

ARMED RESISTANCE FROM THE MOUNTAIN OF FIRE

Jabal Nablus also had, and has, another name, *jabal al-nar*, mountain of fire. It's a name that testifies to passionate regional loyalties and the enthusiasm with which the local inhabitants are willing to take up arms to protect their way of life.

In 1799, Napoleon Bonaparte landed in Cairo, intending to invade Palestine. Shaykh Yusuf Jarrar, the *mutasallim* (an Ottoman appointed official) of Jenin district, wrote a poem in which he exhorted his fellow leaders in Jabal Nablus to unite under one banner against the French forces. Although Shaykh Jarrar was, in part, responding to orders from above, his real commitments were local as expressed in his appeals to the ruling urban households and rural clans.

> House of Tuqan, draw your swords
> And mount your precious saddles.
> House of Nimr, you mighty tigers, straighten your courageous
>   lines.

Muhammed Uthman, mobilize your men,
Mobilize the heroes from all directions.
Ahmad al-Qasim, you bold lion,
Prow of the advancing lines.

'Not once in the twenty-one verses does it [the poem] mention
Ottoman rule, much less the need to protect the empire or the
glory ... of serving the sultan' (Doumani 1995: 17). Shaykh Jarrar
was a member of one of those local ruling families. The Ottomans
had to rely on them to maintain their rule but it also meant that
tensions with the wider power structures of empire were never far
from the surface. The poem illustrates the assumption that the ruling families could mobilise local peasant militias. Although, over
time, these ties would loosen, peasant traditions of regional armed
defence, if anything, would deepen, with serious implications for
the ruling powers of the twentieth century: Britain and Israel.

The *mountain of fire* played a leading role in 1834 against
    invading Egyptian forces,
in the 1936–39 rebellion against British rule,
And in the Palestinian intifada against Israeli occupation that
    exploded in 1987. (Doumani 1995: 22)

GETTING THE CROP TO MARKET: PEASANTS AND MERCHANTS

Nablus was a city, but it was a peasant city. Its

rhythms of life reflected the agricultural calendar of the peasant
community. The hustle and bustle of tons of oil being deposited in the
underground wells of huge soap-factory buildings after the olive harvest in the fall, for instance, were perhaps only surpassed by the com-
motion of raw cotton arriving in the city to be ginned and spun in the
summer. There was no sharp dividing line between city and country.
Nablus was in some ways akin to a very large village: at sunrise many
Nablusis exited the city gates to work on the extensive olive groves,
vineyards and orchards that covered the terraced slopes, as well as in
the fields, vegetable gardens, and grain mills that were scattered
across the valley. In reverse flow, peasants poured into the city to sell
their goods and to search for wedding clothes, work tools, cooking
utensils, rice, coffee and a host of other items ... Many remained in the

> city for a few days ... to become further acquainted with ... the
> hundreds of shops ... the covered markets of the textile merchants ...
> the five central mosques ... the large fortress like compounds of the
> ruling urban families, the Nimrs, Tuqans, Abd al-hadis. (Doumani
> 1995: 26–7)

In the hinterland of Nablus, peasants had learned over the millennia to utilise every topographical feature. Fields were sown with
grain, legumes and vegetables; hills were terraced and planted with
trees; and higher stony land was used for grazing. Until the last
decades of Ottoman rule, most peasants were small landholders,
though their *legal* rights to the land remained ambiguous.[4]

The peasants of the hill regions lived in close-knit village communities which varied in size from a few dozen to a few hundred
inhabitants. Most had an average of two to four constituent clans
and some extended families. The basis of collective solidarity was
the organisation of peasant society into clans, *hamulas*: patrilineal
descent groups believed to be derived from a common ancestor. The
clan system provided a safety net which supported individual families in times of difficulty, and it was well suited to the vagaries of
rain-fed agriculture and the thin soil of hilly regions (Doumani
1995: 27, 28). Codes of behaviour were determined by a deep-rooted
system of customary practice, known as *urf,* which spelled out rights
and responsibilities. Reflecting Bedouin roots, these differed signifi-
cantly from Islamic Shariah law, prevalent in the urban centres. In
other words, even by the nineteenth century, there was a substan-
tial degree of peasant autonomy in legal, moral, personal and financial matters that were clan-based.

Yet, however proud of their independence they might be, the peasants and their clans needed urban merchants to get their produce
beyond the local markets. Chapter 4 illustrated the centuries-old
practice of Arab merchant activities throughout the Mediterranean.
In the nineteenth century a powerful new and rapidly expanding
market came on stream in Europe. The merchants had the know-
how that the peasants needed and of course the peasants had the
produce that the merchants required. Merchant–peasant relations
were carefully cultivated. The merchant had to build trust, and here
religious values were important. These networks were informal; they
were not sanctioned by the Ottoman State and merchants often provided credit. 'Honour', reinforced as an Islamic value, would be built
into attitudes towards debt repayment. Both sides could manoeuvre

around debt, and often did. But a merchant could not afford to fall foul of a rural clan with whom he and his family had spent years, perhaps generations, developing good relationships. Doumani illustrates this with his discussion of peasant weddings.

Weddings were (and are) incredibly important in peasant village life. And the purchase of the wedding wardrobe and other presents was the occasion for a special visit to the city. The wedding celebrations seem to have begun with the visit as the peasants arrived in great style: singing, dancing and bearing gifts (Doumani 1995: 84). They stayed for several days in the house of the merchant with whom they intended to do the most business. It was a point of moral principle, as well as sound commercial practice, for the merchant and his family to show generosity and friendship. Dependent on the timing of the wedding in relation to the harvest, credit would be extended.

Ritual surrounding the collection of the debt was embedded in the local culture. Disputes about the level of the debt were common; the debt collector, often a peasant hired by the merchant, was sent into the countryside. It was a point of honour for the debt collector to be treated with respect. Traditions of peasant hospitality meant that he might stay in a special room in the village square and be provided with food and drink. This did not prevent the peasants exercising skilled tactics at evasion. Whilst ultimately the merchant had more power, the peasant and his clan were past masters at applying pressures for debt 'rescheduling'. However, modernity would upset this delicate balance between town and country.

'THE OLIVE IS THE PHYSICAL DOCUMENT OF HISTORY'

So wrote an astute British observer in the middle of the nineteenth century (Doumani 1995: 178). The ancient olive tree came to serve symbolically not only as a national icon for the Palestinians, reminiscent of a time when they were not refugees or oppressed under colonial rule, but free peasants who lived off the fruits of the land, but also literally as a financial icon. The noble fruit did nothing less than bankroll the arrival of capitalism, and modern social class relations, into the nineteenth-century Palestinian village.[5]

Here is an extract from a letter written by Mahmud Beik Abd al-Hadi, leader of the Nablus advisory council, to the Ottoman governor of Jerusalem in 1851:

> I have relayed to the council your noble order containing the petition
> of the people of Jaba [village] ... in which they accuse the shayks of
> their own village of forcing them to sign promissory notes for this
> year worth 1200 jars of oil and for next year 1400 jars ... (Doumani
> 1995: 146)

Explaining the 'promissory notes' to the governor, Abd al-Hadi
pointed out that it was 'usual practice among people of the villages ...
to sell their future crop of olive oil in advance for reduced prices
through a (salam) contract for the amount of taxes due from their
village' (Doumani 1995: 147).

Now Doumani exhibits ingenious forensic skills in breaking down
these extraordinary documents which arrived in the Islamic courts
of Ottoman Palestine. He also made himself expert in both the use,
and the changing character, of the *salam* moneylending contracts
which dominated relations between peasants and merchants and
sometimes between entire peasant villages and the tax-collecting
authorities in this period.

A *salam* contract was a cash loan to a peasant advanced by a
merchant with an agreed claim on the amount of a crop, usually
olive oil, then owed by the peasant, irrespective of future harvest
yield, weather conditions, etc. Tax payments could also be delayed
or renegotiated on the same basis, where an agreement is made on
the amount to be paid in the form of olive oil at a later date.
Obviously, this system was open to abuse. The local oil merchants
who began to control the city council also collected taxes on behalf
of the Ottoman State! The agreement might also contain hidden
interest charges. Default on the debt could force a peasant to surrender his land, or land rights, to a merchant. It seems 'futures' trading on the global stock exchanges of our own times has surprising
antecedents.

These arguments are developed fully in Doumani's chapter, 'The
Political Economy of Olive Oil', which he insists are essential to
understanding the Palestinian economy at this time. It is a master-
piece and we can hardly do it justice here. Still a basic outline must be
attempted to demonstrate the speed with which the Palestinian peasant economy had to come to terms with a rapidly changing world.

Of course, the plight of the bond-indebted peasants is nothing
new. We find these exploitative relations on the land deep in

historical antiquity. But what is interesting here is the way these moneylending contracts, and the conflicts they generated, became vehicles for modernisation.

Returning to the governor's letter: the idea that peasants could petition the governor was itself new. For generations the peasants had ignored the urban courts. They were used to settling disputes through the strength of their rural clans. Now they ignored their clans, bypassed the local Nablus council and its leader (and oil merchant) Abd al-Hadi who was leaning on the village shayks to collect the taxes, and went to Jerusalem in search of justice.

The new economics also split the clans. The petition attacked their own clan leaders for cheating them, and this suggests a fundamental change. The clan leaders were, consciously or otherwise, anticipating the formation of what Doumani calls a rural middle class. They were following the urban merchants in seeing the moneylending contracts as a mechanism for generating funds for personal profit as well as for investment. At the same time the village peasants were having to organise independently to protect their interests, peaceful petitioning first to be followed if necessary, as we shall see, by more aggressive tactics. The villages also produced would-be entrepreneurs who were not clan leaders. In other words, social class differentiation at several levels was evolving in the countryside.

The story of Abd al-Rahman, a Nablus peasant from Aqraba village, brings together many of these themes. He signed a *salam* contract with a Christian merchant from Jaffa in 1851, who had access to the expanding European market for Palestinian sesame. The peasant-entrepreneur travelled to Jaffa to make the deal with the merchant, bypassing village elders and Nablus merchants alike.

This development was far from unique and it undermines much scholarship which continues to view Palestinian peasants 'during the Ottoman period living in isolated villages and engaged solely in subsistence agriculture ... [many] Palestinian peasants were sharply attuned to the fickle changes of international demand and acted accordingly' (Doumani 1995: 141). Other examples include peasant business partnerships, cutting across village, clan and even, as here, religious lines, and setting up *salam* moneylending facilities for other local peasants (Doumani 1995: 167).

Abd al-Rahman's contract is particularly interesting because of its contradictory features. It contained two incentives: it covered transport costs from the village to the Mediterranean port, and it included a profit-sharing arrangement: 'The *salam* contract could encourage trade, help meet needs for local capital, increase invest-ment in agricultural production, promote economic growth ... and even benefit both parties' (Doumani 1995: 142).

On the other hand, these contracts, including this one, always had the potential to destroy the peasant's livelihood to the advan-tage of the merchant in the wake of debt default. This is exactly what happened to Abd al-Rahman, who was forced to sell his land to the Christian merchant when he was unable to fulfil his side of the contract (Doumani 1995: 163).

Thus, the contracts facilitated capitalism in a classical manner. Merchants could gain access to local crops for the expanding over-seas market with the bonus that a debt default could give them con-trol of prime agricultural land in the Palestinian interior. A minority of peasants could play the game too and wouldn't always be the los-ers. For it is clear that the new export trade brought tangible wealth to some Palestinian villages, which seems to have irritated the British Consul in Jerusalem. In 1856 he reported to London that the villagers were exporting grain 'and greedily grasp the coin in return'. Two years later, it seems that profits were enabling the peasants to 'purchase arms and decorate their women' (Scholch 1982: 19).

CLASS CONFLICT

By the middle of the nineteenth century, the oil merchants of Nablus had accumulated sufficient profits from the peasants to allow them to undertake a massive expansion of the olive oil-based soap-making factories in the city. It became the most successful local industry in the region, and one which brooked no European com-petition. Unfortunately space allows only the briefest of discussion.

Nablus soap had a reputation throughout the Mediterranean, going back as far as the fourteenth century. Several decades into the twentieth century, Palestinians would discover, as with their Jaffa orange, a new way in which the reputation of its produce would be recommended to a wider world when Jewish businessmen marketed their own settlement-made soap as being of 'Nablus quality' (Doumani 1995: 185).

Doumani includes graphic descriptions of the soap-making facto-ries in Nablus. One striking characteristic undermines the classic

Orientalist stereotype of the Bedouin as marauders and remote desert nomads. Alongside the peasants delivering the olive oil to the vast underground wells of the factories, the Bedouin proved themselves to be a vital 'factor of production'. Every year they would gather the barilla plant, burn it and then transport 3,000 camelloads of barilla ashes, the *qilw*, to Nablus. In return they received money, rice, tobacco, sugar, soap and coffee (Doumani 1995: 204).

Bitter struggles developed over control of the soap factories as the oil merchants, newly rich on the basis of their *salam* contracts, displaced the traditional ruling families. At the same time, Ottoman officials insisted on imposing a much harsher tax regime. The soap factory owners rebelled. Using their base on the Nablus city council, which they dominated, in 1853 they organised a tax strike: 'What these merchants objected to the most was the Ottoman government's attempt to ... cut into their material base without providing any real protection against European hegemony' (Doumani 1995: 231). An embryonic Palestinian bourgeoisie was flexing its muscles against outside interference.

We do not know whether the peasants supported the tax strike, for they hugely resented the oil merchants becoming rich at their expense by means of the *salam* contracts. A year before the tax strike, Nablus council had had to explain to the Ottoman authorities in Jerusalem why they had imprisoned some people in the village of Asira who had pelted a representative of an oil merchant with stones and broken his sword and a pistol (Doumani 1995: 173).

'Politically, the heightened tensions acquired, dare one say, some characteristics of class struggle' (Doumani 1995: 180). The peasants of Talluza village summed it all up with a satirical song.

> God is Great when the fezzes [merchants] gather [on the village grounds] ... and the voices of the debt collectors raised.
> The moneylenders listen for the sounds of the returning sheep, then they jump with their friend[s] the police, looking for a victim to fleece ...
> God is Great when the people of the villages greet the coming of Blessed and Auspicious olive season. They go to the city markets to buy their provisions ... But the debtor [sic] demands his due, or the loan is renewed for twice the fee ... The poor soul is forced to submit and God is Great, God is Great ... (Doumani 1995: 94; emphasis added)

ARTICULATING PALESTINIAN IDENTITY:
JERUSALEM'S FIRST MAYOR

At what point did Palestine crystallise as a national identity in the minds of the people who lived there? Until now we have been discussing the modernisation of a society which was a part of the Ottoman Empire. In the latter half of the nineteenth century, independently-minded urban Palestinian intellectuals from traditionalist backgrounds began to emerge in the Empire's political and administrative structure. In this regard the career of Yusuf Diya is instructive (Khalidi 1997: 69–76).[6]

Born in 1842, one of five sons of a senior local official at the Islamic Shariah court in Jerusalem, Yusuf Diya was of that generation of Arabs fascinated and infuriated in equal measure at the seemingly unstoppable advance of all things European. The only way to resist the European was first to understand him, Yusuf concluded. He embarked on a programme of European education, learning French, English and German. He completed his education in Istanbul where he came to the attention of reformist *Tanzimat* Turkish statesmen, who encouraged his political ambitions. Ottoman reorganisation included the promotion of local municipal government. This meant that, in time, Yusuf was able successfully to seek appointment as Jerusalem's first mayor. In this post, he amply demonstrated his modernising credentials by helping to initiate the construction of the first carriage road from Jerusalem to Jaffa, as well as improving the city's water supply. In 1877, he was elected to the Ottoman Parliament.

This was to be only a brief flowering of democracy in the Ottoman Empire. In 1878, the sultan suspended parliament and imposed direct autocratic rule. Nevertheless Yusuf had made his mark as a radical democratic statesman. One American diplomat described him as the 'finest orator and ablest debater in the chamber'. Another likened him to a 'French Republican'. And he had certainly antagonised the sultan. Yusuf was one of several Arab deputies banned for a short period from Istanbul and considered 'most dangerous'.

The Ottoman authorities now kept him under close surveillance and he embarked on an academic career, becoming a professor of Arabic in Vienna, publishing pre-Islamic Arabic poetry and writing a Kurdish–Arabic dictionary. His political ambitions were now thwarted but it is clear that he had fully grasped what was to become the Palestinian political agenda for the twentieth century.

Yusuf compensated for the ban on his political activities with an extensive correspondence with European and Middle Eastern scholarly and public figures. In 1899, via the Chief Rabbi in France, he communicated with Theodor Herzl, Zionism's chief theoretician. He warned Herzl that Palestine was 'heavily populated by non-Jews and was venerated by 390 million Christians and 300 million Muslims'. He asked, 'By what right do the Jews demand it for themselves?' Wealth cannot purchase Palestine, 'which can only be taken over by the force of cannons and warships'.

THE PEASANT WAR ON THE ZIONIST SETTLERS IN PALESTINE

Yusuf Diya would have known that peasant clashes with Zionist settlers had already begun. At the battle at Petach-Tiva, which occurred as early as 1886, Ottoman troops intervened and arrested many peasants, after a Jewish settler had been killed and several others wounded in an attack from the neighbouring Arab village of Yahudiyya. The peasants were aggrieved because land they had considered their own had been sold to the settlers after they had forfeited it to Jaffa moneylenders and local authorities. For Palestinians the twentieth century began at Petach-Tiva (Khalidi 1997: 96–115).

It is telling that Herzl never once mentions Arabs in his most famous work, *The Jewish State*, as though they did not exist. Yet one famous Jewish writer, Ahad Ha-Am, admitted after a three-month visit to Palestine in 1891 that it was 'difficult to find fields that were not sown' by Arab peasants. He added that there *was* unclaimed land, sand dunes and stony mountains, that would grow fruit trees, but it needed 'hard labour, clearing and reclamation' (Khalidi 1997: 96–115).

Which brings us to the story the famous Jaffa orange. The Zionists have long claimed the Jaffa orange as their own, a result of land reclamation 'turning the desert green'. The facts tell a different story.

It was Arab 'hard labour' which transformed the sandy soil on the coastal plain, from north of Gaza to about half-way to Haifa, preparing it for citrus, in the second half of the nineteenth century. Marshlands and swamps too were drained. The results were staggering and helped shift the economic focus away from Jabal Nablus. The introduction of steam navigation brought this export crop, which by 1880 was being grown in about 500 orange groves in the Jaffa region, to the world market. Further expansion ensured that, by 1913, no fewer than 1.6 million cases of oranges were being exported from Jaffa, making it Palestine's most valuable export crop.

Meanwhile a sinister development was occurring on the Zionist settlements in the Galilee area. In 1907, the Ottoman authorities allowed the settlers to arm and defend themselves against increasing attacks by dispossessed peasants. A secret Jewish organisation, *Bar Giora*, was formed which exhorted the slogan 'Hebrew Labour' and gave rise to a paramilitary organisation, the *Hashomer*. We will examine the racist political implications of the Hebrew Labour slogan more closely in the next chapter. Later in the twentieth century, many years after the creation of the State of Israel, General Yigael Allon made it clear in his book *The Making of Israel's Army*, that *Hashomer* was the forerunner of the Israeli armed forces.

By now, the clashes between the peasants and Zionist settlers were becoming much more effectively, and publicly, politicised by the intervention of Arab politicians on behalf of the peasants. The sale to Zionists of the village lands of al-Fula, half-way between Nazareth and Jenin on the famous Marj Ibn Amir plain, by the same Lebanese Sourouk merchant family mentioned earlier, brought matters to a head. This time the sale was made to the Jewish National Fund (JNF), a new institution of the Zionist movement devoted to land purchase, and headed by Arthur Ruppin. Ruppin was another Zionist who knew well that there was no such place as a 'land without people'. He later admitted that there was hardly any unsettled arable land and following land purchase from absentee landlords, we had to 'remove the peasants who cultivated the land'.

The Ottoman-appointed official for Nazareth, Shukri al-'Asali, a member of a prominent Damascus family, was a well-known public speaker and journalist. He refused to hand over the title deeds of the land to the new owners, despite instructions from the Ottoman authorities. Al-'Asali took advantage of the greater freedom now permitted by the renewed phase of constitutional reforms and attacked the sale, and Zionism generally, in a Damascus newspaper under the pseudonym Saladin. His articles were reprinted in Beirut and Haifa newspapers. When *Hashomer* sent 30 armed men to occupy the land, al-'Asali ordered troops to drive them away. However, his superiors quickly countermanded his order and the sale was enforced. Nevertheless the stakes had been dramatically raised and raids by the dispossessed peasants on the land were frequent and sometimes bloody. A much more political atmosphere was developing. Al-'Asali stood as a candidate in Damascus for the reconvened Ottoman parliament, on a programme to fight Zionism 'to his last drop of blood'. He won the seat and his victory galvanised both other Arab deputies and the Arab press to hail peasant resistance to Zionism as a *cause célèbre* for the Arab people.

Thus a new type of political liberation movement was in the making when the British seized Palestine after the First World War. It was a movement which

> united peasants, who tried desperately to cling to their land, or retaliated against the Zionist settlers in a violent fashion if they lost it ... with the urban intellectuals and notables ... In 1935, the funeral in Haifa of the first public apostle of armed resistance, the Syrian Shaykh 'Iz al-Din al-Qassam, who lived and worked for fifteen years among landless *fellahin* [peasants], had migrated to the Haifa slums, and died in combat with British troops, became an enormous public demonstration. This in turn helped to spark the 1936 general strike and the 1936–39 Palestinian Arab revolt. In the words of the best study of al-Qassam, ... his death *electrified the Palestinian people*. (Khalidi 1997: 114–15)

The *mountain of fire* had come of age.

6

'... for a People without Land'

By 1880, the majority of a world population of nearly eight million Jews, were living in Eastern Europe, for the reasons explained in Chapter 3. Some four million lived in territories that had been acquired by the Tsarist empire as it expanded westwards in the eighteenth and nineteenth centuries. This region, which stretched from Lithuania in the north to the Black Sea in the south, and from Poland in the west to 'White Russia' and the Ukraine, in the east, became known as the Pale of Settlement.

Hostile policies of the successive Tsars had concentrated the Jews inside the Pale. According to a very pervasive Zionist myth, these Jews constituted a 'people without land'.

This arena acted as a vast distillery for all the emerging Jewish social trends and political movements: assimilation; mass migration westwards, especially to America; the huge Jewish participation in the rapidly growing socialist parties; and the growth of the Zionist movement. One event above all others, looming on the horizon with an awesome inevitability, would act as yeast, fermenting all these trends and movements, albeit in contradictory directions: the Russian Revolution. The French Revolution of 1789 had held out the promise of a final and lasting emancipation to the Jews of Western Europe. Far from being a people without land, if the promise was fulfilled, they were to be stakeholders, legal citizens with equal rights in the lands of settlement, the lands of their birth. Of course, there was still anti-Semitism. Nevertheless, these Jews felt a new confidence and security rooted in a democratic constitution or parliamentary legislation. At the end of the nineteenth century, the Russian Revolution would make the same promise to the Jews of Eastern Europe.

True, it took many decades for the first anticipatory ripples of this world-shaking historical drama to make an impact on the Pale of Settlement. Yet, modernisation and capitalism, the motors of the revolution, in the form of industrialisation, had made a slow and faulty start in the Pale. Thousands of impoverished rural Jews, redundant artisans, former tavern-keepers, petty merchants, peddlers, paupers, the *luftmenschen* of Yiddish folklore (Deutscher 1968: 62)[1] flocked to the new towns and cities. The centuries-long tradition of Jewish craft skills meant that it was the artisans who adapted most easily to an urban environment. The rest struggled as best they could. But one thing was clear: the medieval Eastern European Jewish economic infrastructure was rapidly disappearing.

The Zionist historian David Vital takes up the story (Vital 1975: 31–60). At the start of the nineteenth century, no single Jewish community numbered more than 10,000 in the Pale. By the end, there were 40 such communities totalling 1.5 million, about a third of the total Jewish population.

In itself this process of internal migration would not necessarily have radicalised the population. These compact, self-contained communities, where Yiddish was the mother-tongue for 98 per cent, could more or less re-establish themselves in an urban environment. But the Tsars imposed one specific and hateful policy which 'burned deep into the social and political consciousness': conscription.

Jews had to provide ten youngsters per 1,000 Jewish inhabitants for military service in the empire, compared to seven per 1,000 for the non-Jewish population. And for Jews the age limit was lowered from 18 to 12. The child and adolescent conscripts were placed in special preparatory establishments for military training where they were subject to special education which for the Jewish youngsters included a disciplinary regime designed to impel them to accept the Christian faith. The policy had one unintended consequence, however. It prepared a minority of Jews for armed struggle against the regime itself.

Conscription was detested throughout empire. 'It was like death – to think about the soldier at home was to tear one's heart out uselessly,' wrote the great Russian novelist, Leo Tolstoi.

Hatred of conscription fuelled a general discontent with the tsars. Across the empire, for all peoples, nationalities and social classes, apart from the most entrenched elements of the aristocracy, it combined with a growing awareness of the freedoms achieved in Western Europe in the wake of the French Revolution. Great hope rested on the 'reforming' Tsar Alexander II in the 1860s.

The ideals of the Jewish Emancipation movement in Western Europe began to capture the imagination of Jews in the Pale.

One minor but representative literary figure in the Pale was moved to write:

> Awake, Israel, and Judah, arise!
> Shake off the dust, open wide thine eyes!
> Justice sprouteth, righteousness is here,
> Thy sin is forgot, thou has naught to fear!
> (Vital 1975: 43)

It is interesting that this early secular adaptation of biblical prose, which would soon become the hallmark of Zionist propaganda, was at first put in the service of the assimilationist movement modelled on Western Europe. Sir Moses Montefiore, a leader of British Jewry, confidently predicted successful democratic reform would free his co-religionists in the Russian Empire.

It was not to be. Tsarist enthusiasm for reforming Russia's medieval landowning empire proved far too slow and inconsistent for its burgeoning revolutionary democratic movement. In 1881 Tsar Alexander was assassinated by the Narodniks.

The assassination was a turning point in Russia in every sense. It symbolised the view of Russia's growing intelligentsia that revolution was indeed the only means of transforming the Tsarist system. The great writers of the period, Tolstoi, Chekhov, Dostoevsky, captured the mood of anticipation, both menacing and exciting. The Tsarist rulers sensed the game was up and prepared the ground for the most massive *reaction*; in a word, *counter-revolution*.

POGROMS

1881 was also the year in which the long-term social effects of the mismanaged emancipation of the serfs, famine, agricultural and industrial unemployment ... had all combined to swell the growing 'barefoot army' of pauperized peasants and lumpenproletariat, particularly in southern Russia ... The regime ... [wanted] to channel the explosive energy latent in the barely controllable mass of restless and impoverished peasantry away from themselves.

At the same time ... fear of the peasantry was increasingly combined with a tendency to view them, the *narod*, the quintessential people, in highly sentimental ... terms, which were similar ... to ... the revolutionary populists. (Vital 1975: 49–50)

The revolutionary populists, the Narodniks, were the first to challenge the autocracy. Drawing their cadre mainly from students, they complemented a strategy of assassinating government targets with a perspective of *going to the peasantry*, hoping to mobilise them for the revolution. The regime, based as it was upon the peasants' principal antagonist, the landlord aristocracy, saw a way of out-flanking the Narodniks, as well as drawing fire away from themselves: target the anger and the energy against the Jews. (The Narodniks, too, had seen the Jews as a legitimate target of peasant hostility, but quickly changed their stand to one of principled condemnation (Frankel 1981: 120).)

> The Jews were admirably suited to the role ... They were loathed not only by the peasants, with whom their relations were mostly on the basis of the Jews' function in the economy at large as petty traders, middlemen, innkeepers, estate agents and moneylenders, but loathed overwhelmingly by the men of position in Russia – the bureaucrats, the military, the Church ... the Tsar himself. (Vital 1975: 51)

Here, then, was that degenerate political culture of the Tsar regime in its death throes. A culture which set the Black Hundred pogromist gangs on the Jews, and which would later forge a docu-ment, a favourite of Hitler incidentally, the *Protocols of the Elders of Zion*, the fabled Tsarist fantasy which alleged a Jewish 'conspiracy' to rule the world.

By the end of 1881 over 200 Jewish communities had been attacked by gangs of peasants and petty criminals, with the police and the army turning a blind eye.

The pogroms generally unfolded according to a common pattern. The Paris newspaper *Le Temps* recorded a particularly bloody one which took place at the south Russian town of Balta during Passover, April 1882:

> The riot began in the afternoon; the Jewish inhabitants prepared to defend themselves; whereupon the municipal authorities had them dispersed by troops who beat them with rifle butts. [The following morning], 600 peasants from the surrounding country recommenced the attack and maintained it without further obstacle. It was a scene of pillage, arson, murder and rape to make one tremble with horror ... 211 were injured 9 were killed, girls were raped ... most houses were demolished ... (Vital 1975: 52–3)

The pogroms broke once and for all the 'deeply ingrained immo-bilism and fatalism' of the Jews (Vital 1975: 59). Panic combined with a determination to find answers to this particularly virulent species of anti-Jewish hatred with its systemic roots in the Russian rulers' defence of their feudal privileges. This was then an explicitly political crisis demanding political solutions. Vital sees the 'genesis of the Zionist movement' (Vital 1975: 65) in this period. Indeed the rest of his writings are devoted to how the Zionist movement then evolved.

Yet, the *emigration fever*, in search of a land where the emancipation of the Jews might finally become a reality, certainly wasn't directed to Palestine, as Vital is the first to admit. Rather, it was America, which 'took on a symbolic quality, suggesting a fresh departure, a new life, and unlimited horizons that it was not to lose for seventy years' (Vital 1975: 61–2). The migration statistics speak for themselves. In 1880, there were fewer than 250,000 Jews in America. Fifty years later the numbers were nearly five million, migration from Eastern Europe combining with natural population growth (Eban 1984: 260).

But in some ways an even more important development occurred after the pogroms. Most Jews did not, or could not, emigrate, and many of them discovered renewed hopes for their emancipation in the land of their birth in the rising revolutionary movement that began to sweep the length and breadth of the Russian empire. The socialists, especially the Jewish socialist Bund, erupted onto the scene in the Pale. Overshadowing the Zionists 'in its mass appeal at least until 1905' (Mendelsohn 1970: vi), the Bund was committed to a Jewish stake in the lands of settlement. It was an uncompromising and ferocious opponent of Zionist emigration schemes to Palestine. It is sadly typical that Vital's book, with nearly 400 pages on the origins of Zionism in the Pale of Settlement, affords the Bund just two pages.

SELF-EMANCIPATION

1881 transformed the way Jews now viewed emancipation. In the past, reliance on others – government authority and the established Jewish leaders – was seen as the mechanism for protecting Jewish interests. 1881 changed all that. Ordinary Jews now became directly involved, and active, in their own interests:

> Jewish politics should strive to become autonomous. The most influential slogan to emerge from the crisis was made famous by

Pinsker: *self-emancipation*. The goal should no longer be adaptation to the environment but rather the creation of an environment radically new ...

The concept of mass organization ... took hold. Party politics, nationalist on the one hand, socialist on the other emerged as a permanent aspect of Russian-Jewish life. (Frankel 1981: 51)[2]

This idea took root in the mass involvement and organisation required to defend beleaguered Jewish communities against the pogromists. But it also reflected the way the wider Russian revolutionary movement now began to permeate the Jewish communities. Far from Jewish self-emancipation being a purely Jewish affair, its evolution was intimately bound up with the deepening expectation of self-emancipation in the wider society.

The carrier of the revolutionary idea to the poor Jewish communities was the assimilated middle-class Russian Jewish student. This was a conscious adaptation of the *going to the people* perspective of the Narodniks.

One of the students, the Jewish writer later known as Ben Ami, recorded the impact they had on synagogue congregations in Odessa:

The mere idea that here were educated persons, whom the masses regarded with pride, but also as beyond their reach, were thinking of them – this alone raised their fallen spirits, raised their feelings of human dignity ... Everywhere, absolutely everywhere, the youth met only with the most profound gratitude and – more important – absolute trust and the promise to do everything that the youth would propose ... To this day I see before me the picture of a venerable, almost seventy year old man who ... laid his hands on my head to bless me ... and burst into tears. (Frankel 1981: 54)

These students pulled no punches. They provided training and guns for the newly formed self-defence committees.

From now on the Jewish intelligentsia would have not just a large audience amongst poor Jews, but one ready to take action in response to its ideas for emancipation. The youth in the poor communities also threw up new leaders ready to challenge the old ways. However, it wasn't just the pogroms that induced mass activity. Urbanisation itself had made a dramatic impact on the Jewish communities. It fostered an unexpected spirit of revolt amongst the new generation of Jewish manual workers in the Pale of Settlement.

There was a real irony here. Jewish emancipation political circles identified the roots of peasant anti-Semitism in the 'middleman' role Jews had played in the medieval economy. Thus Pavel Axelrod, a Jewish political leader who would play a major role in the Russian revolutionary political party, the Mensheviks, identified a link between the intensity of the pogroms in areas where there was a disproportionate number of Jews in non-productive occupations. Even a starving innkeeper, such as his father, was regarded as an exploiter of peasants: 'However great the poverty suffered by the Jewish masses', Axelrod noted, '… the fact remains that taken overall … the non-productive sit astride the neck of the lower classes in Russia' (Frankel 1981: 105). One answer was to persuade the 'non-productive elements' to become manual workers. This was turned into a communist ideal and indeed some Jewish émigrés set off for America in order to establish agricultural communes (Frankel 1981: 55). The colonisation of Palestine with the specific intention of establishing such communes, the 'kibbutzim', has its origins in this period.

But thousands of Jews became manual workers, including incidentally former starving inn-keepers, and even those unpopular 'walking price lists' (Chapter 3) finding themselves without goods to sell, not through intellectual choice or political idealism but through bare necessity. It was the only way to avoid starvation.

Not that manual work could guarantee much more than bare subsistence. Brief employment was often followed by prolonged periods of unemployment: 'From 10 weeks work we must live 52 weeks', was echoed by thousands (Mendelsohn 1970: 13). Jewish workers described the conditions in the new cities of Belorussia-Luthuania at the end of the nineteenth century:

The majority lived in the semi-darkness of cellars or similar hovels that had wet walls and halls and were crammed together in an oppressive and stupefying atmosphere … 10 people living in a room … when a worker's family had a room to themselves it was a luxury. (Mendelsohn 1970: 13–14)

Urban conditions in the Pale were thus appalling. Furthermore, technological innovation was painfully slow, most workplaces were tiny, not employing more than 50 people and often just a handful. Thus the 'textile industry' hired weavers for their ageing wooden handlooms, working 16–18 hours a day in cramped, 'airless' spaces.

Jews were rarely employed in the mechanised firms which had
better conditions. Jews were also employed as manual workers in
carpentry, locksmithing, hosiery, tanning, cigarette and matches
factories (which hired large numbers of women, and children as
young as six), and bristle-making: industries hardly destined to be
the core of the new economy and society of the Russian Empire. Yet
these Jewish workers were to make an outstanding attempt at economic, social and political emancipation, for themselves and for the
rest of their communities. They proved themselves ready to take
collective action against their appalling conditions and helped
spread the idea, far beyond their own ranks, of the mass strike as a
political weapon of liberation.[3]

THE JEWISH WORKERS' STRIKE MOVEMENT

Why were Jews not hired in the more mechanised factories? Anti-
Semitism played a part, of course, but the main reason is quite
astonishing:

> Most employers (Jewish and non-Jewish) preferred Christian to Jewish
> workers because the former were more reliable. The Jewish strike
> movement in the Pale ... struck terror in the hearts of the employers.
> In Smorgon, a Jewish factory owner explained: 'The Jews are good
> workers but they are capable of organizing revolts ... against the
> employer, the regime, the Tsar himself' ... Socialist and non-Socialist
> observers alike agreed that the Bialystok employers' fear of the Jewish
> workers revolutionary potential led them to prefer the relative stability
> of the non-Jewish labour force. (Mendelsohn 1970: 22)

The Jewish workers' strike movement across the Pale, and especially
Belorussia-Lithuania, fully deserved its reputation:

> Artisans ... formed the first cadres of worker-agitators. Gradually, as
> the movement proliferated, the more backward workers of the large
> cigarette and matches factories were drawn into the wave of protest.
> (The cultural level [here] was very low ... the majority in the enormous
> factory in Grodno were illiterate). In Vilna the first strike by factory
> workers occurred in 1895, three years after the artisans had begun
> their organized attack. A strike by several hundred workers at the cig-
> arette plant, the largest establishment in Vilna, marked a new stage in

the development of the city's labour movement. It was in fact the first time a major industrialist, rather than the owner of a small shop, had been challenged ... in Bialystok girls employed at the cigarette factory were organised by an agitator from Vilna, a veteran of the Minsk 'circle' movement.

The strike wave spread from the shops to the factories, and from the large centres to the smaller towns. Generally the labour movement in the small communities was sparked by the arrival of workers from the nearby cities ... experienced in the techniques of agitation ... In Disna, a town in Vilna province, the idea of class struggle was introduced by several bristle workers ... The labour movement in Ihumen was sparked by an agitator from Minsk, who came equipped with a suitcase full of illegal literature; and in Drohiczyn the first strikes broke out after several members of the Bund in Pinsk ... had a meeting in the local synagogue. (Mendelsohn 1970: 82–4)

The movements' agitators and leaders were invariably members of the Bund, which expanded rapidly during this period into a mass revolutionary political party. The Zionist leader, Chaim Weizmann, writing in 1903, conceded its strength: 'Our hardest struggle everywhere is against the Bund ... this movement consumes much energy and heroism. ... children are in open revolt against their parents' (Frankel 1981: 141). The strike movement earned the Bund a special, albeit controversial, place alongside the main revolutionary parties challenging the Russian Empire, the Social Revolutionaries (heirs of the Narodniks), the Mensheviks and the Bolsheviks, as well as the nationalist parties. The Bund produced a large number of working-class socialist cadres, many of whom took their ideas abroad as migrants and would make impressive contributions to the spread of socialist movements throughout the industrialising world. The Bund regarded socialist education as important as staging strikes for better pay and conditions. The bristle workers in the town of Mezrich (Miedzrzyec), one of the most militant groups, were asked by their weary employer what they would do with their 'leisure' time, after they had forced him to reduce the number of working hours (to a twelve hour day). They showed him socialist literature issued by the Bund and replied, 'This is our Torah – we shall study it in our free time' (Mendelsohn 1970: 86).

This remark was not made tongue in cheek. And it wasn't just the Jewish employers who were perturbed by it. The rabbis were increasingly worried about *The Communist Manifesto* replacing the Torah, and sometimes in the most unlikely places:

> Many hundreds of young men left the *yeshiva*, Jewish religious schools, and plunged into the exhilarating secular world. The process involved a wrenching break with many of the values inherited from the world of their fathers, such as the decided preference for the life of religious study ... The acuteness of the rupture with the past was most vividly illustrated when ... *yeshiva* [students] ... consciously shifted from the study bench to the work bench, there to be exposed to the eye-heart-and-mind opening message of social emancipation expounded by the Bund. (Medem 1979: 217n.1)

This passage is from the memoir of Vladimir Medem, one of the Bund's leaders in the Pale of Settlement. Introducing the memoir, Professor Sam Portnoy explains the psychology of the new Jewish worker, 'having waged and won the struggle with himself – with his own passivity and fears', he now emerged as a revolutionary ready to 'repudiate the system of institutionalized timidity' that dominated the old Jewish congregational leadership (Medem 1979: xiv).

Fellow Bundist Abe Cahan has left us a vivid portrait of the young Medem himself, the Jewish Narodnik, a brave Russian aristocratic student from a family which had converted to Christianity, ever ready to face death as a deportee in Siberia, learning Yiddish 'beautifully', the language of the Jewish poor, routinely dismissed as 'jargon' by the assimilated Russian Jew (Medem 1979: xxxiii–xxxv).

We join Medem on the *birzha*, the street in every city 'designated as the site where the agitators would come together with the crowd'. The crowd offered a cover from police surveillance as ties were established 'with a fresh contact with some workshop or other'. 'The *birzha* literally teemed with hundreds of persons every night, all of them youthful worker types ... the familiar faces of the activists ... the new zestful people at the initial stage of imbibing the fresh wonderful teachings' (Medem 1979: 159).

Medem also shows the way the revolutionary movement was beginning to overturn anti-Semitism. He had studied at the University of Minsk. Shocked by the intervention of a lone anti-Semite, the revolutionary students seize the anti-Semite, put him on trial for two days, when a 'mass meeting of the whole university was convened' (Medem 1979: 108).

He describes a remarkable event in the city of Riga in 1905 when the revolution finally erupted. Its fate depended upon the strategically vital, and most definitely non-Jewish, railway workers there joining the general strike. They had shouted *zhid* ('kike', an offensive term for a Jew) at speakers, even those who were not Jewish, yet 'Maxim', the Bund speaker, 'pale, thin, with a dark beard ... hardly the horny-handed gentile proletarian', won them round (Medem 1979: 430n.6).

The Bund's expectations seemed about to come true in the 1905 revolution. Briefly, it looked as though the ideals of the French Revolution were to be carried by a multi-ethnic, co-religious social-ist workers movement, bringing emancipation for everyone as the Tsarist Empire came tumbling down, even if the price was great sacrifice:

> On June 5th in Lodz [Poland's second largest city] a demonstration, in which the supporters of the Bund and the Polish socialist parties merged, was fired upon and two days later some 50,000 people marched in the funeral procession. A general strike was called ... and that night barricades were raised in the Jewish quarter and elsewhere in the city. Pitched battles were fought with the cavalry and all during the night and into the next day.
>
> Hundreds were killed, [the] majority were Jews. The correspondent for the Russian revolutionary newspaper, *Iskra*, reported:
>
> 'I cannot but emphasise the great respect in which ... Christian Lodz holds the Jews. The heroic conduct of the Jews in the clashes with the police and the army arouses admiration everywhere ... Legends are circulating about yesterday's battle between the Jews and the Cossacks – legends which describe the Jews as some kind of Samsons.' (Frankel 1981: 146)

The normally cautious and moderate Jewish newspaper *Voskhod* noted the general trend everywhere, 'never has the Christian population of the Pale felt such solidarity with the Jews' (Frankel 1981: 147).

The long years of preparation by the Bund and by Jews acting as individual members of the Russian and Polish socialist parties had paid off. It meant that when the revolution came,

> it was seen by large sections of the Jewish people as part of the natu-ral order of things: revenge for twenty-five years of humiliation and victimization, and *the long overdue entry of Russia into Europe.* (Frankel 1981: 142; emphasis added)

REVOLUTION DEFEATED: THE STRUGGLE FOR
THE SOUL OF JEWISH LABOUR

However, the revolution failed. And a new wave of pogroms launched in October 1905 threw the movement massively on to the defensive. Leon Trotsky,[4] the leader of the soviet, the workers revolutionary council in Petersburg, dominated by the militant metalworkers, spelled out their significance:

> A hundred Russian towns and townlets were transformed into hells. A veil of smoke was drawn across the sun. Fires devoured entire streets with their houses and inhabitants. This was the old order's revenge for its humiliation. (Trotsky 1972: 131)

The Bund was thrown into crisis. On its right, Zionist leaders like Vladimir Jabotinsky baited it for its preoccupation with Jewish *workers*, for refusing to take seriously the need to unite all social classes in the Jewish community, for refusing to see the 'Jewish nation' (Frankel 1981: 253). On its left, the demand came from rank-and-file Jewish workers to unite the Bund in a single party with the Bolsheviks and Mensheviks (Frankel 1981: 256).[5]

This was an old argument. Much to Lenin's fury, it had split away from a united revolutionary party in 1903 on the grounds that it alone could and should represent Jewish workers. The Bund demanded national cultural autonomy for the Jewish people within the context of the revolution. But what did this really mean? Recognition of Yiddish as a language was readily conceded by the Bolsheviks (much more willingly than the Zionists conceded it). But recognition of a Jewish nation? This would make the Bund 'seasick Zionists', according to the veteran revolutionary, Georgi Plekhanov (Frankel 1981: 255). Lenin's view was that Jewish workers were potentially so advanced that they could overcome the limitations of national consciousness. He pointed to New York, where Jewish worker migrants were heavily involved with building multi-ethnic trade unions and the international socialist movement (Lenin 1972: 20, 27–33).

In 1903 this argument had split the Bund congress down the middle. The leadership was so embarrassed that it expunged the debate from the minutes (Medem 1979: 281).

There was a further factor noted by the 'Zionist Marxist' Ben Borochov. The Jewish workers could not fight alone forever. On the one hand, in terms of numbers of strikes, the Jewish strike movement of the Pale showed a greater intensity than anywhere in the world. On the other hand, the strike statistics were highly misleading. Mostly they took place in tiny workplaces so that a strike by three tailors in Minsk counted as the equivalent of a strike by 3,000 steelworkers in Pittsburgh (Mendelsohn 1970: 85). Borochov's conclusion was to emigrate to Palestine; Lenin's was to integrate the Jewish workers' movement into the wider workers' movement and to make the fight for Jewish equal rights, and unequivocal hostility to all forms of anti-Semitism, an integral part of the revolutionary programme.

It is interesting that even Ben-Gurion was forced to admit that Lenin and the Bolsheviks were absolutely uncompromising in their determination to destroy anti-Semitism. Only Lenin's 'administration can summon the strength to defend the Jews' from their enemies, he was to write after the 1917 revolution (Teveth 1987: 232).

*   *   *

After 1905, battle had been joined between the Bund and the Zionists, as one writer put it 'for the hearts and minds of every Jewish youth and maid in every city and every *shtetel* [Jewish village]' (Frankel 1981: 156).

A measure of the impact of Marxist politics, and the centrality of the Jewish worker as revolutionary fighter, Bundist or non-Bundist, was the way the Zionist movement itself was forced to accommodate it. Ben-Gurion was a unique witness.

When the 1905 revolution broke out, Ben-Gurion was living in Warsaw, 60 kilometres from his home town of Plonsk. According to Shabtai Teveth, his sympathetic biographer, Ben-Gurion regarded those Jews, whom he saw in its vanguard, as wasting their lives for a hopeless cause. Jewish 'salvation would only be found in *Eretz Israel* [i.e. Palestine] ... the revolution might liberate Russia (and Poland) but not the Jewish people' (Teveth 1987: 25–6).

Yet Ben-Gurion understood the impact of Marxist ideas on the youthful Jewish radical imagination. In Warsaw, he came across the 'Zionist-Marxist' party, Poale Zion, which tried to adapt Marxist ideas to the Zionist cause. Ben-Gurion felt compelled to join Poale Zion even though he did not espouse its ideas (Teveth 1987: 30). The Zionists could compete with the revolutionary parties only by playing them at their own game and Poale Zion was their chosen instrument. Ben-Gurion had first-hand experience of what this meant. Whilst in Warsaw, the Bund had organised defence squads against anticipated pogrom attacks in Plonsk which Ben-Gurion knew of and was very impressed by. Ben-Gurion returned home determined to defeat the Bund. Teveth's description of what happened next could have been of any *shtetl*, town or city in the Pale.

Ben-Gurion and Poale Zion challenged the Bund to a public debate in the town's Great Synagogue. The Bund sent a leading orator. Shops were closed for the occasion and 'out of respect for the synagogue, their handguns were placed on the table' (Teveth 1987: 32). Teveth assures us that Ben-Gurion easily won the argument, but the Bund press seems to have regarded it as something of a pyrrhic victory when they reported him threatening to turn his guns on Bund members. It is also interesting that Ben-Gurion felt compelled to consolidate his base in the town by organising trade unions there (Teveth 1987: 33).

CRACKED REFLECTION: THE IMPACT OF 1905 ON THE ZIONIST MOVEMENT IN PALESTINE

Ben-Gurion's generation of young Zionists in the Pale of Settlement were deeply affected by the experience of the 1905 revolution. It provided a very special cadre for Zionism's mission to Palestine. It is even argued that a Jewish State could not have been created

> without their intrusion into the *Yishuv* ... The hard core within the immigrant youth, perhaps no more than two or three hundred, were charged with an exceptional degree with political energy – an energy drawing its force from the Russian revolutionary experience, on the one hand, and from Jewish messianism, on the other ...
>
> They were anticlerical, often atheist, but their vision of the world remained largely messianic – shaped by *heder* [youth education] and *yeshiva*, by the Hasidic upbringing or by their deeply emotional involvement with Herzl, as the harbinger of the long awaited Redemption, the End of Days ...
>
> Those of the immigrant youth whose attachment to Zionism was rooted in socio-revolutionary concepts alone without the admixture of national myth rarely stayed in the country ... Ben-Gurion put the figure as low as 10 per cent, remaining in the country. (Frankel 1981: 366–8)

An attempt was made to create a coherent socialist ideology out of this peculiar way the Russian revolution energised what we might call the religious nostalgia of a minority of Jewish youth, as the basis for a modern Jewish nationalism in Palestine. Although, as for the Bund, Jewish workers were cast as the social agency for transformation of Jewish national life, this argument took on a completely different meaning when it was grounded in the realities of the Arab world. Socialist ideas constantly surrendered to the Jewish nationalism inherent in an ideological focus on *Jewish* labour.

At the Congress of Poale Zion in Jaffa in 1906, Ben-Gurion vigorously opposed the more orthodox Marxist minority, who naively believed that Jewish socialists should support and even help Arab workers to organise trade unions, instead of struggling for exclusive Jewish labour. This argument was soon to be put to a severe test during a strike against starvation wages by Arab orange grove workers from the village of Petach-Tiva. The same Marxist minority attempted to organise solidarity with those whom they believed to be their Arab brothers in struggle. 'The Ottoman administration, the Jewish settlers and the Zionist labour leaders immediately closed ranks against the orange grove workers. The strikers were arrested and tortured but refused to betray their Jewish comrades' (Weinstock 1979: 87).[6]

From the Zionist viewpoint, the problem with the Petach-Tiva Arab workers wasn't just that they went on strike, it was that they had jobs at all in the 'Jewish economy'. An ominous new slogan appeared. It appeared to be 'socialist', but in practice was the very antithesis of socialism in that it exposed the virulent anti-Arab sentiment which was to be the hallmark of the Zionist trade union movement, the Histadruth. The slogan was the 'conquest of labour' (Weinstock 1979: 133), for which read the 'conquest by Jews of jobs from Arabs'.

The Histadruth was always more than just a trade union. In the early days under the British Mandate it was the largest employer after the government:

> This policy tended to equip the developing Jewish working class in Palestine with an indispensable economic infrastructure: its producer co-operatives created jobs for Jewish immigrants and its sales companies ensured the marketing of Zionist production ... The counterpart of the trade union watchword *Jewish Labour* was the slogan *Jewish Produce* ...

> Zionist economic 'apartheid' was inherent in the Histadruth ... Every member had to pay two compulsory levies (1) for Jewish Labour – funds for organizing pickets etc. against the employment of Arab workers. (2) for Jewish Produce – for organizing the boycott of Arab produce ... (Weinstock 1979: 184)[7]

Thus, ideas traditionally associated with trade union and socialist struggle, like *picketing* and *boycotting*, are turned inside out and take on meanings exactly the opposite of their intention: in other words, to destroy, rather than to promote, solidarity between Arabs and Jews. These 'principles' of the Jewish trade union movement in Palestine anticipated the foundations of the Israeli state itself: the institutionalised separation of Arab and Jew, privileging the Jew at the expense of the Arab.

HERZL: THE REACTIONARY MESSIAH FROM THE WEST

Arab realities in Palestine made explicit and hardened the Jewish *isolationism* implicit in the Zionist enterprise. In truth, though, the original theoreticians of Zionism, like its main inspiration, Theodor Herzl, had already made a virtue of that sense of Jewish isolation induced by European anti-Semitism. It is this dimension of Zionism which gives its ideology such a deeply reactionary character, long before its inevitable confrontation with Arab Palestine.

A recent sympathetic portrait of Herzl, by the Zionist writer Robert Wistrich, reminds us that it was in Paris in 1892 that Herzl began to see anti-Semitism as a universal phenomenon. He claimed that the people 'in republican, modern, civilized France, one hundred years after the Declaration of the Rights of Man' had spontaneously revoked the edict of the Great Revolution (Wistrich and Ohana 1995: 17–18). This was his response to the trial of Alfred Dreyfus, the French Jewish army officer, who had falsely been accused of treason. The trial became a *cause célèbre* for both the Right and the Left, made famous by the French novelist, Emile Zola, and his rallying cry, *'J'Accuse!'*, mobilizing the Left on behalf of Dreyfus. But Herzl could see France only through the eyes of the nationalist Right, which is where his own political sympathies lay (Shapira 1992: 12). He surrendered to its view that anti-Semitism would capture the majority of its people. He was to say that it was the trial that turned him into a Zionist.

Wistrich, retelling this story, ignores the way the Dreyfus trial was also a watershed for the Left. It acted as a wake-up call, in the words of French Socialist leader, Jean Jaurès, 'to take sides in the conflicts among various bourgeois factions ... to save political liberty ... as in the Dreyfus affair, to defend humanity' (Jacobs 1992: 15). As in Russia, the growing Socialist movement now had to carry forward the ideals inscribed on the banner of the French Revolution. And from now on the Left would see anti-Semitism 'as its most dangerous opponent'[8] (Jacobs 1992: 12). The Left committed itself to challenging the prejudices amongst its growing working-class supporters. Interestingly enough, Dreyfus himself would side with the socialists, rejecting Zionism as an 'anachronism' (Burns 1992: 302).

Herzl now developed a frankly shocking attitude to anti-Semitism. He wrote that he was ready to 'understand and *pardon*' it (Wistrich and Ohana 1995: 11). Pardoning anti-Semitism allowed him to develop a perverse diplomatic initiative in Russia, which shook many even in the Zionist camp. Several months after one of the most bloody pogroms ever, at Kishinev in 1903, when nearly 50 Jews were killed, Herzl held a meeting with Siacheslav Konstantovich Pleve, the Tsarist minister held responsible for the Black Hundred pogromists. Far from being on the defensive, Pleve and his fellow ministers told Herzl that the problem was the Jews threatening revolution. Pleve claimed that young Jews comprised up to half of the membership of the revolutionary parties.

Herzl listened sympathetically. He reported to the sixth Zionist Congress that year that his supporters in Russia who backed revolution should start behaving 'calmly and legally'. Socialist-inclined youth at the Congress regarded his remarks as virtually treasonable, producing a rebellious pamphlet 'Neither Calmly nor Legally' (Frankel 1981: 279). The Bund hardened the accusation of treason. It was 'direct collaboration ... to have the regime disgorge its unwanted Jews' (Medem 1979: xv).

Still, we should not underestimate Herzl's appeal in the Pale. After his visit to Pleve he was able to draw vast crowds, even in the Bundist heartland of Vilna (Frankel 1981: 179). His messianic appeal (he picked up the epithet 'King of the Jews' in the Pale) offered a momentary, comforting and, above all, a very clever illusion. Here was a famous European aesthete – as a playwright and journalist he had been the darling of the Jewish bourgeoisie in Vienna – playing upon ancient Judaic themes and emotions, for a people struggling in the here and now against stifling and hateful conditions. Here was a dream ticket back to the future. He was saying, 'Look at me, I'm a Jew who has made it in the modern world, you can too if you follow me to Palestine, to build a modern nation in our ancient homeland.' He forgot to tell them about the Arab people who were already living there. 'Herzl had a unique talent for weaving the illusion of power, for creating the mood then forcing the will for nationhood on a demoralized and dispersed people' (Wistrich and Ohana 1995: 16).

Herzl had been ready to help protect the Tsarist status quo because he wanted the Tsar to put pressure on the sultan, the head of the Ottoman Empire, to let more Russian Jews into Palestine. He had already made a highly offensive and demagogic appeal to the sultan where, aiding and abetting those voices already gleefully exaggerating and raising allegations about Jewish financial power, Herzl had offered Jewish regulation of the sultan's finances in return for letting the Jews into Palestine. The sultan had politely refused.

Herzl's appeal to the sultan was revealing in another regard. It would set the seal on Zionist strategy for the rest of the twentieth century, to be explored in detail in the rest of this book, as the instrument for Great Power domination of the Arab world. 'We would form a portion of a rampart of Europe against Asia, an outpost of civilization against barbarism' (Vital 1975: 266).

A PEOPLE WITHOUT LAND?

One hundred years later we are able to make a full assessment of this myth, perhaps the only one with a genuine resonance in reality. This is because all three possible routes to emancipation facing Jews in the Pale of Settlement at the beginning of the twentieth century – emigration to America, emigration to Palestine or emancipation through struggle to overthrow the Tsarist Empire – were to be put to the severest of tests. Though a successful implementation of the Bolshevik programme, following the second revolution in 1917 in Russia, would have brought about far-reaching Jewish emancipation, it was not to be. The long years of Stalinism periodically revived and manipulated anti-Semitic sentiment to such an extent, that as the Soviet Union disintegrated at the end of the 1980s, there was a massive exodus of over a million Soviet Jews.

But here was the test. Would they choose America or Israel? In overwhelming numbers, they chose America, where possible, using the Israeli visas they had obtained. In 1989 this was stopped

(Beit Hallahmi 1992: 198).[9] The right-wing Israeli leader, Yitzak Shamir, had panicked. Here was the Zionist theory of Jewish history being overturned before the eyes of the world. Shamir approached President Reagan for a deal: help us redirect these Jewish migrants to Israel and we will be even more your friend and pursue your policies in the Middle East with even greater vigour. Reagan obligingly agreed. A later chapter will explore in much greater detail US–Israeli relations at this time. Here we need conclude only that the US was playing the Zionist game to serve its own interests. As for the Soviet Jews, their conception of emancipation was well and truly thwarted as they found themselves pawns of US foreign policy in the Middle East and forced to live in the least safe place for Jews anywhere in the world.

7
Plucky Little Israel or Great Power Protégé? I: Britain and the Zionist Colony in Palestine

Zionist propaganda has often portrayed the struggle for a Jewish state in Palestine with the Old Testament's David and Goliath fable hovering as metaphor in the background: a heroic, downtrodden and isolated people battling against overwhelming odds for a national home of their own. Success would depend exclusively upon the Jews, on their initiative and moral and physical courage. Such an outcome would be nothing less than a modern miracle. Jewish independence and freedom would be realised at last.

It is a powerful and persuasive myth, but at root it is fundamentally flawed. The processes set in train, which took thousands of Jewish settlers to Palestine, reproduced a modern version of Jewish dependency upon autocracy (as well as producing a modern autocratic Jewish ideology), so characteristic of medieval and even ancient times. In the past Jews sold their services to rulers in return for the protection of their religion. Now they would serve the interests of the Great Powers in return for the protection of their right to occupy the land belonging to another people. Zionist ideology would develop as distinctively autocratic, as least as far as its responses to the native population of Palestine were concerned.

This chapter explores in detail how Britain became the first Great Power officially to endorse and implement a Jewish claim on Palestine and how it expected to benefit in return. Naked imperialist ambition combined with disturbingly strong undercurrents of anti-Semitism in the minds of Britain's rulers as they began their embrace of the Zionist creed during the First World War. It was not a very attractive beginning for the much trumpeted 'Return to Zion', the long awaited rebirth of the Jewish people in the land of their origin. Moreover, it was a beginning that would leave forever a curse and a scar on Zionist politics, an emblem that it came to Palestine as a politics of oppression.

The chapter ends with historical confirmation of this proposition: the great Palestinian national uprising, the first *intifada*, a classic anti-imperialist and anti-colonial movement, which so sharply exposed the British and the Zionists as oppressor colonists.

A later chapter will explore what happened when the United States replaced Britain as sponsor and began to use the newly-created State of Israel to pursue its imperialist designs. This would so enlarge Zionism as a politics of oppression that, by the beginning of the twenty-first century, it was reeling from world-wide condemnation.

HOW BRITAIN DECLARED FOR ZIONISM: THE BALFOUR DECLARATION

Theodor Herzl had always argued that the creation of a Zionist colony in Palestine would need the backing of a Great Power. At a critical point during the First World War, Britain's rulers persuaded themselves that this was a cause for them; indeed a cause of the highest order of nobility and honour, both politically and even spiritually; a cause entirely in keeping with those who aspired to rule the greatest empire the world had ever seen. It also had the merit that it might simultaneously assist the allied war effort as well as secure Palestine for the British Empire once the war was over. Some of them, the most famous names in early twentieth-century British imperial history, David Lloyd George, Winston Churchill, Arthur Balfour, even declared themselves converts to Zionism. Curiously, though, these same men were also known to harbour some extremely peculiar, if not downright hostile, attitudes towards Jews. How do we explain this bizarre development?

We need to comprehend fully the British imperial tradition, or at least capture its mood. No one has come closer to doing just that than the poet, Percy Bysshe Shelley. A hundred years earlier he had penned the *Mask of Anarchy* about some famous statesmen in early nineteenth-century imperial history.

> I met Murder on the way
> He had a face like Castlereagh
> Very smooth he looked yet grim:
> Seven bloodhounds followed him.

Next came Fraud, and he had on,
Like Eldon, an ermined gown;
His big tears, for he wept well,
Turned to millstones as they fell;

Clothed with the Bible, as with light,
And the shadows of the night,
like Sidmouth next, Hypocrisy
On a crocodile rode by,

And many more Destructions played
In this ghastly masquerade,
All disguised, even to the eyes,
Like Bishops, lawyers, peers or spies.

(abridged)[1]

One of the most notorious minor imperial players, a Destruction if
ever there was one, during the First World War was Mark Sykes, aris-
tocrat, High Tory, Roman Catholic, roving diplomat, vulgar anti-
Semite. Together with Georges Picot, his opposite number in France,
Great Britain's principal ally in the 'machine for massacre', Eric
Hobsbawm's (1994) apt description of the First World War, he had
cast his greedy eyes on the 'Levant' (the Middle East) including, of
course, Palestine. The Ottoman Empire was crumbling; soon it
would be up for grabs. In 1916, on behalf of their respective imperial masters, Sykes and Picot met to reflect on its downfall and to
consider the distribution of the spoils of war. As Sykes put it:

> it was clear that an Arab rising was sooner or later to take place, and
> that the French and ourselves ought to be on better terms if the rising
> was not to be a curse instead of a blessing. (Said 1995: 221)

Sykes also became a Zionist sympathiser. Within a year the entire
Imperial War Cabinet would commit itself to Zionism and publish
the famous Balfour Declaration, Arthur Balfour's statement, on
behalf of the British government, which guaranteed a national
home for the Jewish people in Palestine.

We have one very special witness to this strange metamorphosis:
Chaim Weizmann. Weizmann was *de facto* Herzl's successor, at least
as far as the promotion of the Zionist cause in Britain was concerned. A Jewish migrant from Russia and trained scientist, when
war broke out Weizmann was working as an explosives expert for

the British government. Is it not highly appropriate that the man who would help convert the Imperial War Cabinet to Zionism was also hired to improve the efficiency of its death machine? Indeed, Lloyd George once quipped that the Balfour Declaration was his gift to Weizmann in return for his services to the war effort (Segev 2000: 43–4). Weizmann's most effective role, though, was to pander to the prejudices of the Imperial War Cabinet and the ugly way it judged what is sometimes called the Jewish Question.

WHAT A GANG! THE BRITISH IMPERIAL ZIONISTS

No. 1 David Lloyd George

When Lloyd George became prime minister at the end of 1916 he reaffirmed the dismantling of the Ottoman Empire as a 'major war aim' (Vital 1987: 209). He also insisted that the British occupy Palestine. This was in flagrant breach of the Sykes–Picot agreement, which had promised France a major stake in Palestine. He had the backing of C.P. Scott, editor of the *Manchester Guardian* and one of Lloyd George's staunchest supporters. Just before Lloyd George took office, the paper's military correspondent had written that 'the whole future of the British Empire as a Sea Empire' depended upon Palestine becoming a buffer state inhabited 'by an intensely patriotic race' (Fromkin 1989: 271). This concurred with Weizmann's view: 'a Jewish Palestine would be a safeguard to England, in particular in respect to the Suez Canal' (Weinstock 1979: 96). Scott had learned about Zionism and its alleged possibilities from Weizmann.

Sentimental accounts of Lloyd George's Zionism always stress his biblical affiliations. It was said that he was a true believer in restoring Jews to Zion (Fromkin 1989: 268) in that curious tradition of Protestant philosemitism. Yet there was also a darker and more ominous attitude. He had a grotesquely inflated view of 'Jewish power', to such an extent that it led him to the view that the Jews of Russia could prevent that country breaking ranks with the allied war effort in the year of the Russian Revolution, 1917. There is a plausible argument, which we will examine later, that this determined the timing, if not the fact, of the Balfour Declaration. Lloyd George referred to the 'Jewish race', 'world Jewry' and the 'Zionists' as if they were the same thing, and Weizmann worked hard to encourage such a view (Segev 2000: 42). Herbert Asquith, British prime minister immediately prior to Lloyd George, had probably the truest view of his successor. 'Lloyd George', Asquith had noted, 'does not care a damn for the Jews or their past or their future.' But he did care about Palestine (Vital 1987: 233).

No. 2 Arthur Balfour

Balfour, the statesman who signed the famous declaration, was also prime minister at the time of the infamous Aliens Act of 1905. This legislation had slammed the door in the face of Eastern European Jewish migrants fleeing the waves of pogroms in the Russian Empire. Balfour had personally piloted the Bill through the House of Commons. He insisted, nevertheless, that he was a vigorous opponent of anti-Semitism. Even the *Jewish Chronicle*, then as today a conservative commentator on public affairs, expressed surprise at this breathtaking display of hypocrisy (Stein 1961: 149–50).[2] That splendid acronym, NIMBY (Not In My Back Yard) had yet to be coined, but it fits perfectly with Balfour's attitude. Jews were not welcome in Britain's backyard, but Britain would welcome them in the front garden of the Palestinian Arabs, with or without the Arabs' approval.

In fact, Balfour had admitted anti-Semitic sympathies to no lesser a personage than Weizmann himself. He had told Weizmann of conversations he had had with Cosima Wagner, widow of the notoriously anti-Semitic German composer, Richard Wagner. But the Zionists also subscribed to 'cultural anti-Semitism', Weizmann reassured Balfour. Zionists also believed that those German Jews who had identified themselves as Germans 'of the Mosaic faith', i.e. Germans in terms of nationality and Jewish in terms of religion, were 'an undesirable, demoralizing phenomenon' (Segev 2000: 41).

Balfour epitomised this anti-Semitic strand in British Imperial thought now allied to Zionism. It didn't like the real Jews that it saw, and in many ways neither did the Zionist leaders. British imperialism subscribed to the Zionist conception of re-ordering Jewish life to fit a crude blueprint of reviving the Old Testament Jew in modern guise. Here was a really exciting, romantic experiment for the British Empire to revive continuity in Western civilisation, which was after all rooted in the Judaeo-Christian tradition, and at the same time strengthen its presence in the Arab world. It had about it a unique moral and spiritual quality on a plane simply not accessible to the Arab mentality. Georges Antonius, a prominent, Jerusalem-based Palestinian Christian Arab, shrewdly observed that Balfour saw Palestine as 'a historico-intellectual exercise and diversion'.

Balfour himself would say, 'Zionism, be it right or wrong ... is of far profounder import than the desires and prejudices of the 700,000 Arabs who now inhabit that ancient land' (Segev 2000: 45).

No. 3 Winston Churchill

The idea that Zionism might re-order Jewish life had particular appeal to Churchill, who became Colonial Secretary after the war and hence the minister directly responsible for the implementation of the Balfour Declaration. Churchill had been profoundly disturbed by the Russian Revolution and was convinced that the 'International Jew' was behind it. He called the Bolsheviks 'a bacillus', an expression frequently applied to Jews in anti-Semitic publications. This reinforced his Zionist convictions. He believed that the Zionists 'would provide the antidote to this sinister conspiracy and bestow stability instead of chaos on the Western world' (Segev 2000: 158).

Churchill seems to have believed that there were three types of politically active Jew: those who participated in the political life of the country in which they lived, of whom he wholeheartedly approved and whose immigrant co-religionists he was ready to encourage (in 1905 he had opposed Balfour's Aliens Act); those who became subversives, especially in the Russian Empire where a majority of the world's Jews lived; and those who became Zionists.

Britain could do the world a favour and stem the subversive tendencies of the Jews of Russia by offering them a national home of their own in Palestine, now part of the British Empire. As he wrote just before taking office as Colonial Secretary in 1920:

> If, as well may happen, there should be created in our own life time by the banks of the Jordan a Jewish State under the protection of the British Crown ... an event will have occurred in the history of the world which from every point of view would be beneficial and would be especially in harmony with the interests of the British Empire. (Fromkin 1989: 519)

Even Weizmann was amazed at Churchill's readiness to encourage the Zionists. Weizmann once admitted to the new Colonial Secretary that the Zionists were smuggling arms into Palestine in response to rising Arab hostility. Churchill told him, 'We don't mind, but don't speak of it' (Segev 2000: 194).

No. 4 Mark Sykes

The transformation of Sykes from anti-Semite into Zionist is a clear case-study of this perverse phenomenon. Sykes loathed the Jews. The Jew was 'the archetype of the cosmopolitan financier ... rootless moneygrubbers, all the more contemptible when they tried to disguise themselves as something else'. In his youth he had even drawn 'hideous Jewish types' (Stein 1961: 272). And yet Sykes too would become hooked on Zionism and see it as a grand social experiment. He told the pope in 1917 that it would raise 'the racial self-respect of the Jewish people' and produce a 'virtuous and simple agrarian population' in Palestine (Stein 1961: 275). However, this did not mean that Sykes was any less an anti-Semite. On the contrary, he saw Zionism as a counterweight to international Jewish finance, which, he believed, was backing the German war effort (Stein 1961: 276). And like Churchill he also viewed Zionism as a counterweight to those international Jewish subversives who saw 'Karl Marx as the only prophet of Israel' (Stein 1961: 275). These subversives could also damage the allied war effort because they could withdraw Russia from the war.

Sykes represented, in concentrated form, the British Imperial view that Zionism could, reform the behaviour of 'international Jewry'; secure the support of 'international Jewry' for the allied war effort; and secure Palestine for the British Empire after the war.

In reality, it was the last two assumptions that mattered most. It was upon these assumptions that Lloyd George would encourage Sykes to sabotage the agreement he had reached with Georges Picot. Sykes would play the 'Zionist card' to intimidate the French into dropping their claims on Palestine. But before turning to the despicable antics of Lloyd George and Sykes we must first briefly give voice to a rather more honourable and forgotten view, that of British Jewish anti-Zionism.

'THE ANTI-SEMITISM OF THE PRESENT GOVERNMENT'

This was the title of a Cabinet paper, written by Edwin Montagu in August 1917 (Vital 1987: 282). Newly appointed Secretary of State for India, Montagu could hardly be accused of not having the interests of the British Empire at heart. However, though he was the only Jew in the British Cabinet and hence his views had to be taken rather seriously, by an odd quirk of fate, his cousin Herbert Samuel, the first professing Jew ever to serve in a British Cabinet, was only recently out of office. Samuel was a staunch Zionist and so undermined any claims that Montagu might make that he, rather than the Zionists, represented the true interests of Britain's Jewish community.[3] Nevertheless, the force of Montagu's argument touched a raw nerve. Wouldn't Zionism create two national identities for Jews? Wouldn't this encourage anti-Semites everywhere to call for Jews to be deported to Palestine? Didn't this mean that Palestine would become a modern Jewish ghetto? Wouldn't Zionism itself, far from alleviating anti-Semitism, inadvertently promote it?[4]

As Segev has noted, this is precisely what the Zionists wanted. 'The anti-Semites will become our most loyal friends, the anti-Semitic nations will become our allies,' Herzl had written in his diary (Segev 2000: 47).

What is remarkable is how sophisticated was the response of the War Cabinet, now fully committed to the Zionist cause. They went to great lengths to convince Montagu that he was mistaken. A Foreign Office paper was specially commissioned to refute Montagu point by point. Balfour, of all people, led the War Cabinet discussions, insisting that the assimilation of Jews in Britain or elsewhere would not be affected. It was a measure of just how committed the War Cabinet now was to Zionism, and Montagu's challenge was seen off (Vital 1987: 280–6).

KEEPING FRANCE OUT OF PALESTINE: THE LLOYD GEORGE–SYKES 'ZIONIST PLOT'

That the 'Zionists might be useful allies in the effort to overturn the Anglo-French Agreement was certainly the chief cause of the reappearance of the Palestine idea on the Government's agenda' in the early months of 1917 (Vital 1987: 213). Vital, who has paid scrupulous attention to this phase of the War Cabinet's attachment to Zionism, chooses his words with care: 'To employ the Zionists in this way made good sense to people (among them Curzon ...) who had no particular sympathy for their cause or for Jews in general' (Vital 1987: 214).[5] Here we see the precise relation between the rulers of the British Empire and Zionism. Shorn of sentimentality, Zionism was to be a useful and worthy *tool* (Vital 1987: 222), to enhance British interests.

Indeed, as the Zionist leaders were drawn into the plot to break up the Anglo-French Agreement, they were kept in the dark about its true intentions. The agreement was, after all, a wartime secret, to divide the spoils of war long before the war had actually been won. In any case, Zionist considerations had not figured in it all (Vital 1987: 202); this was not something that Sykes or Lloyd George would care to let the Zionists realise. But now the situation was completely different. Not only were Zionist aspirations suddenly *useful*, they were to be actively encouraged. Sykes had Lloyd George's full support as he began, in his words, to get the Zionists 'fired up' (Vital 1987: 224). This was a critical moment for the Zionists in Britain. Overnight their status was transformed. Now they were the favoured ones in the eyes of the government. The traditional leaders of the Anglo-Jewry, sceptical to say the least about the Zionists' plans, had to take a back seat. The Zionists were now, according to Weizmann, closer to the 'heart of the matter' than ever before (Vital 1987: 238). They were called to special meeting where Sykes lectured the Zionists on French policy. He expressed his sympathies for the idea of a 'Jewish Palestine', but said the French were putting obstacles in the way. They needed to be convinced about the merits of Zionism. Who better to do that than the Zionists themselves (Vital 1987: 238–40)?

It was agreed that Nahum Sokolov, a Zionist leader from Russia, should put the case to the French. Thus the trap was laid for the French, without the Zionists fully understanding its true intent. The French were impressed with the Zionists' case. Sokolov met Picot and other high-ranking French officials over a period of weeks. But when the French made the obvious offer that they, the French, might be ready to sponsor a Zionist colony in the event of France occupying Palestine, Sokolov explained that British sponsorship was preferred. In other words, it began to dawn on the French that Zionism came as part of a larger package, with its British sponsors already in place. Given that it would be the British rather than the French that would seize Palestine militarily, the French were in a weak position. Sykes then again met Picot to stress 'the importance of meeting Jewish demands' and to realise the implications of the Zionists favouring 'British suzerainty' (Vital 1987: 243).

Sykes was understandably well pleased with himself. He wrote to Balfour, 'As regards Zionism … the French are beginning to realize they are up against a big thing and they cannot close their eyes to it' (Vital 1987: 244).

Yet why did both the British and the French see Zionism as a 'big thing'? At one point in the discussions between Picot and Sokolov,

Picot had urged that 'It would be of great use to their cause if the Jews would make their devotion to the Entente [between France and Britain] more evident' (Vital 1987: 241).

It seems that Zionism carried something rather more in the eyes of the allies than just its claim on Palestine.

ZIONISM: THE 'BIG THING'

In his *War Memoirs*, Lloyd George wrote:

> Russian Jews had become the chief agents of German pacifist propaganda in Russia. By 1917, the Russian Jews had done much in preparing for the general disintegration of Russian society ... It was believed that if Great Britain declared for the fulfillment of Zionist aims in Palestine ... the effect would be to bring Russian Jewry to the cause of the Entente. (Levene 1992b: 70)

The fall of Tsar Nicholas in February 1917 had indeed raised the possibility that Russia might pull out of the allied war effort. But the idea that Russia's Jews were ultimately responsible and that they might be persuaded to keep Russia in the war if Zionist aims were conceded is perverse in the extreme. Yet we have already seen that some of these sentiments were being voiced by Lloyd George's war colleagues. It was also a view endorsed by sections of the British military establishment. Lieutenant General Sir George Macmunn and Captain Cyril Falls in their history of the First World War claimed that 'the imperative pressure of allied needs, and the international power of the Jewish race, had made desirable the recognition of Jewish aspirations for a "National Home" in Palestine' (Vital 1987: 297).

Weizmann had worked long and hard to encourage such a view. He pieced together a political fantasy about the Jews in the Russian Revolution and the impact they could have on both the allied *and* the German war effort. It was a fantasy that played directly on those anti-Semitic prejudices in the Imperial War Cabinet which were preoccupied with 'Jewish power'.

According to Weizmann, Russian Jews were now rallying to the Zionist cause. He made this claim despite the fact that the overthrow of the Tsar regime meant that, for the first time in Russia's history, full Jewish emancipation was a real possibility, endorsed by a clear commitment from all of Russia's revolutionary parties.

Again, Weizmann claimed that Russia's Zionists had the power to marshal Russia's Jews behind the allied war efforts, despite admitting privately the difficulty he was having persuading Russia's Zionists to give up their policy of *neutrality* towards the war (Levene 1992b: 74). Finally, Weizmann talked wildly about how a declaration for Zionism would make for 'friendship with the Jews of the world ... not a *thing* to be blown upon ... a thing that matters a great deal, even for a mighty empire like the British' (Levene 1992b: 73).[6] Weizmann was playing on a very specific fear. Germany was occupying Poland and parts of Lithuania, parts of the old Pale of Settlement, and Germany was beginning to make promises about a Jewish Palestine. Britain had better get in first.

History itself would very quickly burst the fantasy bubble about Zionist power to affect Jewish support for the allied war effort. By a wonderful irony, the very same week that the Balfour Declaration was published in October 1917, the Bolsheviks seized power in Russia and pulled the country out of the war. The Jewish conspiracy theorists everywhere were confounded. After all, the Jews were supposed to keep Russia *in* the war, now that the allies had promised them a Jewish home in Palestine. Still, our satisfaction at seeing the conspiracy theorists so easily mocked and routed in this way should be tempered by the sheer depth of the underlying anti-Semitism that has been exposed. Levene has pointed to remarks at the beginning of Volume IV of Leon Poliakov's, *The History of Anti-Semitism*, that early twentieth-century European high society's obsession with Jews has now been largely forgotten (Levene 1992b: 76). Yet this obsession played a part in imposing the Zionist colony on the Palestinians: an obsession, anti-Semitic at its core, which the Jewish Zionist leaders had no desire whatsoever to challenge.

IMPERIALIST, RACIST AND ZIONIST: CHURCHILL AMONG THE JEWS AND ARABS IN PALESTINE

Churchill became Colonial Secretary in February 1921, with direct responsibility for the Middle East. Within three months the most serious anti-Zionist Arab riots yet encountered broke out across Palestine (Fromkin 1989: 515). Herbert Samuel, formerly the War Cabinet's only Jewish Zionist, now the British High Commissioner for Palestine, responded by suspending any further Jewish immigration. This provoked a major crisis for Zionism and threatened to undermine the very basis of the Balfour Declaration. Ben-Gurion would denounce Samuel as a 'traitor' (Segev 2000: 492). Churchill was expected to clear up the mess.

Churchill made clear that the British government had no intention of reneging on the Balfour Declaration. He had told a Palestinian Arab delegation in Cairo that Zionism was 'good for the world, good for the Jews, good for the British Empire, but also good for the Arabs' (Fromkin 1989: 519). Following the riots, in the summer of 1921, he repeated the point to a Palestinian Arab delegation in London: 'The British Government mean to carry out the Balfour Declaration. I've told you so again and again' (Fromkin 1989: 524). Jewish immigration to Palestine was eventually resumed.

In practice, Churchill had a profound contempt for the Arabs. His chief adviser on 'Arab affairs' was the legendary British military agent 'Lawrence of Arabia'. The legend sometimes gives the impression of a genuine British affection for all things Arabic. Over the years there has been much talk of the 'Arabists' in the Foreign Office, allegedly heirs to the Lawrence tradition, always ready to undermine Britain's overall commitment to Zionism. But this displays a deep misunderstanding of Lawrence and 'British Arabism'. In one sense 'British Arabism' was like its imperial counterpart, 'British Zionism'. The English ruling classes conjured up an ideal type of 'Arab' in the same way that they had invented an ideal type of 'Jew'. The ideal Jew was a 'new Jew', a superior brand, just the sort of chap to help rule the empire. But the ideal Arab was the Orientalist image presented by the desert Bedouin from the Arabian peninsula, an 'old Arab' from the *Arabian Nights*, quick-witted and selfless. By contrast, the Palestinian Arabs were, according to Lawrence 'stupid, materialist ... bankrupt' (Cohen 1985: 77). In fact, there was some doubt whether they were real Arabs at all. Gilbert Clayton, first head of the British Military Administration in Palestine immediately after the war, wrote that Palestinian Arabs were of 'mixed race and questionable character ... the so-called Arabs of Palestine are not to be compared with the real Arabs of the Desert' (Cohen 1985: 77).

Churchill absorbed these attitudes by the bucket-load. Many years later he had to give evidence to the Peel Commission investigating the causes of the 1936 Arab revolt in Palestine. He later forbade the Commission to print them, belatedly realising their inflammatory content. In fact, we understand that he had spewed up the most extreme type of Zionist prejudice against the Arabs. Insisting that the Jewish national home would eventually cover the whole of

Palestine, Churchill said that this was no injustice to the Arabs. 'The injustice', he said, 'is when those who lived in the country leave it to be desert for thousands of years.' Responding to a suggestion that the Jews could be seen as foreigners who had invaded Palestine in the twentieth century, Churchill countered that originally it was the Arabs had come to Palestine after the Jews, and that it was the 'great hordes of Islam' who had 'smashed' up Palestine. Reminded of the great Arab civilisation that had stretched as far as Spain, Churchill retorted that he was glad they had been thrown out; it was for the good of the world (Cohen 1985: 79).

Earlier, Churchill had become so nauseated with his colonial responsibilities for the Arab world that he proposed pulling out altogether. He had been having great trouble controlling the newly appointed Iraqi puppet king, Feisel, who had begun to demand real independence. Lloyd George, the prime minister, wouldn't hear of it. He reminded Churchill of the widely-held belief that large reserves of oil might be discovered in the area: 'If we leave we may find in a year or two ... that we have handed over to the French and the Americans some of the richest oil fields in the world' (Fromkin 1989: 509).

BRITAIN, ZIONISM AND THE 1936–39 PALESTINIAN ARAB ANTI-COLONIAL REVOLT[7]

Another very famous British name, who would also become a Second World War hero, followed Churchill into Palestine: Field Marshal Montgomery. In 1938 he arrived in Palestine to crush the Arab revolt against British rule and defend British backing for the rapidly expanding Zionist colony. Montgomery's attitude to Arabs more than matched Churchill's. He gave his men simple orders on how to handle the rebels: kill them, especially as they were, in his words, 'gangs of professional bandits' (Segev 2000: 432). Montgomery was preoccupied with how the British had lost control of most of Ireland. He thought far too many concessions had been made to Sinn Féin. Ruthless obliteration of nationalist identity was the order of the day.

Thus he ordered any Arab caught wearing the peasant *kufiya*, the celebrated Palestinian headscarf, which owes its origins as a symbol of resistance to this revolt, to be 'caged' (Swedenburg 1995: 34). The British political authorities had to restrain him.

Caging the Arabs was one idea; chaining their legs was another. Sir Ronald Storrs, a former British Governor of Jerusalem, has left us this insight into the British colonial mentality from his autobiography. Storrs was playing tennis when the Arab ball boy 'emitted a curious clank. Looking closer I discovered that he and his colleagues at the other end of the court were long-term criminals, heavily chained by the ankles, whom the local police officer had sent up from the jail to act as ball boys' (Storrs 1939: 446).

One senior British army officer in Palestine, Orde Wingate, was sometimes known as the 'Lawrence of the Jews'. He organised Jews for military service; more than any other leading figure, he stepped across the line allegedly separating British and Zionist interests. The Israeli Ministry of Defence, many years after his death, proclaimed him as a role model, underlining his influence on the Israeli army's 'combat doctrine' (Segev 2000: 430).

He had set up what was virtually a private army, mostly of Jews, which pursued 'terrorists' at night. These 'Special Night Squads' had one absolutely vital and highly symbolic duty: protecting the railways and the oil pipeline, which ran from Kirkuk in Iraq to the Palestinian port of Haifa. Wingate was unambiguous about his wider political aims. He was, he said 'establishing the foundations of the Army of Zion' (Marshall 1989: 42).

There are many appalling stories about the Special Night Squads which do indeed read like the activities of the Israeli army today on the West Bank and Gaza. Random killings and beatings in Arab villages suddenly entered without warning. Phoney 'trials' and 'courts' set up at whim in the villages, followed by executions. Many of Wingate's own troops thought he was mad. It's not difficult to see why. He had a penchant for crackpot schemes of provocation. On one occasion he wanted his Jewish soldiers to dress up as Arabs, go to the Arab market in Haifa and start shooting (Segev 2000: 431).

However, it is difficult to separate Wingate's excesses from the wider British apparatus of repression of the revolt. Torture of suspected rebels was routine. Thousands were held in administrative detention without trial in overcrowded camps with inadequate sanitation. Between 1938 and 1939 at least one Arab was sentenced to death every week (Segev 2000: 417).

Furthermore, the principle of *collective* punishment imposed on entire villages, so beloved by the Israeli army, was pioneered by the British. A British doctor named Elliot Forster documented in his diary an operation in Halhoul, a village near Hebron, in May 1939. Villagers had been herded into open-air pens, one for men and one for women, during a heat wave, and deprived of food and drink. The women were allowed to leave the pen after two days, but many of the men were kept for much longer and at least ten died. Forster concluded that the British could probably teach Hitler a thing or two about running concentration camps (Segev 2000: 421–2).

Nor should we see Wingate as exceptional in the way he integrated the British soldiers and armed Zionist settlers in the same military units. The British authorities were compelled by the Arab revolt to expand the colonial police force. Thousands of Jewish settlers enlisted. The Zionist leader Moshe Shertok was not slow to draw the conclusion that the future Jewish army would be dependent on their success (Segev 2000: 427). In fact, the British even asked the Zionist leaders to share the burden of the policemen's salaries and pay for the uniforms! The construction company Solel Boneh, specifically set up by the Histradut to facilitate Zionist colonisation, was commissioned to put up a barbed wire fence along the northern border as well as build new police stations (Segev 2000: 428–9).

THE REVOLT

Zionist histories gloss over the Palestinian Arab revolt. They echo Montgomery's contemptuous dismissal of the rebel nationalists as murderous 'bandits'. But privately they knew the truth and occasionally were ready to admit it. Indeed, it was the right-wing Zionist extremist leader, Jabotinsky, an admirer of the Italian fascist leader, Benito Mussolini, who had coined the ominous phrase the 'Iron Wall' in the 1920s, for dealing with the inevitable upsurge of Palestinian nationalism. The Iron Wall was a metaphor for the overwhelming military force the Zionists would need to impose their nationalism on Palestine and break the will of Palestinian nationalism. Jabotinsky also reaffirmed Herzl's principle that the European Jewish settlers should understand themselves as culturally superior to the natives, an outpost of European civilisation. Avi Shlaim, the dissident Israeli historian, in his brilliant book *The Iron Wall*, has shown conclusively how nearly all the Zionist leaders, especially the so-called 'left-wing' leaders like Ben-Gurion and, much later, the 'peace-maker', Rabin, signed up to Jabotinsky's 'Iron Wall' philosophy. Ben-Gurion witnessed the 1936–39 revolt. He had no doubt that it was a legitimate nationalist movement. But that conclusion only hardened his resolve. It prepared him for measures to enforce the compulsory transfer of Arabs from a future Jewish state (Swedenburg 1995: 14).

Nevertheless, Zionism's official position was and remains in denial over the revolt. It hardly features in the history taught in Israeli schools. And this applies wherever Israel has controlled the teaching of history to Palestinian schoolchildren. Since 1967 Israel has banned literally thousands of books on the West Bank and Gaza. Yet Israel has been unable to eradicate the Palestinian memory. In recent years the relation between history and memory has come to form virtually a new dimension in scholarship. And despite Israel's best efforts, the Palestinian memory has also been a beneficiary of this innovatory form of research.

Swedenburg's book of outstanding interviews with surviving participants of the revolt published in the 1980s, is a superb example of the genre. And whilst we cannot do it justice here, we can at least confirm that the *al-thawra al-kubra*, the great revolt, was the 'most significant anticolonial insurgency in the Arab East in the interwar period' (Swedenburg 1995: xix).

The revolt was inevitable and its ultimate cause lay with British protection for the expansion of Jewish immigration which had increased almost six-fold from the date of the Balfour Declaration, growing particularly rapidly in the 1930s. Jews were almost a third of the total Palestinian population at the outbreak of the revolt (65,000 Jews in 1917, 384,078 in 1936) (Gilbert 1998: 47, 80).

The Palestinian peasants could not understand why their land should be used as a refuge for European Jews fleeing anti-Semitism in Europe. These were not the Jews of Arab lands who had been their neighbours for centuries. The peasants saw exactly what Jabotinsky saw: a European coloniser, moreover one protected by the armed might of the British Empire. The peasants had the nerve to declare war on the British Empire in order to protect their land, in that great tradition that we met earlier with the *mountain of fire*.

THROUGH PALESTINIAN EYES

It took Swedenburg a long time to persuade Ali Husayn Baytam to talk to him (Swedenburg 1995: 107–9). The old fighter placed a condition on the interview. Swedenburg would have to publish the names of his comrades killed by the British after nine soldiers had been blown up in a land mine planted by a peasant militia. Ali then described the massacre as the British army took revenge on an entire village. Ali had kept the list of names for 40 years. He had waited all that time to achieve recognition for unknown fallen martyrs. It was a principle and a mood that Swedenburg encountered time after time amongst the old peasant fighters. They knew something really important had happened. But somehow it had missed its official place in that means of memorising called written history.

Ali described himself as both a Muslim and a communist and insisted that there was no contradiction. Moreover, whilst Ali was one of the most sophisticated of the former local peasant leaders Swedenburg interviewed, his insistence that the villages formed the backbone of the resistance, with improvised and daring military initiative and leadership, overwhelms all the accounts. The untold story is that the British, let alone the Zionists, were in danger of losing control of the Palestinian countryside. At the least a very violent military stalemate ensued which could be broken only by serious political concessions from the ruling power. As an official British archive put it: 'the heavily booted British soldiers are no match for lightly clad natives who, at any moment, can drop their weapons and become peaceful ploughmen and goatherds' (Swedenburg 1995: 126).

Remarkably, Swedenburg reports on a virtual peasant-Palestinian state-in-waiting. Perhaps this is an exaggeration, and it certainly begs all kinds of questions about the palpable tensions, etched very deep in the old peasant mind, even after 40 years, between the rebel villages and the deeply divided upper-class Palestinian leadership in the towns and cities. That subject is way beyond the remit of this book. Still, there are too many examples of a court and justice system emerging (as well as printed stamps, receipts on taxes collected), for this notion to be readily dismissed. In any case, there are one or two independent witnesses. Dr Forster, whom we met earlier, observed the rebel courts and recorded: 'their justice and common sense does not appear to me to be inferior and their expedition is demonstrably superior to that of H.M.G.' (Swedenburg 1995: 135).

Ali Husayn Baytam had another list of names in his head: cousins, uncles, other relatives killed over 40 years later during the Israeli-backed massacre of unarmed Palestinians at the refugee camps at Sabra and Shatila in Beirut in 1982. Swedenburg reports how he and a Palestinian colleague 'felt in awe of the fierce spirit burning so brightly in the diminutive man who repeated the names of the dead, as if that act could arrest the storm of progress'.

A quotation suddenly came into Swedenburg's mind: 'one single catastrophe which keeps piling wreckage upon wreckage and hurls it in front of his feet' (Swedenburg 1995: 137). It was so apt for Ali, and yet the quotation is from that mysterious Jewish philosopher, Walter Benjamin, as he was anticipating the Holocaust.

8

'The Nazi Holocaust Proved the Urgency for a Jewish State'

The use of the Holocaust to justify Israel's existence as a Jewish state was made explicit in Israel's Declaration of Independence in 1948:

> The Nazi Holocaust, which engulfed millions of Jews in Europe, proved anew the urgency of the re-establishment of the Jewish state, which would solve the problem of Jewish homelessness by opening the gates to all Jews and lifting the Jewish people to equality in the family of nations. (Mendes-Flohr and Reinharz 1995: 629)

At face value it would seem almost impossible to argue with this statement. After all, the Nazi Holocaust was intended to bring about the destruction of the Jewish people in Hitler's so-called Final Solution. (Or rather this was the intention of the *Judeocide* at the core of the Holocaust. We must never forget the millions of other victims of the Holocaust: the Romani, the gays, the disabled, the millions of Slavs and other nationalities, the Soviet prisoners of war and the political dissidents, including the socialists and the communists.) Yet the foundation of the Jewish State meant uprooting and excluding another people, the Palestinians, seizing their land and reducing many of them to penury. For Palestinians this was *Naqba*, the Catastrophe.

The new Jewish State then recast Palestinian land as 'Jewish' land ... This chapter explores the case for the Jewish State in the overlapping shadows of the Holocaust and the *Naqba*. It attempts to answer some very difficult questions. Is it legitimate to use the Holocaust to draw political conclusions? How do we draw the correct political conclusions? Has Israel drawn the correct political conclusions? These questions are addressed in three ways, first, through the work of Lawrence Langer, a leading scholar of Holocaust testimony and art; second, through testing the usefulness of the concept of *Imperialism* as part of a debate on the Marxist Left about how to explain the

Holocaust; and third, through the controversy over some Zionist attitudes to rescue from, and resistance to, the Holocaust. It is argued that each approach yields important *insights* about the Holocaust with implicit *warnings* about the political judgements needed to respond to it.

The last section of the chapter attempts to draw together these insights and warnings as a means of considering the connection between the Holocaust and the *Naqba*. A final critical comment is offered on Israel's use of the Holocaust.

When discussing the Holocaust in these ways there is always a danger of *intellectualising* it, abstracting it. To some extent this is inevitable; nevertheless, it makes anyone who tackles this subject feel uneasy. Even so I would like to think that this chapter may make a modest contribution to the

> incessant anxious dialogue about how our civilization may absorb into reasonable hopes about the future the disabling outburst of unreason we name the Holocaust, as it continues to assault memory and imagination with immeasurable sorrow and undiminished force. (Langer 1998: xix)

WHAT WAS THE HOLOCAUST?

This may seem an absurd, even an insulting, question. Yet it is doubtful whether any of the thousands of scholars, artists, journalists and other writers, including Holocaust survivors, who have been struggling with an answer over the years are entirely satisfied with their conclusions. Bitter and acrimonious disputes have often erupted over claims to have made sense of the Holocaust. Indeed, there is a plausible school of thought that places the Holocaust *beyond* our understanding. When, for example, the highly respected Holocaust historian, Raul Hilburg, was asked if the Holocaust had any meaning, he replied, 'I hope not.' Hannah Arendt, famously interpreted evidence from the Jerusalem trial in 1961 of Adolf Eichmann, a leading Nazi bureaucrat responsible for implementing the Holocaust, as a 'banality of evil'. One senses here simple yet profound truths suggesting the limits of our understanding. Yet in reality, and perhaps in some cases despite themselves, nearly all writers find themselves struggling with sophisticated interpretations as well as drawing political lessons.

LAWRENCE LANGER'S *ALARMED VISION*

Langer is one of the most accomplished interpreters of Holocaust survivor testimony and Holocaust art and literature. His guide was Primo Levi, arguably one of the best known writers on the Holocaust and himself a Holocaust survivor, who turned to writing to make sense of his experiences.

Levi was appalled at attempts to explain the Holocaust by the 'universalising' argument that what the Germans did only 'reflected a capacity for violence and evil buried in human nature everywhere' (Langer 1998: 33). For Levi this was evasion. In *The Drowned and the Saved*, Levi made it plain that the Germans must accept their specific responsibility for Nazi crimes.

Yet despite devoting the introduction of his book, *Pre-empting the Holocaust*, to an immensely persuasive endorsement of Levi's remarks about the dangers of 'universalising' the Holocaust, Langer's most hard-hitting essay, 'The Alarmed Vision', is a master-piece of Holocaust writing articulating a 'universalist' message. In this essay Langer is engaged in a detailed analysis of the testimony of Holocaust survivors. He has stumbled upon a terrifying and sad truth about these survivors: they inhabit two worlds simultaneously, one fixed in chronological time, our time, and one fixed in what he calls durational time. Durational time fixes the survivor's being at the death camp forever. Not only is the past frozen and relived again and again, there is an acute sense of 'having missed one's intended destiny by surviving one's own death' (Langer 1998: 72–3). Holocaust survivors carry an overwhelming burden of death experience that is very difficult for us to comprehend fully.

At this point in his essay, the force of what he is understanding seems to impact like an electric shock and Langer drops resistance to the problems of 'universalising' the Holocaust. He changes mode completely, though there is no signposting and the reader is unprepared:

> narratives like hers threaten our dependence on coherence, reason, order, the moral and psychological balance that constitutes for us civilised being ... Testimony like this should summon us not to the healing victims but to a revision of the myth of the civilised being. Human nature can no longer be set in opposition to inhuman nature, as if one were the norm and the other a correctable aberration. Atrocity in the form of violence that maims and kills others has become

a 'normal' rather than a pathological expression of self ... (Langer
1998: 74)

Langer concludes that we do indeed live in an *age of atrocity*. This is
at the core of his *alarmed vision*. Earlier in the essay, he generalises
from the Holocaust, where the Jew died so that the German could
live, to suggest what seems to be a 'principle' in the age of atrocity:
he writes that we are living in a world

where the goal of life so often appears to be the death of others,
we are forced to regard the reversal of expectations rather than the
fulfilment of dreams as a model for being and behaviour in some
communities. (Langer 1998: 68)

Now Langer's vision is bleak indeed. He offers neither an explana-
tory framework nor a solution and indeed implies that they may
not be available at all (Langer 1998: 202n.7). Nevertheless his
deduction that in the age of atrocity life sometimes depends upon
the death of others, casts a ghastly glow across the contemporary
global political landscape. We have here a truly alarming *insight*
and surely a *warning* about the need to take action to respond
urgently.

This idea of a life-based-on-death principle is precisely the subtext
for a key argument in Hobsbawm's widely acclaimed history of the
short twentieth century, *The Age of Extremes*.

The Second World War, which had Auschwitz at its core, had
Hiroshima at its conclusion: 'The dropping of the atom bomb was
not justified as indispensable for victory, but as a means of saving
American lives' (Hobsbawm 1994: 27). In other words, live
Americans depended upon dead Japanese. It comes as no surprise
that Levi is one of Hobsbawm's first witnesses in *The Age of Extremes*
(Hobsbawm 1994: 1).[1]

If this is true, if this 'life-for-death' principle really is a feature of
our age, the age of atrocity, then Zionism and Zionists need to think
very carefully about the lessons they are drawing from the
Holocaust. Hasn't the Zionist enterprise been based, at least in part,
on saving Jewish lives at the expense, if necessary, of dead
Palestinians? I return to this theme later in the chapter.

IMPERIALISM AND THE GENOCIDE WE CALL
THE HOLOCAUST

'*The giant empire in the east is ripe for collapse*', wrote Adolf Hitler in *Mein Kampf* in 1925. '*And the end of Jewish rule in Russia will also be the end of Russia as a state* [emphasis added]'.

Ian Kershaw, arguably Hitler's most accomplished biographer, has described how, with this statement, the two key components of Hitler's 'personalized world-view' – 'the destruction of the Jews' and acquisition of 'living-space' – came together.

> War against Russia would, through the annihilation of Jewish Bolshevism, at the same time deliver Germany its salvation by providing new 'living-space'. Crude, simplistic, barbaric: but this invocation of late nineteenth century imperialism, racism and anti-Semitism, transposed into Eastern Europe in the twentieth century, was a heady brew for those ready to consume it. (Kershaw 1998: 250)

If we leave aside the conditions that allowed Hitler and the National Socialist Party to come to power in Germany, we have here a starting point for trying to understand some of the processes which led to the Holocaust.

That the processes were to be genocidal is not in doubt. *Mein Kampf* is punctuated with genocidal threats to the Jews. These 'international poisoners of the masses' would have to be 'exterminated' (Kershaw 1998: 244). Of course, the exact form of the genocide is not spelled out. In any case the war against Russia and its Slav population posed a more general genocidal threat to all its peoples.

That the Slavs were also *Untermenschen*, sub-human, was a taken-for-granted assumption, with deep roots in German pan-nationalist *volkist* culture (Kershaw 1998: 79).

Just before the Nazi invasion of Russia in early 1941, Himmler told SS leaders that there would have to be a reduction of some *30 million* Slavs. Hitler called it a 'war of annihilation' (Kershaw 2000: 353, 339). And it was. Tens of millions were slaughtered. There is no agreement on even an approximate figure, but we do know it included no fewer than *3.3 million* Russian prisoners of war (Hobsbawm 1994: 43). It is certainly possible to understand the twentieth-century Nazi genocide as an adaptation, albeit with its own terrifying peculiarities, of good old-fashioned European imperialism and its nineteenth-century theories of biological race science. This is why Jewish philosophers and writers as diverse as Hannah Arendt, George Steiner and Saul Friedlander do not quite get it right when they argue that the Holocaust is unique because the Nazis could choose who should live and who should die on the basis of race selection (Traverso 1999: 67). The Holocaust is unique, but this is not the reason.

European imperialism had already practised what Steiner calls 'ontological massacre' (Traverso 1999: 67) – eliminating victims not because of their acts, but because they existed.

Native Americans were virtually wiped out because they existed in the way of European living space in North America. Hitler sometimes compared the war on Russia with the European struggle in North America 'against the Red Indians' (*Hitler's Table Talk* 2000: 621).

As early as 1830, Sir George Murray, a relatively enlightened British Secretary of State for the Colonies, observed that his own government might have embarked on a policy of eliminating an entire 'race', the Aboriginal peoples of Australia. He warned that 'the extinction of the Native race could not fail to leave an indelible stain upon the character of the British government' (Reynolds 2001: 4).

In India too, the scale of British genocide is breathtaking. In Bengal alone, up to 20 million people were slaughtered at the end of the eighteenth century (Davidson 1999: 25). Hitler was fascinated by, and deeply jealous of, the experience of the British in India. He referred to it many times, explaining why it proved that Germany could easily dominate Russia (*Hitler's Table Talk* 2000: 15).

The genocidal significance of our age of imperialism had shaken many writers, from the Left and the Right, long before the Nazis came to power. Here is Rosa Luxemburg:

> Engels once said, 'capitalist society faces a dilemma, either an advance to socialism or a revision to barbarism'. Thus we stand today before the awful proposition: either the triumph of imperialism and the destruction of all culture ... depopulation, desolation, degeneration, a vast cemetery; or the victory of socialism. (cited Rees 1998: 160)

These lines were written before the twentieth century had revealed the names of the Somme, Auschwitz, the Gulag or Hiroshima. In similar mood, the conservative sociologist Max Weber predicted 'a polar night of icy darkness and hardness' (Traverso 1999: 75). Earlier, Marx had conjured up this stunning image from British rule in India, 'the hideous pagan idol who would not drink the nectar but from the skulls of the slain' (Traverso 1999: 25).

Traverso's very stimulating *Understanding the Nazi Genocide, Marxism after Auschwitz* considers the implications of the argument for the Judeophobia at the core of the Holocaust. He warns that the argument fails fully to grasp the enormity of the crime. First, a colonial war carried out in Europe, in the midst of the twentieth century, using the tools of destruction of a developed industrial society, concentrated the genocide over just a few years rather than centuries or even decades. Second, he argues that the Jews 'were not like Africans or Native Americans, a colonial people, but a people at the origins of Western civilization'. Now, in fairness to Traverso, he is aware of the dangers of this type of argument. He goes on to insist that he is not introducing 'a hierarchical scale in the history of genocide'. Instead, the Holocaust indicated 'a new stage attained by the violence of capitalism: no longer destruction by a conquering imperialism imposing the rule of Western civilization on the extra European world, but the beginning of this civilization's collapse (what Adorno and Horkheimer called the "self-destruction of reason")' (Traverso 1999: 126).

Intriguing though this insight is – and it deserves more consideration than is possible here – it is not satisfactory. Gandhi's quip immediately comes to mind. Asked what he thought about Western civilisation, Gandhi replied that he was looking forward to it. In any case, civilisation in its Western variant, or more generally, did not collapse; the Nazi regime did. It would be better to say that the Holocaust served on the rest of us a terrible warning about what kind of politics does indeed threaten civilisation.

The British Marxist writer Alex Callinicos has observed a further weakness with Traverso's promotion of Adorno and Horkheimer. By treating the Holocaust only as a symptom of a more general civilisational disorder which destroys the 'age of reason', the specific causes of the Nazi genocide are ignored (Callinicos 2001: 387). There is an irony here because Traverso, along with another Marxist writer, Norman Geras, have charged that Marxism itself is too prone to these kind of generalisations and is not capable of analysing the specific causes of the Nazi barbarity. This argument echoes Levi's thesis discussed earlier. In 'Plumbing the Depths: Marxism and the Holocaust', Callinicos seeks to demonstrate that Marxism can indeed rise to the challenge.

Two very different aspects of Callinicos's essay deserve our attention here and attempt to grapple with the really terrifyingly *specific* and *unique* components of the Holocaust. The first is the centrality of bio-logical race science and the Nazi obsession with the Jews. Callinicos sees Hitler's remark to Himmler in 1942 as particularly poignant:

> The discovery of the Jewish virus is one of the greatest revolutions that have taken place in the world. The battle in which we are engaged is of the same sort as the battle waged, during the last century, by Pasteur and Koch. How many diseases have their origin in the Jewish virus! ... We shall regain our health only by eliminating the Jew. (Callinicos 2001: 402)

The Jews weren't the only 'unfit race' or social group that had to be eliminated. But the Jews were at the head of the list in the hierarchy because this most degenerate of races had such immense power in the world. The scale of Nazi anti-Semitic ideological fanaticism here should never be underestimated. The Jewish 'virus' had the entirety of 'Western civilization' in its deadly grip. After all, according to Hitler, Jews had invented Christianity as well as capitalism and communism. But what were the events that precipitated the Nazis giving the ultimate practical expression to their Judeophobia?

Scholars agree that Hitler's invasion of Russia provided the con-text for the Holocaust. However, there remains an unresolved argu-ment about the immediate trigger. (The infamous Wannsee conference in January 1942 left no written record of the intention to use death camps for the 'Final Solution'.)

Christopher Browning, for example, sees Hitler taking the decision in the 'euphoria of victory' in Russia between mid-September and mid-October 1941. Martin Broszat, on the other hand, sees Hitler's looming defeat in Russia, in the period immediately after this, as the key that opened the death camps (Cesarani 1994: 14, 7).

Callinicos's spirited defence of Broszat's position introduces a further possible insight into the processes that led to that specific form of genocide we call the Holocaust. Broszat argues that the more it became obvious that Nazi ideological dogma could not be converted 'to the tasks of constructive re-organisation' in Russia, 'the more exclusively that ideological policy focused only on the negative policies and aims' (Callinicos 2001: 404).

That 'constructive re-organisation' was based on the Nazi 'vision' of a racially pure, socially homogeneous German 'community', the

Volksgemeinschaft (Callinicos 2001: 394, 398), which would have stretched from Germany into Russia where the new German colonist would 'live on handsome, spacious farms' (*Hitler's Table Talk* 2000: 24). Now the vision was in ruins as the Nazi onslaught finally stalled at the end of 1941 in the face of the stubborn resistance of the Russian army. In addition, the prospects of deporting Jews to the more inhospitable regions of the Soviet Union where most would certainly have perished (this would also have been a Nazi genocide of the Jews but in a different form) was no longer possible (Callinicos 2001: 401) (Kershaw (2000: 493) argues that Wannsee reflected this 'dilemma' for the Nazis). Jew hatred intensified. Nazi exterminationist resolve is likely to have hardened even more with the entry of the US into the war at the end of 1941, for which Hitler blamed the Jews: 'Germany no longer held the initiative ... Though it would not become fully plain for some months, Hitler's gamble, on which he had staked nothing less than the future of the nation, had disastrously failed' (Kershaw 2000: 457). By the end of the year, four million Jews had been slaughtered (Kershaw 2000: 493).

If the above sketch is at all accurate, what insights can we draw?

The unique aspects of German Nazi imperialism should not blind us to some truisms about imperialist conquest. It is *always* prone to genocidal behaviour and attempts to legitimate it are always rooted in variations of race and ethnicity hatreds. Genocidal prospects increase if military force is contemplated to clear land for 'living space' of an allegedly inferior ethnic group in favour of an allegedly 'superior' ethnic group. Utopian ideologies, which justify land clearance by force in the name of ethnic superiority, may become ever more fanatical, and genocidal, in the face of failure.

Zionism is *not* the same as Nazism. It did not have an exterminationist intention at its core, though, as we shall see Zionism has been, and is, capable of genocidal outbursts. But Zionism *is* rooted in the traditions of European imperialism. That truth alone is sufficient to serve urgent warnings about the implications of Zionism's ruthless colonial ambitions in Palestine.

BEFORE THE DELUGE: ZIONIST ATTITUDES TO RESCUE
AND RESISTANCE

I want now to turn to a very different argument concerning Zionist attitudes before the Holocaust. One would have thought that after

the Nazis came to power in Germany in 1933, the Zionists would
have been in the forefront of organising resistance to the Nazis as
well as rescuing Jews from them. Yet there was often a troubling
ambiguity about this, especially amongst some of the Zionist
leaders, which does cast doubt on Zionism's moral credibility in the
very arena where there should be no doubt. This also raises the
'universalist' and 'particular' question in a quite dramatic way. For
the question posed is whether the particular needs of the Jewish
state-in- waiting, as perceived by the leaders of the Jewish colony in
Palestine under British control at the time, should take priority over
the need for a universalist response to the imminent Jewish crisis
brought about by the Nazi threat.

The way some leading Zionists judged rescue priorities was highlighted by the Evian Conference in 1938. This was an initiative by
President Roosevelt to co-ordinate an international solution for the
increasingly large number of Jewish refugees seeking to escape from
Nazi control. Whilst the intentions of Evian were no doubt honourable, the results were far less than impressive (Wasserstein 1988:
8–9). However, this was not at all obvious to many of the participants, who took the conference's intentions very seriously indeed.
This was particularly true of the Zionist delegates, some of whom
were worried that the outcome of conference might be very
successful!

This strange and disturbing attitude was articulated with great
passion by none other than Ben-Gurion. At a meeting of Jewish
leaders, Zionist and non-Zionist, drawn from Jewish communities
in different parts of the world, he warned of 'damage, danger and
disaster that could be expected from the Evian Conference. It could
remove Palestine from the international agenda as a factor in the
solution of the Jewish question.' The reason was, he went on, that
'in the eyes of the world, Palestine now resembles Spain [where a
civil war raging] ... there are riots ... every day bombs are thrown'.
Here he was quite correct. The Palestinians had indeed declared a
national liberation 'war' on the British occupiers and their Zionist
allies. There was no way Britain could now open Palestine to Jewish
refugees. An alternative solution was urgently required. As Ben-
Gurion himself noted, Roosevelt had drawn the same conclusion.
Ben-Gurion reported that Roosevelt had said that 'Palestine could
not solve the Jewish question and that a different way had to be
sought'. In other words, Jewish refugees should be absorbed elsewhere. But for Ben-Gurion this was a disaster; he wanted Evian to

fail. As he put it: 'We must see to it that this dangerous tendency does not find expression at the conference' (Beit Zvi 1991: 228).[2]

Ben-Gurion wasn't a crank. On the contrary, as we have noted several times, he was Zionism's most outstanding leader in the twentieth century. We are entitled to make judgements about Zionism from this man's attitudes and behaviour. Yet these attitudes displayed a narrow, and surely a debased, nationalism at the heart of the Zionist enterprise, which was ready to put Jewish lives at risk on the 'eve' of the Holocaust. This is not an overstatement. Nor was it an aberration on Ben-Gurion's behalf. He repeated such sentiments in even more abhorrent form. In a letter to the Zionist executive, in the same year as the Evian Conference, he wrote:

> If Jews will have to choose between the refugees, saving Jews from concentration camps, and assisting a national museum in Palestine, mercy will have the upper hand and the whole energy of the people will be channelled into saving Jews from various countries. Zionism will be struck off the agenda ... If we allow a separation between the refugee problem and the Palestine problem, we are risking the existence of Zionism. (Bober 1972: 171)[3]

Ben-Gurion's attitude had real life-and-death implications. Again in the same year, he *opposed* a British plan to allow migration to the UK of several thousand German Jewish children:

> If I knew that it would be possible to save all the children in Germany by bringing them over to England, and only half of them to Eretz Israel [Palestine] then I would opt for the second alternative. For we must weigh not only the lives of those children but also the history of the people of Israel. (Brenner 1983: 149)

The assertion of the alleged needs of the Jewish state-in-waiting over the priority of rescue was paralleled in the ways this attitude could not only compromise resistance to the Nazis, but even suggest collaboration. When Hitler took power in 1933, the Zionist Federation of Germany sent him a memorandum, which 70 years later has not lost its power to shock:

> May we therefore be permitted to present our views, which, in our opinion, make possible a solution in keeping with the principles of the new German State of National Awakening, and which at the same time

> might signify for Jews a new ordering of the conditions of their existence ... which consists above all in an abnormal occupational pattern, and in the fault of an intellectual and moral posture not rooted in one's own tradition ... (Brenner 2002: 42-3)

The memorandum goes on to reassure Hitler that the Zionists would *oppose* the world-wide anti-Nazi campaign demanding a boycott of German goods. A later justification for this extraordinary behaviour was the notorious pre-war 'Transfer' agreement. Here German Jews and some of their belongings were allowed to leave Germany for Palestine. At the same time German goods would be sold to Jews in Palestine. Non-Zionist Jews as well as some Zionist Jews were appalled at such collaboration.[4]

One strand in Zionism even seemed to many observers to be inspired by the Nazis. The present-day Likud Party, the major governing party in Israel at the time of writing, rarely admits this ghost from its past. Yet when one of its most famous leaders, and a man who would become prime minister, Menachem Begin, visited New York at the end of 1948, he and his political organisation faced an attack from the world's most famous Jewish scientist, Albert Einstein. Einstein, as well as many leading American Jews, denounced Begin in the *New York Times* for leading a party 'akin in its organisation, methods, political philosophy and social appeal to the Nazi and Fascist parties' (Brenner 2002: 184).

The *insights* and *warnings* are self-evident here. In the period that Brenner calls *Zionism in the Age of the Dictators*,[5] Zionism displayed a troubling and chameleon-like trait, a readiness to prioritise its particular nationalist needs over the self-evident universal case for rescue, a capacity to mimic aspects of the totalitarian behaviour of its tormentor.

THE HOLOCAUST, ITS SURVIVORS AND THE *NAQBA*

As the truth about the Holocaust began to dawn after the war, it became the most convincing case for Zionism yet mounted, frankly dwarfing the pre-war and wartime behaviour, and the poor judgements, of some of its leaders.

One very specific and practical consequence of the Holocaust began to press itself with increasing urgency on the victorious wartime allies, especially Britain. Where would its survivors now live?

War had exhausted Britain. The demands for national independence were loud and clear throughout the empire. The pre-war Palestinian Arab national revolt might have been temporarily curtailed, but British policy-makers knew only too well that it was unfinished business, and likely to flare again at any time. Now they faced a new threat: independent Zionist militias were ready to confront the occupying British army over the question of migration to Palestine of Holocaust survivors (Pappe 2001: 21). In reality, British policy ignominiously collapsed and the future of Palestine passed to the United Nations.

This is not the place to discuss the merits or effectiveness of what was then a very new international organisation established, in the aftermath of the world's most bloody and horrific conflict, to discharge – at least at the level of rhetoric – international justice and to establish the mechanisms for keeping the world's peace. But Pappe, one of Israel's very few anti-Zionist scholars, has noticed something very revealing about the UN's initial response to the Palestine crisis. For reasons to do with the interplay of Big Power politics at the UN, particularly between the US and the Soviet Union (Pappe 2001: 17–18), its intervention in Palestine has left us with a unique window on events.

A United Nations Special Committee on Palestine (UNSCOP) was established to investigate the situation in Palestine and report back. The US, in an effort to minimise Soviet influence on UNSCOP, to some extent, allowed the composition of the committee to slip out of the hands of the main powers. This gave representatives from smaller countries, including those from the developing world, a greater say than perhaps otherwise they might have had. Many of the committee members had no prior knowledge of the conflict. This gave UNSCOP a freshness, a naiveté even, in the way it came to understand the situation in Palestine. But it also meant that it was susceptible to immediate pressures without fully understanding their context.

This last point was dramatically highlighted by the arrival of the *Exodus*, the famous ship carrying Jewish refugees to the shores of Palestine coincidentally during the period that the UNSCOP team were conducting their deliberations. They watched with amazement as the British authorities, still the governing power, intercepted the ship, refused to let its passengers land and refused, moreover, to take any responsibility for them. This included a refusal to consider the obvious option of at least a temporary stay in Britain itself.

Instead, the ship was sent back to Germany! No event, before or after, would so decisively play into the hands of the Zionists. The fate of the *Exodus* immediately became the stuff of legend.[6] It seemed so unequivocally to confirm the Zionist case.

The *Exodus* affair overwhelmed the UNSCOP team. Zionist leaders had already carefully cultivated them, whereas, rightly or wrongly, Palestinian Arab leaders had boycotted the committee (Pappe 2001: 23). The UNSCOP priority now became

> the fate of the Jewish survivors instead of the Arab demand to determine the future of Palestine according to the demographic reality of 1947. The outcome was that the committee decided to accept the link between the fate of European Jewry and that of Palestine. (Pappe 2001: 25)

Here was a critical turning point in the struggle for the foundation of the Jewish state. The Zionists had won the propaganda war long before the first bullet was fired in the real war for control of Palestine, a year later, in 1948.[7] UNSCOM's role as 'honest broker' to world-wide public opinion, *de facto* now a conduit for the Zionist case, was sealed by the *Exodus* affair.

The two principal victorious wartime allies, Britain and the US, were responsible for this situation. Whilst they did absorb many survivors, they were certainly not prepared to offer the rest permission to settle in their own countries (Pappe 2001: 276n.32). They were not even ready to build on the intentions of the pre-war international conference at Evian and use the United Nations as the obvious postwar vehicle for an honourable international response to the Jewish refugee crisis. Suddenly the Zionist case looked like an admirable means of solving the 'problem'. This was a re-run of the very low moral standards of international behaviour personified by the British politician Balfour, described in the last chapter: dump the unwanted Jews in Palestine.

Possibly some 'farsighted' American politicians already recognised just how much a new Jewish state might come to serve US interests. Certainly we know that US military chiefs of staff were impressed by Israel's victory in 1948 in the so-called 'war of independence' against the Arabs. They were to describe the new state as the major regional power after Turkey, offering the US the means to gain 'strategic advantage in the Middle East that would offset the effects of the decline of British power in the region' (Chomsky 1996: 204). But this is to anticipate the argument of the next chapter.

Where did the Holocaust survivors themselves want to settle? General Clay, the US Military Governor of Germany, told the UNSCOP team that in his experience camp survivors were choosing to go to Palestine, but he added, 'Of course I do not know how this would stand up against the opening up of other countries for immigration' (Pappe 2001: 27). And that is the problem. We do not know because it was never put to the test. We do know, however, how successfully the Zionists operated in the displaced persons camps, the camps set up for the survivors. They were able to co-ordinate the testimony of survivors before the UNSCOP committee. Refugees chosen at random by the committee for interview were well versed in Zionist propaganda and terminology.

By the end of 1949, just one year after the foundation of the Jewish State, there were almost 350,000 Holocaust survivors living in Israel, almost a third of the population (Segev 1993: 154). In the 1948 war, almost a third of the soldiers were Holocaust survivors (Segev 1993: 176).

The moral justification for the foundation of Israel appeared to be reinforced by this living remnant of the Holocaust. And yet on the scales of morality, we must immediately contrast this immensely important fact with another. In early 1947, Jews owned 7 per cent of the land in Palestine; three years later, they had seized 92 per cent of land within the new state, including Arab homes and buildings of every kind (Kimmerling 1983: 143). As Anderson has noted, this constituted a colonial occupation on a scale, and with a speed, without precedence in colonial history (Anderson 2001: 12). In a sense that is very difficult to define, there is a connection between the enormity of the crime of the Holocaust perpetrated on its principal victims and the intensity of colonial occupation that was carried out in the name of those victims. There was also a ferocity, with genocidal implications, at the heart of the colonial drive that similarly disturbs.

DEIR YASSIN AND THE *NAQBA*

On 9 April 1948, during the war which had by then begun between the Zionists and the Arabs, a particularly fanatical Zionist militia, led by Menachem Begin, entered the Palestinian Arab village of Deir Yassin and massacred most of its 400 inhabitants. The gruesome details were recorded by Jacques de Reynier of the International Red Cross (Hirst 1977: 128). Deir Yassin quickly came to symbolise the intensity of terror the Zionists were ready to use to force Palestinians to flee their homes. Deir Yassin and the *Naqba*, which is how all Palestinians have come to remember the forced expulsion from their homeland of 750,000 mostly Palestinian Arab villagers, also in some uncertain way is connected to the enormity of the crime of the Holocaust. Just how this is the case forms the conclusion of this chapter. In recent years, some progressive-minded Jews in Britain and their Palestinian and other Arab friends have started to commemorate Deir Yassin. This has opened a major debate within the Jewish community. Afif Safieh, the Palestinian Delegate-General in the UK, effectively the Palestinian ambassador, found himself embroiled in the debate in the letters pages of the *Jewish Chronicle*, with a little known British rabbi who was unwilling to accept the interpretation of Deir Yassin outlined above. Afif Safieh's response is extremely pertinent here:

London April 10, 2001
Rabbi Dr Sidney Brichto (Letters, March 30) seems annoyed at Chaim Weizmann's being quoted in the pamphlet on 'Deir Yassin Remembered' as saying 'it was a miraculous clearing of the land'. But he does not dispute the authenticity or the accuracy of the quotation.
    On the massive flight of the Palestinians in 1948, Ben-Gurion also said 'it was a miraculous simplification of the problem'. I would hope one day to know Dr Brichto's reaction, as a spiritual leader, on the frequent use of the word 'miraculous'. As for myself, I have always considered God to be innocent. Palestinian historians have now documented 537 villages leveled to the ground in 1948 by the Israeli authorities so as to prevent any possible return of Palestinian refugees. As for Deir Yassin, the late Menachem Begin boasted in his 1952 memoirs, 'La Révolte', that, without Deir Yassin, there wouldn't have been an Israel and that, after Deir Yassin, the Zionist forces could advance 'like a hot knife in butter'. He was later advised to remove this from subsequent editions of his memoirs.
    The Israeli political establishment inflicted on Palestinians four types of denial. First came the denial of our very existence. Then followed the denial of our rights. All this was accompanied by the denial of our sufferings and the denial of their moral and historical responsibility for this suffering. Dr Brichto's Naqba (catastrophe) denial is equally disturbing.
    I have never 'likened' the *Naqba* to the Holocaust. My conviction has always been that there is no need for comparisons and historical analogies.

No one people has a monopoly on human suffering and every ethnic tragedy stands on its own. If I were a Jew or a Gypsy, Nazi barbarity would be the most atrocious events in history. If I were a Black
African, it would be slavery and apartheid. If I were a native American,
it would be the discovery of the New World by European explorers and
settlers that resulted in near-total extermination. If I were an Armenian,
it would be the Ottoman massacres. I happen to be a Palestinian, and
for me it is the *Naqba*. Humanity should consider all the above repug-
nant. I do not consider it advisable to debate hierarchies of suffering. I
do not know how to quantify pain or measure suffering. I do know that
we are not children of a lesser God.

Afif Safieh

Launching a personal memoir of the *Naqba*[8] at a packed meeting at
the Egyptian Cultural Centre in London in early 2003, the radical
writer and broadcaster Tariq Ali described the victims of the *Naqba*
as additional victims of the Holocaust. The *insights* and *warnings* we
have been discussing in this chapter confirm the truth of this
proposition.

INSIGHTS AND WARNINGS FROM THE HOLOCAUST
AND THE *NAQBA*

In the age of atrocity, Palestinian lives have been sacrificed to create
space for Jewish lives on Palestinian land renamed Jewish land. For
a generation, the attempt to construct a Zionist Jewish identity
explicity denied Palestinian identity. The long confrontation with
the Palestinians has fostered those not infrequent Zionist outbursts
that have parallels with the genocidal racism and the unbridled use
of violence of the Nazi era.

Dr Baruch Goldstein, the American-born Zionist settler who
opened fire with a Galil assault rifle issued to him by the Israeli
army (Shlaim 2000: 524), killing 29 Muslim worshippers in the
Tomb of the Patriarchs in Hebron on the West Bank, is hailed as a
visionary in some Zionist settler circles.

Writing in the aftermath of the assassination of Israeli prime minister, Yitzak Rabin, by another right-wing fanatical Zionist, the
Israeli novelist David Grossman warned his fellow countrymen that
they would continue to ignore, at their peril, the 'depth of the internal poison that our huge use of violence causes us' (*Jewish Chronicle*,
10 November 1995).

Sometimes Holocaust survivors themselves are compelled to draw the parallels. Dr Shlomo Shmelzman went on hunger strike during the Israeli invasion of West Beirut in Lebanon in 1982. In his letter of explanation, he wrote:

> In my childhood I have suffered fear, hunger and humiliation when I passed from the Warsaw Ghetto ... to Buchenwald ... I hear too many familiar sounds today ... I hear 'dirty Arabs' and I remember 'dirty Jews'. I hear about 'closed areas' and I remember ghettos and camps. I hear 'two-legged beasts' and I remember 'Untermenschen', 'Subhumans', ... Too many things in Israel remind me of my childhood. (Chomsky 1999: 257)

It was during the Israeli siege of Beirut that a Christian fascist *Phalangist* militia, supported by the Israeli Defence Forces which had sealed off the two Palestinian refugee camps at Sabra and Shatila, 'entered the camps and methodically slaughtered the inhabitants ... under the observation of the Israeli military a few hundred yards away' (Chomsky 1999: 364–5).

The massacres at Sabra and Shatila shocked the world. It was described as a war crime. The very concept *war crime* is itself an outcome of attempts to define a new legal system of international justice in the shadow of the Nazi era.

We are dealing here with *insights* and *warnings* from the Holocaust. We are *not* discussing *equivalence* between Nazism and Zionism. But a blind ideological refusal to realise that Zionism and the legitimate aspirations of the Palestinian people are incompatible could continue to radicalise Zionism and release even greater displays of genocidal violence. A vortex could open up where the civilisational norms, which still exercise some restraint, could finally collapse. We don't fully understand just what triggers such an ultimate degeneration into barbarism.[9]

Fortunately, there is still time to avoid it. The apartheid regime in South Africa pulled back from the brink, disbanded itself, and isolated and confronted its own home-grown Boer Nazis. Whether the development of 'post-Zionism' in Israel suggests the possibility of a similar honourable retreat will be considered briefly in the conclusion.

*   *   *

This chapter has tried to challenge the way the Israeli State has used the Holocaust for its own political legitimation. It has been suggested that the *insights* and *warnings* that issue from exploring the tensions between universal and particular aspects of the Holocaust point in a very different direction. In a sense these *insights* and *warnings* are well understood. They coincide with, and have contributed to, what is now a well-founded universalist or international discourse on justice, human rights and citizens' rights, with its unconditional objection to colonial occupation, racism in all its forms, and its defence of the universal rights of refugees.[10] In a very real sense a new international morality is being coded. This underpins the hostile response of international public opinion to the way contemporary Israeli governments conceive of their narrowly defined particularistic needs in the face of the needs of the Palestinian people. The wider implications will be considered in the final chapter.

DON'T LET THE SCAR DO THE WORK OF
THE WOUND

Peter Novick has left us with a final *insight* and *warning* on the use of memory about deep grievances. He cites a passage from a writer, and the son of a Holocaust survivor, called Leon Wieseltier, who warns that the collective memory of oppression can instil

> an isolating sense of ... apartness. It transforms experiences into traditions ... Because it abolishes time and dissolves place, collective memory ... leaves the individual and the group too sceptical about change; does not ready them for discontinuity ... Don't be fooled, it teaches, there is only repetition ...
>
> In the memory of oppression, oppression outlives itself. The scar does the work of the wound ... Injustice retains the power to distort long after it has ceased to be real. It is a posthumous victory for the oppressors, when pain becomes a tradition. (Novick 1999: 281)[11]

9

Plucky Little Israel or Great Power Protégé? II: How Israel became the *Strategic Asset* for the United States

This chapter unashamedly owes its origins to arguably the most important book written about Israel in the latter half of the twentieth century: Noam Chomsky's *The Fateful Triangle, The United States, Israel and the Palestinians*. As Said wrote in the introduction to the book's most recent edition:

> *Fateful Triangle* may be the most ambitious book ever attempted on the conflict between Zionism and the Palestinians viewed as centrally involving the United States. It is a dogged exposure of human corruption, greed and intellectual dishonesty ... [It] can be read as a protracted war between fact and a series of myths – Israeli democracy, Israeli purity of arms, the benign occupation, no racism against Arabs in Israel, Palestinian terrorism ... Having rehearsed the official narrative, he then blows it away with vast amounts of counter evidence. (Chomsky 1999: vii)[1]

There was a very simple reason why the United States might need a *strategic asset* (Chomsky 1999: 20) in the Middle East in the years following the Second World War. This was the region, according to a US State Department analysis in 1945, that contained 'one of the greatest material prizes in world history' (Chomsky 1999: 17): *oil*. Israel could play its part in helping encase the region in a military structure, which would protect Western oil supplies.

In time Israel would be in receipt of more military[2] and civilian aid than any other client-state of the United States, which by the end of the twentieth century totalled nearly $100 billion.

American presidents rarely admit the real reasons for so much aid. But President Reagan broke diplomatic cover when, in 1981, he blurted out:

> with a combat experienced military, Israel is a force in the Middle East that actually is a benefit to us. If there were not Israel with that force, we'd have to supply that with our own, so this isn't just altruism on our part. (Aruri 2003: 39)

But it is important to realise that Israel had both to earn and learn this role. Previous chapters have described how Zionism, from its earliest days, understood that its success would be entirely dependent upon Great Power sponsorship. Within just three years of its foundation, its ideologues were ready to tie Israel's survival to the predatory intentions of the 'Western powers'.

Gershom Shocken, editor and publisher of *Ha'aretz*, arguably Israel's most serious newspaper, wrote in 1951 what would effectively become Israel's *mission statement*.

> Strengthening Israel helps the Western powers to maintain equilibrium and stability in the Middle East. Israel is to become the watchdog. There is no fear that Israel will undertake any aggressive policy towards the Arab states when this would explicitly contradict the wishes of US and Britain. But if for any reasons the Western powers should sometimes wish to close their eyes, Israel could be relied upon to punish one or several neighbouring states whose discourtesy to the west went beyond the bounds of the permissible. (*Ha'aretz*, 30 September 1951; cited Bober 1972: 16–17)

1951 also just happened to be the year that Dr Mossadeq, Iran's new radical nationalist leader, nationalised British oil interests. Radical nationalism was poised to sweep across the Middle East. Israel's statement of intent could hardly have been more prescient. Israel would indeed become the watchdog.

ISRAEL'S PART IN THE SUEZ ADVENTURE AND ITS THREAT TO ALGERIA'S LIBERATION

Within eight years of its foundation, in 1956, the Jewish State was taking part in a military and imperialist adventure, alongside Britain and France, in an effort to overthrow President Nasser, Egypt's radical nationalist leader. In 1956 Nasser nationalised the Suez Canal, that great symbolic and global artery for oil tankers bound for the West, an immensely popular act throughout the Middle East and beyond. When Britain, France and Israel declared war on Egypt, they provoked world-wide outrage that forced even the United States to call for restraint.

These basic facts are well known. Less well known is how in these early days it was France that had become Israel's military sponsor.

At the time, France was engaged in one of the most bitter anti-colonial wars of the twentieth century. It was determined to hold on to its North African colonies, especially Algeria, whatever the cost. The rebels led by the Front de Libération Nationale (FLN) came to symbolise the demand of the developing world, or the 'third world', that colonial oppression must be overthrown once and for all. The struggle inspired Franz Fanon's *The Wretched of the Earth*, a book legitimating revolutionary violence, which would become a virtual manifesto for all anti-colonial struggles.

When Nasser came to power in Egypt, France panicked. Nasser had promised aid to the FLN. France now became obsessed with Nasser and began to conspire with Israel to seek his removal. A secret deal between the two countries, made in 1955, provided planes, tanks and ammunition for Israel on a scale that began to make a reality of its offensive regional pretensions. The agreement also called for joint operations such as blowing up transmitters that disseminated Egyptian propaganda throughout the Arab world, as well as striking at FLN bases in Libya (Shlaim 2000: 164–5). It was France, also, that provided Israel with nuclear technology (Shlaim 2000: 175–6).

Israel had placed itself unambiguously not only on the side of the Western colonial powers but also alongside the deeply racist French *colons* in Algeria, who would later provide inspiration and cadre for the neo-Nazi National Front in France.

These events were to make a deep impression on the United States. Suez had demonstrated that Britain and France were clapped-out colonisers. At the same time, Israel was proving itself to be a serious military player in the field. A US National Security Council Memorandum in 1958 noted that a 'logical corollary' of opposition to radical Arab nationalism 'would be to support Israel as the only strong pro-West power left in the near East'. Israel's secret pact with Turkey, Iran and Ethiopia at this time, the 'periphery pact', was encouraged by the US (Chomsky 1999: 21).

1967–73: OUSTING NASSER AND THE EMERGENCE OF PRESIDENT NIXON, ISRAEL'S UNEXPECTED BUT GREATEST FRIEND

But it was the 1967 Israeli–Arab war that finally clinched Israel's role as the US's *strategic asset* in the Middle East. Israel humiliated Nasser and his Arab allies. Nasser never really recovered from this defeat. Radical Arab nationalism itself was undermined and militant Islamic politics began to replace it as the principal anti-imperialist force in the region. Israel seized huge amounts of new territory, including the whole of Jerusalem, the West Bank, Gaza and Syria's Golan Heights. A US State Department document now made clear its recognition of Israel's capacity to represent its interests:

> Israel has probably done more for the US in the Middle East in relation to money and effort invested than any of our so-called allies and friends elsewhere around the world since the Second World War. In the Far East we can get almost nobody to help us in Vietnam. Here the Israelis won the war, single-handedly, have taken us off the hook, and have served our interests as well as theirs. (Bonds et al. 1977: 116)

Now the US began to send Israel highly sophisticated weapons, including supersonic Phantom fighter planes which would be unleashed on Egypt four years later with US approval (Shlaim 2000: 293). In those four years Israel would receive $1.5 billion military aid from the US – ten times the amount sent in the previous twenty years.

But this period also saw Israel's military prowess tested to the limit. In 1973, Anwar Sadat, Nasser's successor, together with Syria, launched a surprise attack on Israel, the so-called Yom Kippur War (Shlaim 2000: 318). This war exposed just how close relations between Israel and the United States had become. Now the US had to do rather more than simply look on approvingly as Israel used US weaponry to batter their Arab foes into submission. The US calculated that there was a serious prospect that Israel might actually *lose* this war, a prospect that it was simply not prepared to tolerate under any circumstances.

This is the period in the aftermath of the military defeat of the US in Vietnam. An oil boycott was gathering pace, temporarily uniting the most radical oil-producing countries like Colonel Gadaffi's Libya with the two most reactionary oil producers, Saudi Arabia and Iran.

The oil boycott was aimed mainly at tilting the oil market more favourably in the direction of the oil producers and would help make OPEC, the cartel of the Oil-Producing Exporting Countries, a global political and economic player to be reckoned with. But the leaders of the oil boycott were also openly calling on the US to restrain Israel. The long-suspected connection between the US bid to control Middle East oil and US support for Israel was now out in the open. The crisis was given added poignancy because of the Watergate corruption scandal which was engulfing Nixon.

Henry Kissinger, Secretary of State and Nixon's infamous Middle East adviser, had no doubts about US strategy. An Israeli victory was essential. Restraint of Israel was out of the question. This was part of what became known as the Nixon Doctrine. As Kissinger explained:

> The United States saved Israel from collapse at the end of the first week by our arms supply ... Some have claimed it was American strategy to produce a stalemate in the 1973 war. This is absolutely wrong. What we wanted was the most massive Arab defeat possible ... we sought to break up the Arab united front. (MERIP Report 1981)[3]

Egypt, historically, was the leader of that Arab united front against Israel. As Aruri has noted, the military defeat allowed Kissinger to detach Egypt altogether from the Arab opposition to Israel in return for truckloads of US dollars. Egypt became so ensnared in a US diplomatic trap that 'Israel was granted time to consolidate the occupation [of Palestinian territory seized after the 1967 war] and build up its offensive capability vis a vis the (remaining) Arab states on the eastern front' (Aruri 2003: 22).

THE NIXON DOCTRINE: NO NEED OF THE 'JEWISH LOBBY'

The Nixon Doctrine was forged as a response to the US débâcle in Vietnam. Of course, US interests would still have to be protected in the developing world, but from now on 'proxies' would be used (Shlaim 2000: 309): locally based regional powers devoted to upholding the US definition of the status quo. Israel was admirably suited to this role.

Hence Nixon became the first US president to endorse comprehensively Israel's *raison d'être*: its perception of itself as 'watchdog' of the Western Powers. At first sight, Nixon, a right-wing Republican, seems a most unlikely White House candidate to underwrite the regional pretensions of the Jewish state. After all, here was an American president who used to *boast* about how he ignored the so-called Jewish lobby in America. He was not in any way dependent upon Jewish votes. In fact, according to Kissinger, Nixon took it for granted that the Jews were politically hostile to him:

> The President was convinced that most leaders of the Jewish community had opposed him throughout his political career. The small percentage of Jews who voted for him, he would joke, had to be so crazy that they would probably stick with him even if he turned on Israel. He delighted in telling associates and visitors that the 'Jewish lobby' had no effect on him. (Organski 1990: 25)

Organski, a political scientist, who cites this and similar passages, from Kissinger's memoirs, is very dismissive of the impact of the 'Jewish lobby' on US–Israeli relations. His careful empirical investigations show how Jewish votes and financial campaign contributions have made little difference to the political behaviour of American Senators and Congressmen and Congresswomen over the years. He focuses attention upon the majority of American politicians who are in no way indebted to Jewish support. He discovers that they support Israel in a not dissimilar way to those politicians who might be considered to be influenced by Jewish votes or campaign contributions. What matters to them is their perception of Israel's behaviour in the region. And they see a bargain. Unlike aid to many other countries, 'economic aid does at least some good for Israel's people while military aid does a lot of good for America's technological and power image' (Organski 1990: 82). The title of Organski's study is *The 36 Billion Dollar Bargain*. American politicians see an aid package to Israel, in the fashionable jargon of neo-liberalism, that's both value for money and good for America.

CRUSHING THE PLO: HOW THE US SUPPORTED ISRAEL'S INVASION OF LEBANON IN 1982

At the beginning of the early 1980s, the Palestine Liberation Organisation (PLO) had its headquarters in West Beirut. Armed Palestinian fighters were on the streets of the city. Palestinian welfare services attempted to bring aid to the thousands of Palestinian refugees living in Lebanon. It was as though an embryonic, albeit displaced, Palestinian state had emerged inside Lebanon's southern border with Israel. Israel was waiting for the opportunity to crush it.

Both the United States and Israel agreed that destroying the PLO, or at least severely damaging it, was a precondition for the US–Israeli version of how 'peace' might come to the Middle East. Here was the direct application of the 'Iron Wall' perspective, pioneered by the right-wing Zionist Jabotinsky in the 1920s and applied by successive Israeli governments (Shlaim 2000). Now the United States was Israel's willing partner in the need to break the will of Palestinian nationalism.

Immediately prior to the Israeli invasion, Sharon visited Washington where, he claims, he warned the US Administration that Israel would have to 'act in Lebanon'. Pentagon figures reveal a massive surge of military supplies from the United States to Israel in the first three months of 1982, as Israel was planning the invasion. These deliveries continued through June and included so-called 'smart bombs', one of which caused the destruction of an entire building killing 100 people in an apparent effort to kill the PLO leader Yasser Arafat, who was thought to be there (Chomsky 1999: 214).

The figures for US military and civilian aid to Israel at this time are staggering. For the fiscal years 1978 through 1982, Israel received 48 per cent of all US military aid and 35 per cent of US economic aid world-wide. For 1983 the Reagan Administration requested almost $2.5 billion for Israel out of a total aid budget of $8.1 billion (Chomsky 1999: 10).

Israel killed tens of thousands of Lebanese and Palestinians during its invasion. Not only had Israel been armed by the US, Prime Minister Begin boasted that Israel was testing secret weapons made in Israel, on behalf of the US. Such a weapon, he told an audience in America, had enabled Israeli jet aircraft to knock out Russian-made Sam-6 and Sam-8 missile batteries in Syria without losing a single aircraft (*Washington Post*, 6 August 1982).

Israel's Lebanese invasion finally provoked world-wide condemnation following the massacres of hundreds of unarmed men, women and children by Lebanese Christian Phalange militias at the Palestinian refugee camps of Sabra and Shatila in West Beirut. The Israeli army, and especially War Minister Sharon, were exposed as complicit in the massacre (Chapter 8). But the United States itself cannot claim to be an innocent bystander.

Before the Sabra and Shatila massacres, the combined pressure of the United States and Israel had forced the PLO to agree to evacuate

West Beirut. A US peacekeeping force was sent to Beirut with the dual responsibility of overseeing the departure of the PLO and safeguarding the remaining civilian population. Chomsky cites the formal statement issued to that effect:

> The governments of Lebanon and the United States will provide appropriate guarantees of safety ... of law-abiding Palestinian noncombatants left in Beirut, including the families of those who have departed ... The US will provide its guarantees on the basis of assurances received from the Government of Israel and the leaders of certain Lebanese groups with which it has been in contact. (1999: 389)

But the US peacekeepers *withdrew* after the PLO fighters had left Beirut, two weeks before the original mandate had run out, effectively ending the US commitment to protect Palestinian civilians. Shortly after the Israel Defence Forces were able to surround the Sabra and Shatila camps, providing cover for the Christian Phalange militia. As the Israel writer, Amos Elon, put it, 'a man who puts a snake into a child's bed and says: "I'm sorry, I told the snake not to bite ..." this man's a war criminal' (Chomsky 1999: 392).

THE OSLO ACCORDS: THE GREAT US–ISRAELI 'PEACE' SWINDLE

The enduring image of the Oslo Peace Accords (so-called, because Oslo was the venue for the secret Israeli–Palestinian 'peace' negotiations) is surely that of the famous handshake between Israeli premier Rabin, and PLO leader Arafat, on the lawns of the White House, hosted by US President Clinton in 1993. Readers who recall the TV footage may also remember the reluctance of Rabin to shake Arafat's hand. That he finally did so helped clinch the emotional impact of it all. Arafat would call it the 'peace of the brave'. It appeared that the Palestinian *intifada*, which had erupted in the late 1980s, had finally wrung some concessions from Israel. Rabin was assassinated shortly afterwards by a right-wing Zionist fanatic, who accused him of selling out the 'land of Israel'. In a ferocious exchange, Rabin's widow, Leah, accused the right-wing Likud Party, the main alternative Israeli political party to Labour, of providing ideological succour to her husband's killer.

The murder, paradoxically, gave added credibility to the Oslo Agreement. Here was Zionism fatally divided, and it seemed that its

more rational and pragmatic wing was now ready to recognise the
legitimate aspirations of the Palestinian people.

Alas, this was not so. Shlaim, whose book *The Iron Wall* has
several times been recommended on these pages, is a particularly
important witness here. Shlaim is a left-wing Israeli historian who
was at the time a fervent believer in the two-state solution. He
hoped against hope that Oslo represented a genuine step forward,
that a genuine Palestinian state would emerge on the West Bank
and Gaza. But he had to conclude reluctantly that it represented the
opposite. As he put it, Israel's intention was to 'repackage rather
than end Israel's military occupation' (2000: 524). He went on to
give a particularly succinct summary of the fraud at the core of Oslo:

> Worst of all, Israeli settlements continued to be built on Palestinian
> land in palpable violation of the spirit, if not the letter, of the Oslo
> accords. In the Gaza Strip, home to only five thousand Jewish settlers,
> Israel controlled a third of the land and most of the scarce water
> resources desperately needed by its one million Palestinian inhabitants.
> In the West Bank, Israel retained control over the water resources and
> over three quarters of the land. The building of settlements through-
> out the West Bank and especially in East Jerusalem continued
> unabated, and a network of bypass roads seemed designed to
> preempt the possibility of Palestinian statehood. (2000: 530)

Herein, alongside the hundreds of road blocks impeding the movement of Palestinians between the West Bank, Gaza and Israel, lie the
roots of the second *intifada* that erupted in September 2000. In the
period between Oslo and the *intifada*, the number of Jewish settlers
on the West Bank and Gaza had doubled to over 400,000. However
what Shlaim omits in his account is the deep complicity of the US
in this treachery. The US had a continuing interest in a strong Israel.
It wasn't ready to force serious compromises on its ally.

It might be thought that with the collapse of the Soviet Union
and the obvious victory of the US as the world's only superpower,
US reliance on Israel to supervise its interests in the Middle East
might have waned. Not so, according to General Shlomo Gazit, formerly Head of Israeli Military Intelligence, a senior official of the
military administration of the occupied territories, and who was
also a leading participant of the secret meetings that developed
the security arrangements for implementing the Oslo agreement.

According to Gazit:

> Israel's main task has not changed at all, and it remains of crucial importance. Its location at the centre of the Arab Muslim East predestines Israel to be a devoted guardian of stability in all the countries surrounding it ... to protect the existing regimes ... halt the processes of radicalization and block the expansion of fundamentalist religious bigotry. (Chomsky 1996: 235)

That Oslo represented a humiliation for Arafat and the PLO was gratuitously celebrated in the American press. Typically, Thomas Friedman, veteran Middle East correspondent for the *New York Times*, described Arafat's letter to Rabin recognising Israel as 'not simply a statement of recognition. It is a letter of surrender, a typewritten white flag in which the PLO chairman renounced every political position on Israel he has held since the PLO's foundation in 1964' (Chomsky 1996: 265). US contempt for Arafat was palpable. It was made very plain in the earlier Reagan Administration, which had paved the way for the 'peace process'. George Shultz, Reagan's Secretary of State, delighted in mocking Arafat in his memoir, *Turmoil and Triumph*. Shultz describes Arafat jumping through hoops to learn just who was boss, by making him utter what Shultz called the 'magic words'. He reports that he told Reagan in December 1988 that Arafat was saying in one place 'Unc, unc, unc', and in another he was saying 'cle, cle, cle', but nowhere will he yet bring himself to say 'Uncle' (Chomsky 1996: 228).

The Israeli journalist Danny Rubenstein had all too accurately predicted what the 'autonomy', which the US and Israel were ready to accept for the Palestinians, really meant. It was the autonomy 'of a POW camp, where the prisoners are autonomous to cook their meals without interference and to organize cultural events' (Chomsky 1996: 223).

Within just a few months of the Oslo Agreement, the Israeli press was reporting

> secret government plans to extend the integration of greater Jerusalem virtually to Jericho, with vast construction projects, plans for tourist sites along the northern shore of the Dead sea, some 700 million dollars of investment in new roads to connect settlements with Israel, bypassing Palestinian villages and towns ... (Chomsky 1996: 264)

The US turned a proverbial blind eye. US–Israeli links tightened. Water has remained a dominant factor in the Israeli seizure of Palestinian land. One of Israel's leading specialists on the topic, Professor Haim Gvitzman, also happened to be a consultant for the US Defense Department.

He has described how the patterns of settlements on the West Bank have been determined by access to water. Commenting before Oslo on water resources, he warned that any peace deal must safe-guard the 500 million out of the 600 million cubic metres of water taken annually from 'Judaea and Samaria', the words he used to describe the West Bank, apparently without embarrassment. This is theft on a breathtaking scale – Palestinian water pumped to Israel from the subterranean aquifer under the occupied territories. Water from the West Bank satisfies about a 'third of the water require-ments of citizens of Israel' (for urban communities, irrigation, etc.). It was Gvitzman's view that the 'autonomy authorities must never be given any power over the water resources of their areas' (Chomsky 1996: 210). Even the *Financial Times* choked on the grotesque unfairness of it all when Oslo reinforced these patterns of water seizure: 'Nothing symbolizes the inequality of water con-sumption more than the fresh green lawns, irrigated flower beds, blooming gardens and swimming pools of Jewish settlements in the West Bank' (8 August 1995). Meanwhile nearby Palestinian villages were denied the right to drill wells.

The refugee question also exposed just how compromised the United States was by the Oslo Agreement. The refugee question was shelved by Oslo until so-called final status talks. Now it is common knowledge that Israel has absolutely no intention of conceding the Palestinian refugee right of return. President Clinton lent support to this Israeli position by cynically manipulating the Oslo Accord. Because the issue would be *talked about*, here was a fig leaf to try to undermine 50 years of UN policy on the matter.

Clinton reversed longstanding US support for UN Resolution 194 of 11 December 1948 which affirms the right of Palestinian refugees who had fled or had been expelled during the fighting to return to their homes. For the first time the US joined Israel in opposing the resolution, reaffirmed by a vote of 127 to 2.

Resolution 194 was a direct application of Article 13 of the Universal Declaration of Human Rights, adopted unanimously by the United Nations the day before (10 December 1948). Article 13 states that 'everyone has the right to leave any country, including his own, and return to his country'. The Universal Declaration is recognised in US courts and elsewhere as 'customary international law' and the 'authoritative definition of human rights'.

The Clinton Administration's argument at the UN in 1993 was that, following Oslo, past resolutions were 'obsolete and anachronistic'. Washington even called for the abolition of the UN Special Committee on Palestinian Rights, which it termed 'biased, superfluous and unnecessary' (Chomsky 1996: 219).

A ZIONIST CONSPIRACY? THE SECOND *INTIFADA*, 9/11 AND PRESIDENT GEORGE BUSH'S US WAR ON TERROR

There is a widely-held view that the right-wing Republican Administration of President George Bush developed much closer links with Israel, at the beginning of the twenty-first century, than any previous US government. Indeed, there is even a view that, far from the US directing Israeli policy, the relationship was reversed and Israel began to direct US policy in the Middle East.

Certainly, there was a perception of an overbearing Zionist influence in Washington. In much of the Arab and Islamic world, this, in turn, was seen as a Zionist conspiracy.

Now the phrase 'Zionist conspiracy' is emotionally and historically loaded, especially in Europe and America. It resonates with memories of European anti-Semitism's classical handbook, the infamous forgery *The Protocols of the Elders of Zion* (see Chapter 6), which accused the Jews of secretly conspiring to control the world. Only, this was not what was meant. Here, the accusation was that an Israeli government was conspiring with the US to seize even more Palestinian land and at the same time overthrow most of the Arab and Islamic regimes in the region. Of course, if you were not careful, there was a slippery slope from one position to the other. Because Israeli governments claim to speak on behalf of all Jews, and because the US is the world's only superpower, it could be argued, from this perspective, that the Jews were using the US to weaken Israel's enemies and to increase their power in the world. Add to this the Zionist claim that all Palestinian land truly belongs to the Jews, and you have a highly combustible mixture.

It was why the Arabic translation of the *Protocols of Zion* found an audience.[4] Of course, the argument is rotten to the core just as it always was. There is not, and never was, a unified Jewish global bloc. Israel's power is contingent on America's, and certainly not on some imagined world Jewish power. In addition, a large and growing minority of Jews across the world have been nauseated by Israel's behaviour. To give just one example: a quarter of the supporters of the International Solidarity Movement are Jewish. This is a radical pacifist American-European-Israeli group, whose members have been killed by the Israeli army for demonstrating their support for the Palestinians in the occupied territories. Whether Jewish community leaders around the world have done enough to articulate this discontent is another matter, which will be discussed in the concluding chapter; and whether there was a 'Zionist conspiracy' in the more restricted sense of a joint US–Israeli plan, led by committed Zionists, to increase joint US–Israeli power in the Middle East remains a legitimate question.

*   *   *

Clearly, then, at the beginning of the twenty-first century, the Israeli–Palestinian conflict was becoming ensnared in a very different, and much more disturbing, political climate. To gain an accurate picture of what was really happening, we needed, and need, a cool and clear retelling of the established facts.

When Bush became president in January 2001, the Oslo peace process had broken down for the reasons explained earlier, and the second *intifada* was raging. Within just a few weeks Ariel Sharon was elected Israel's prime minister on the platform of the Likud Party of using maximum force to crush the *intifada*. Later that same year Bush launched his war on terror, following the conflagration that has become known as 9/11, when thousands of Americans were killed as hijacked planes crashed into New York's World Trade Center and the Pentagon.

When the Sharon government moved to cast Israel's military assault on the Palestinian *intifada* as part of the wider US-led war on terror, it found a receptive audience in Washington.

In fact, the groundwork for an attempt to co-ordinate the ideological offensive and the political and military activities of a right-wing Israeli Likud government and a right-wing Republican US Administration had been laid several years before.

According to *Guardian* journalist Brian Whitaker, in a little noticed but highly innovative investigation, 'Playing Skittles with

Saddam' (2 September 2002, Guardian online):

> Its roots can be traced, at least in part, to a paper, entitled 'A Clean Break', published in 1996 by an Israeli think tank, the 'Institute for Advanced Strategic and Political' Studies. It was intended as a political blueprint for the incoming [Likud] government of Binyamin Netanyahu.

Among other things, it hoped for a breakdown of Oslo and a return to the unabashed land grab of raw Zionism. As the paper put it, 'Our claim to the land – to which we have clung for hope for 2,000 years – is legitimate and noble.' It continued, 'Only the unconditional acceptance by Arabs of our rights, especially in their territorial dimension ... is a solid basis for the future.'

The paper set out a plan by which Israel would 'shape its strategic environment' beginning with the removal of Saddam Hussein.

To succeed, the paper stressed, Israel would have to win broad American support for these new policies, and it advised Netanyahu to formulate them 'in language familiar to the Americans by tapping into themes of American administrations during the cold war which apply well to Israel'.

As Whitaker pointed out, 'At first glance, there's not much to distinguish the 1996 *Clean Break* paper from the outpourings of other right-wing and ultra-Zionist thinktanks ... except for the names of its authors.' These were senior, mainly Jewish, US Republican officials, rather than Israelis, who have become known as neo-conservatives. The paper's author was Richard Perle, Chairman of the Defense Policy Board at the Pentagon in 2002. Also among the eight-person team was Douglas Feith, a neo-conservative lawyer, who would hold one of the top four posts at the Pentagon under Bush, as Under-Secretary of Policy. As Whitaker noted, 'Mr Feith has objected to most of the peace deals made by Israel over the years ... He regarded the Oslo peace process as nothing more than a unilateral withdrawal which raised life-and-death issues for the Jewish state.'

Two other opinion-makers in the team were David Wurmser and his wife, Meyrav, founder of *Memri*, a Washington-based charity that distributes articles translated from Arabic newspapers which, says Whitaker, portray 'Arabs in a bad light'. After working with Perle at the American Enterprise Institute, David Wurmser was at the State Department, as a Special Assistant to John Bolton, the

Under-Secretary for Arms Control and international security. Whitaker continued:

> A fifth member of the team was James Colbert, of the Washington-based *Jewish Institute for National Security Affairs* (JINSA), a bastion of neo-conservative hawkery whose advisory board was previously graced by Dick Cheney, US vice-president in 2002 [and a key architect of the war on Iraq], John Bolton and Douglas Feith ... With several of the *Clean Break* paper's authors holding key positions in Washington in the Bush Administration, the plan for Israel to reshape ... the Middle East looks a good deal more achievable today than it did in 1996.

In fact, since that time, what Whitaker calls the game of 'playing skittles' has regularly hit the headlines, as the US neo-conservatives make no attempt to hide their desire for 'regime change' throughout the Middle East. Certainly Iran, and probably Saudi Arabia, is on the US skittle hit-list.

Two weeks before Whitaker published his article, and many months before the US/UK war on Iraq, Tom Neumann, executive director of JINSA, spelled out the plan, in the *Washington Times*, in clear, cold terms:

> Jordan will likely survive the coming war with U.S. assistance, so will some of the sheikhdoms. The current Saudi regime will likely not. The Iran dissident movement would be helped enormously by the demise of Saddam, and the Palestinians would have to know that the future lies with the West. Syria's Ba'athist dictatorship will likely fall unmourned, liberating Lebanon as well. Israel and Turkey, the only current democracies in the region, will find themselves in a far better neighbourhood. (cited in Whitaker)

Thus it seemed that the Zionist conspiracy theorists had a case. Indeed at times it has looked as though Ariel Sharon is personally directing White House policy. Not only did Bush start calling Sharon a 'man of peace', many commentators, including Israeli journalists and even one of Sharon's Cabinet colleagues, were convinced that a Bush speech, obsessed with 'Palestinian terror', had actually been written by Sharon.[5]

Although I shall argue that the neo-conservatives are not as successful as many people think they are, nevertheless, we do need to pause and comment on their breathtakingly arrogant abuse of power. They have indeed attempted to impose an even more fanatical version of Zionism on US–Israeli policy in order to bring about the total and complete destruction and humiliation of the Palestinian people. They have real influence in the corridors of the world's only superpower as well as influence in the most powerful state in the Middle East. They do indeed represent a serious threat to the Arab world. But they also represent a threat to Jews because they speak so loudly with a Zionist voice. Consider an imaginary anti-Semitic tract which denounced this sinister clique of rich and powerful Dual Loyalty Zionist American Jews which is conspiring to complete the theft of every last acre of Palestinian land and every last drop of Palestinian water, and then ask yourself what it is in the allegation that you disagree with. The answer is that there is nothing to disagree with! Of course, their appalling behaviour most certainly is not in the interests of most Jews, which is where the anti-Semitic allegation falls apart. But this crucial factor can appear to be a subtlety that is missed or at least misunderstood. What this all means is that the neo-conservatives are a contributing factor to anti-Semitism in the Middle East and other parts of the world and that the sooner their clique is isolated and broken up the better.

As it happens, they have not found it easy to implement the central plank of the Likud perspective. This was, it should be recalled, the abandonment of Israeli–Palestinian peacemaking activities which would lead to any talk of a Palestinian state.

Yet George W. Bush began talking about a 'viable Palestinian state'. Indeed that section of the Bush Administration's *National Security Strategy*, dealing with Israel/Palestine, issued in the shadow of 9/11, steers well clear of Likud Zionism. Instead, it extols a rhetoric that could easily have come from the pen of a Clinton or even a UN policy paper. This, it should be remembered, was the Adminstration's most important Statement of Intent, its Anti-Terror Manifesto, with strong hints of its impending the war on Iraq. Yet on Israel/Palestinian the tone is different:

> There can be no peace for either side without freedom for both sides. America stands committed to an independent and democratic Palestine, living beside Israel in peace and security. Like all other people, Palestinians deserve a government that serves their interests

and listens to their voices ... If Palestinians embrace democracy, and the rule of law, confront corruption, and firmly reject terror, they can count on American support for the creation of a Palestinian state.

Israel also has a large stake in the success of a democratic Palestine. Permanent occupation threatens Israel's identity and democracy. So the United States continues to challenge Israeli leaders to take concrete steps to support the emergence of a viable, credible Palestinian state. As there is progress towards security, Israel forces need to withdraw fully to positions they held prior to September 28, 2000 ... Israeli settlement activity in the occupied territories must stop. As violence subsides, freedom of movement should be restored, permitting inno-cent Palestinians to resume work and normal life ... (www.white house.gov/nsc/nsall.html)

Of course, there was no commitment here to force Israel to abandon the settlements on the West Bank and Gaza, let alone any mention of Jerusalem or the refugees. Nevertheless, this was most certainly not the *Clean Break* demanded by the Likudite neo-conservatives at the heart of the Bush Administration. In fact, it takes us back to precisely that point at which Oslo broke down.

Undeniably, however, there was agreement about some of the aims in the wider Middle East context. But the starting point was the global United States interest, rather than Israeli regional interest. One Jewish neo-conservative, Paul Wolfowitz, one of the authors of the *National Security Strategy* statement and deputy to US Defense Secretary, Donald Rumsfeld, in the Bush Administration, had sketched out a global overview for a Republican Administration, in an essay, before Bush came to power.

Comparing the start of the twenty-first century with the begin-ning of the twentieth, Wolfowitz argued that China had the poten-tial to pose the kind of threat to global stability (read US hegemony) that Germany posed (to Britain's hegemony) a hundred years earl-ier. Conclusion: reinforce US superpower status. And what better place to start than in the Middle East, not least because of America's interest in Middle East oil (www.nationalinterest.org).[6]

This was the second factor shaping US global policy: its determi-nation to control and expand its oil supplies. In May 2001 the Bush Administration published its *National Energy Plan* prepared by a team headed by Dick Cheney. It called on oil-producing governments around the world – not least in the Persian Gulf – for a much greater opening up of their oil industries to US oil company involvement.[7]

Oil was a major factor that drove both the US-led wars against Iraq, in 1991 and 2003, in the Gulf. On both occasions Israel was told politely but firmly to stay still and shut up. This exposed the limits of the Israeli role as US proxy. As the US has become directly involved militarily, the wilder Israeli ambitions have, arguably, become something of an embarrassment.

Yes, there was undoubtedly a Likud cuckoo in the Bush nest. But did it control the nest?

In early 2003 the Bush Administration published its Road Map for an Israeli–Palestinian peace. This was the operational expression of the National Security Strategy. Its reception in America revealed both the strengths and limitations of the Likud master plan.

One immediate strength of Likud scheming had been the proliferation of very well-endowed hard-line Zionist think tanks. Whitaker explored this in a separate *Guardian* article, 'US Think Tanks Give Lessons in Foreign Policy' (19 August 2002, Guardian online).[8] Its ideologues had been very successful in capturing column space on the 'oped' pages (i.e. opposite the editorial pages) of the mainstream US press. And it certainly seemed in the summer of 2003 that they had one very prestigious scalp, the domination of the opinion columns of the *Wall Street Journal* (*WSJ*).

In June 2003 these columnists were apoplectic after Bush criticised Sharon for trying to assassinate Abdel Aziz Rantisi, one of the political leaders of the Islamic group Hamas. It was obvious to all sides that the assassination attempt was a brazen bid to wreck the Road Map, obvious, not least because Hamas had been signalling for months that it was ready to consider a ceasefire. The only question was whether the Road Map should be wrecked.

The *WSJ* gave space to Ruth Wisse, a Harvard professor, to explain a few home truths to the president:

[The White House] still tends to treat the regional crisis as a 'conflict of two people over one land' that can be resolved by the creation of a Palestinian state ... Unfortunately, the Arab war against Israel is no more a territorial conflict than was al-Qaeda's strike against America, and it can no more be resolved by the Road Map than anti-Americanism could be appeased by ceding part of the US to an Islamic enclave ... (Jews and Anti-Jews, 16 June 2003)

We were then subjected to what can only be described as a rant or stream-of-consciousness, from which the reader will be spared, concerning her view of the depths of Nazi-style anti-Semitism that now afflicts the entire Arab and Islamic world. Still, Wisse was a model of restraint compared to the columnist who followed her a few days later. Ms Cynthia Ozick, a novelist, apparently identified the Palestinians' real crime: they consider themselves a nation:

> In order to deprive Jews of their patrimony, Palestinians have fabricated a sectarian narrative alien to commonplace knowledge ... [claiming to be] descendants of civilisations that have lived in this land since the Stone Age ... By replacing history with fantasy, the Palestinians have invented a society unlike any other, where hatred trumps bread. They have reared children, unlike any other children, removed from ordinary norms and behaviours ... [recruited] ... to blow themselves up with the aim of destroying as many Jews as possible ...
>
> We now live with an anti-history wherein cause and effect are reversed, protection against attack is equated with the brutality of attack, existential issues are demoted or ignored; cycle-of-violence obfuscations all zealously embraced by the State department and the European Union. ('Where Hate Trumps Bread', 30 June 2003)

Just in case the eloquence of Ms Ozick has passed over the head of the reader, it should be explained that her remarks concerning the cycle-of-violence and protection against attack etc., were about her joining in the general fury that Sharon had not been allowed to assassinate Rantisi.

However, the Likud crazies weren't only dabbling in some US newspaper columns, they had embedded themselves, albeit incompetently, as we will see, in a much more menacing arena of US politics.

* * *

At the time of writing, in the summer of 2003, the fate of the Road Map was far from clear.[9] But the Bush presidency itself was in trouble as more and more Americans were asking why he had dragged the country into war with Iraq. Despite the 'victory' of toppling the Saddam regime, more and more US soldiers were being killed as the US-led war turned into a very unwelcome US-led occupation of the country. The demand to 'bring the boys home' was starting to grow. As in Britain, the American public were also expressing increasing distrust about the major reason advanced by both

governments for going to war: that Iraq possessed the fabled
Weapons of Mass Destruction (WMDs). But WMDs could not be
found. More serious from both governments' point of view,
were the increasing suspicions about the dubious 'intelligence' that
made the claims about WMDs in the first place. In the United States
a potentially explosive row was brewing about the intelligence
claims that had emanated from the 'alternative' intelligence unit,
Office of Special Plans (OSP), set up by Rumsfeld at the Pentagon.
Remarkably, OSP had links to an 'alternative' intelligence unit run
directly from Sharon's office in Israel! These were 'alternative' units
in the sense that the established intelligence organisations, the CIA
in the US and MOSSAD in Israel, were considered unable to supply
the 'intelligence' about Iraq that both governments needed. The co-
ordinator was the US Republican Likudnik official referred to earlier,
Douglas Feith (see Julian Borger's special investigation in the
Guardian, 17 July 2003).

Whether Bush survived the deepening crisis is not really the
point. The argument has been that, despite the much closer links
between his Administration and that of Sharon in Israel, and
despite much of the wilder rhetoric, as well as Likud's conspirator-
ial fun and games, the specific US policy on Israel–Palestine has
remained remarkably consistent with previous US governments.

Not that the Palestinians can draw much comfort from that. If, as
suggested earlier, the Road Map is nothing more than a map with a
road that leads back to that point where Oslo broke down, then
none of the real problems – the Jewish settlements on the West
Bank and Gaza, the status of Jerusalem, the right of return of the
refugees – were going to be addressed.

10
'Us' Jews, 'Them' Arabs II: The Lost Jewish–Arab Symbiosis – In Search of the 'Spark of Hope in the Past'

Within just a few years of the emergence of the Jewish State in 1948, the long and uninterrupted 2,500-year-old history of Jews in lands that had become known as Arab and Islamic came more or less to a close. In 1948, there were roughly 800,000 Jews living in Arab countries (about 6 per cent of the world's total). Twenty-five years later most of these Jews had left.

This chapter will argue that, whilst Zionism was itself the major factor which explains this truly tragic and quite unnecessary ethnic polarisation between Arab and Jew, blame also lies with the broader intervention of European imperialism in the Middle East. This means looking albeit briefly, at how nineteenth-century Europe cynically exacerbated religious tensions in the Middle East. It also means looking, again far too briefly, at how Europe's twentieth-century crisis of imperialism, which led to Hitler's Nazism and Stalin's communism, further compounded the polarisation between Arab and Jew. Brief histories of the struggles for Arab national independence in Iraq and Egypt provide case studies to explore how these different pressures worked themselves out.

It will be argued that twentieth-century politics failed both Arabs and Jews. The chapter concludes by considering some unusual voices seeking routes to Arab–Jewish reconciliation in the twenty-first century.

Two Zionist scholars, Bernard Lewis and Norman Stillman, prove to be rather useful sources. The argument with them here will be not that their evidence is biased; rather that it is too one-sided. Nevertheless, and despite themselves, both help provide powerful arguments for a case they did not intend to make.

174

EUROPEAN IMPERIALISM 'DOOMED THE JEWISH COMMUNITIES' IN ARAB COUNTRIES

Zionist propaganda would have us believe that Jews in Arab countries fared almost as badly under Arab Islamic rule as they did under European Christian rule. But we saw from Goitein's outstanding analysis of medieval Cairo's *Geniza* documents, discussed in Chapter 4, that this was not the case. Even Bernard Lewis, whose judgement on modern Arab history is savaged as Zionist and *Orientalist* by Edward Said (Chapter 5), readily concedes, in his *Jews of Islam*, that the *Dhimmi* rules, maintaining the inferior position of non-Muslim subjects under Islam, were often relaxed. Lewis writes that 'Personal friendships, business partnerships, intellectual discipleships, and other forms of shared activity were normal and indeed common' (1984: 56). In fact he goes much further:

> The medieval symbiosis of Jews and Arabs is far closer to the pattern of modern Western Europe and America and very different from the situation in the Roman, Ottoman and Russian empires. As Professor Goitein has pointed out, this symbiosis produced something that was not merely a Jewish culture in Arabic. It was a Judaeo-Arabic, or one might even say a Judaeo-Islamic, culture. (1984: 77)

In periods of political stress when Islam was threatened, the *Dhimmi* rules would be tightened, and hostility to *Dhimmis* could certainly develop. One British Jewish 'exile' from Arab lands, Lucien Gubbay, captures the duality of this Jewish experience of Islam with the compelling title of his book *Sunlight and Shadow* (Gubbay 1999). (One wonders whether Britain's Muslims and some other ethnic minorities would be so generous about their experience with the ups and downs of racism in modern enlightened Britain.)

Unfortunately, Lewis tells us only of the *Shadow* overhanging Arab Muslim–Jewish relations in the modern period.

Zionism, too, sees only the *Shadow*, and it has claimed the role of saviour for those Jews from Arab and Islamic countries, from which, it claims, they were forced to flee. This is a cynical reversal of cause and effect. Zionism was itself a major factor that undermined the position of the Jews in Arab and Islamic countries. As Norman Stillman puts it in *The Jews of Arab Lands in Modern Times*, the most recent authoritative reference for Jewish scholarship on these matters:

> By the late 1930s, tensions between Jews and the surrounding
> population were mounting everywhere in the Arab world. During the
> last two years leading up to the second world war, there was a rash of
> sabotage incidents aimed at Jewish private and communal property in
> Iraq, Syria, Lebanon, and, for the first time, Egypt. The primary factor
> was the conflict in Palestine, which between 1936 and 1939 had
> degenerated into an open rebellion against the British mandate and
> the Zionist enterprise. (1991: 111–12)

The importance of this perspective is that it calls into question that
favourite Zionist canard 'Arab anti-Semitism'. Tensions between
Arabs and Jews had nothing to do with anti-Semitism in the
European usage of the term (though, as the tensions mounted during this period, anti-Semitism, in its European ideological form,
would find a base. Not least, officials in Hitler's German embassies
in the Arab world made strenuous, and sometimes successful, efforts
to import their own particularly noxious version of the virus).

Those tensions increased in direct proportion to the growth of the
Zionist colony, seen as an increasingly provocative Jewish outpost
of the same British Empire that, alongside the French Empire,
everywhere was dominating Arab lands and the Arab people.
Zionism exacerbated doubts, already growing, about the loyalties of
Jews in Arab countries to the cause of Arab national liberation. Jews
and other non-Islamic minorities, like the Christians, could seem to
be benefiting from foreign rule:

> at the very time that Jews and Christians in most parts of the Islamic
> world were experiencing a growing sense of liberation from the restric-
> tions and disabilities of the past, coupled with expanding horizons of
> opportunity, the Muslim majority – with the exception of the small
> modernizing elite – was feeling itself increasingly on the defensive,
> with its traditions, its social order, and its very independence in dan-
> ger. The very same forces that represented benevolence to most Jews
> and Christians were perceived by most Muslims as the opposite.
> The budding optimism of the minorities stood in marked contrast to
> the dismay and pessimism of the majority. (Stillman 1991: 45)

Lewis is even blunter: 'imperial rule ushered in a new era of Jewish
educational progress and material prosperity. It also ensured the
ultimate doom of these communities' (Lewis 1984: 172–3).

Unfortunately, the scholarship of Stillman and Lewis is limited by their support for the Zionist enterprise. Stillman's book is mainly about the increasing harassment of the Jewish minorities in the oppressive context that he has so accurately described. Rarely does he deal with the efforts of Arab and Jewish radicals in Arab countries determined to find common cause in the struggle for Arab liberation and who found a significant audience in the Jewish communities. The courage of the traditional leaderships of the Jewish communities, who endeavoured to hold the line against Zionist encroachment, receives far too little attention. Nevertheless he has raised an absolutely decisive point about the predatory European colonial powers, which strove to detach the non-Islamic minorities in Middle Eastern countries. This requires further elaboration.

Here is Sir Neville Henderson, Britain's Acting High Commissioner in Egypt, in 1926:

> In itself ... a little xenophobia is not a bad thing, as it inclines the foreigner to acquiesce more readily in the predomination of British control and influence as their only safeguard ... That is surely the ideal position: that the Egyptian should regard us as his friend and protector against the rapacious foreign cuckoo and that the foreigner should consider us to be his only safeguard against the injustice and discrimination of the Egyptian fanatic. (Kramer 1989: 232)

Notice how the Jew in Egypt was defined as a 'foreigner'. It was true that a majority of Egypt's Jews were recent migrants, but Britain had absolutely no interest in seeing these migrants, or for that matter the settled Jewish minority, proud of its deep roots in Egypt,[1] integrate into the newly emerging, and potentially threatening, Egyptian Arab nation.

Everywhere they ruled in the Middle East, Britain and France deliberately widened the gap between the religious minorities, Jews and Christians and the Muslim majority. This had begun as a political device to undermine the Ottoman Empire by offering different forms of 'protection'. Then offers of citizenship turned some Jews and Christians into direct agents of the British and French colonial authorities after they displaced the Ottomans. In Algeria, though an exceptional example, where France had taken control as early as 1830, all of Algeria's Jews had become French citizens by 1870 (Stillman 1991: 17). In Egypt, France attempted to undermine Britain's authority with offers of French citizenship. Other European countries, like Italy, were also playing the game. Between the wars, over a quarter of the Jews in Egypt either had foreign citizenship or foreign 'protection' (Kramer 1989: 31–2).

European Christian and Jewish educational institutions made a similar impact by providing a modern education (in European languages), equipping the non-Islamic minorities with a disproportionate share of modern professional skills. Amongst the Jews, the Paris-based Alliance Israelite Universelle was hugely successful. Inevitably, its activities 'were quickly recognized in official circles as an important extension of what they saw as the cultural mission of France' (Lewis 1984: 162). And in the new colonially created state of Iraq, British officials welcomed the expanding trading activities of the old Arab Jewish merchant class. They reported on their distinctive and rapid adaptation to the increased commercial opportunities in the country. The British Civil Commissioner observed in 1918 that 'the elements we most need to encourage are, firstly, the Jewish community in Baghdad'. Hanna Batatu quotes this Officer Commissioner, serving the British Empire, in his *The Old Social Classes and the Revolutionary Movements of Iraq*, one of the best histories of the struggle for Iraqi independence (1978: 244–6, 311).

Meanwhile, as Europe's twentieth-century ideological and political crisis deepened, it became inevitably intertwined with the growing Arab nationalist and Islamic resistance to British and French colonial domination of their lands. As we have mentioned, there was importation of European anti-Semitism. Though support for Germany in the Second World War should not necessarily be seen in this light. It was much more a question of backing my enemy's enemy as my friend, sometimes combined with a naive, and in some cases plain stupid, belief in Hitler's cynical overtures to the oppressed Arab nation. The telegram of Egypt's King Faruq to Hitler in 1941 is a case in point, looking forward to the arrival of the German army, 'liberators from [the] unbearable English brutal yoke' (Kramer 1989: 156). More astute Arab nationalists would have known about the German Führer who, in 1939, told his army commanders: 'We will continue to stir up unrest in Arabia ... Let us think as masters and let us see in these people lacquered half-apes at best who want to feel the whip' (Kramer 1989: 262n.122).

At the same time, the left wing of the Arab resistance movements discovered that its enthusiastic welcome for Marxism also usually meant support for Stalin and the Soviet Union. This would prove catastrophically divisive. Stalin's and the Arab Communist Parties' support for the creation of the state of Israel strengthened the argument of those right-wing Arab nationalists and Islamists who argued that Judaism, Zionism and communism were essentially the same thing.

An examination of the history of Iraq during these years illustrates how these complicated pressures would play themselves out, antagonising relations between the Jews and the wider society, which Zionism was then able to exploit. Zionism particularly benefited from the mounting popular resentment to Britain's control of Iraq.

JEWS AND THE STRUGGLE FOR THE LIBERATION
OF IRAQ

In 1920, a British Administration estimate of Iraq's total population put a figure of about 1.75 million with a Jewish population of less than 100,000 (their figure of 58,000 is thought to be an underestimate by about 30,000). The majority of the Jews lived in Baghdad and Basra (Shiblak 1986: 18).[2] Iraq's Jewish community was the oldest in the Arab and Islamic world, and extremely proud of its roots in the Babylonia of ancient Mesopotamia. It was not particularly receptive to the appeals of Zionism.

In 1922, Menahem Salih Daniel, a leading Baghdadi notable from an old Jewish family, and later a senator to the Iraqi parliament, had written, politely but firmly, to the Zionists to stay out of Iraq:

> in all Arab countries, the Zionist movement is regarded as a threat to Arab national life ... any sympathy with the Zionist movement is [seen as] nothing short of betrayal of the Arab cause.
>
> ... the Jews in this country hold indeed a conspicuous position. They form one third of the population of the capital, hold the larger part of commerce of the country, and offer a higher standard of literacy than the Moslems ... [the Jew] is regarded by the waking up Moslem as a very lucky person, from whom the country should expect full return for its lavish favours. (Rejwan 1989: 207)

Some Iraqi Jews would make their own contribution to the awakening Iraqi nation. The first modern Iraqi short story in the inter-war period was written by a Jew, Murad Mikhael. It was called *Shahid al-Watan wa-Shahidat al-Hubb*, loosely translated, *He died for His Country, She Died for Love*. Mikhael was one of the first generation of Iraqi Jewish authors who saw themselves as 'Iraqi patriots, who

earnestly hoped for the emergence of a new Iraq, a modern democratic and open state' (Somekh 1989: 14). In this period, nearly a
third of Iraq's top 100 musicians were Jewish (Shiblak 1986: 28).

Anwar Sha'ul was another writer from this generation, born in Hilla,
in southern Iraq. He wrote poetry, fiction and did translations. In 1929
he launched a cultural journal, *Al-Hasid*, one of several newspapers
and journals founded by Jewish writers, which promoted new writers,
Jewish and non-Jewish alike. Sha'ul, highly esteemed by his Muslim
and Christian fellow writers, in 1932, was elected to the committee
that welcomed the world-renowned Indian poet, Tagore, to Baghdad.

Sha'ul's autobiography celebrates Hilla, a site he proudly identi-
fies as part of ancient Babylon on the Euphrates. He writes about his
famous Iraqi Jewish family tree, the Sassoons, but describes the head
of the family as *Shaykh* Sasson, deliberately associating even something as sensitive as authority in family structures with Islamic and
Arabic cultural conceptualisation. His wet nurse (*umm bi'l-ridda'a*,
mother by nursing), was a Muslim who breastfed him alongside her
own son. The two 'brothers by nursing' were to have an emotional
reunion as adults in Baghdad (Somekh 1989: 18).

THE THREAT: THE *FARHUD* AND THE DEFEAT
OF *AL-WATHBAH*

The Second World War, and Britain's determination to drag Iraq into
it against its wishes, undermined Jewish leaders looking to integrate
the community into the movement for Iraqi national independence.
In 1941, British military policy provoked extremely ominous anti-
Jewish riots, sometimes called the *Farhud*, which left hundreds dead.

Perceived Iraqi Jewish support for the British war effort, and the
reappearance of the British army in Iraq, seem to have been a cause
of the riots, though there is no satisfactory account of it. Stillman
points to a particularly mendacious British role, which is still in
need of an investigation, as well as the circulation of openly Nazi
propaganda (1991: 119, 413–16).

Support for Jews from Muslim neighbours in mixed localities,
sometimes at the risk to their own lives, and the progressive position adopted by the spiritual leader of the Islamic Shi'ite community in Baghdad, may have helped to steady the nerves of Iraq's Jews
(Rejwan 1989: 223–4). The Zionists were able to report few short-term
gains (Shiblak 1986: 54). Though there is no doubt that the *Farhud*
was shocking and that it left a deep scar.

Al-Wathbah (the Leap), 'the most formidable insurrection in the history of the monarchy' (Batatu 1978: 545), immediately after the war, was aimed in part at continuing British involvement in the country. It had the potential to heal the wounds left by the *Farhud*. *Al-Wathbah* aroused the whole country, including many of its Jewish citizens. But the *Wathbah*'s gains were compromised by the Arab defeat in the war with the Zionists in Palestine in 1948 and by the behaviour of the Iraqi Communist Party.

During the *Wathbah*, even the Zionist underground movement had to admit that it was an 'era of brotherhood' when the idea of emigrating to the Jewish state in Palestine 'looked so remote' (Shiblak 1986: 55).

The antics of the right-wing Pan-Arab Iraqi Istiqlal Party reflect the shifting political attitudes towards the Jews at this time. When a Jewish youth, Shamran Olwan, was killed by the police during the *Wathbah*, the newspaper *al-Yaqtha*, which supported the Istiqlal Party, described him as 'the martyr of the Iraqi people in their fight for freedom' (5 February 1948). During the following two months *al-Yaqtha* frequently published the names of Jewish contributors to the Arab war effort in Palestine (Shiblak 1986: 55–6). And yet just three months later (3 May 1948) *al-Yaqtha* was denouncing 'the three evils the Communists, the Zionists and the Jews' (Shiblak 1986: 65). The Palestine war had tipped the balance. It gave the Iraqi authorities the excuse to impose martial law and crack down on the radical wing of the *Wathbah*, especially the communists. Three of its leaders were hanged in public. The communists themselves handed a propaganda coup to the right wing by supporting the newly formed state of Israel. They forfeited real, possibly decisive, influence over the direction of the independence movement. The potential guarantor of Iraqi nationalism resisting anti-Semitism had failed an all-important test: uncompromising opposition to Zionism:

> The decision gravely compromised the Communists in the eyes of the popular mass, deepened the gulf between them and nationalists of all shades, and brought terrible confusion into the party's own ranks. (Batatu 1978: 566)

Meanwhile, the Istiqlal Party was incorporated into government.

Anti-Semitism came to be used, just as it had been in Europe, as a mechanism for social control, crushing the opposition and diverting attention away from government failure. Israel's victory in the

1948 war underlined the menacing sense of failure. Jews were
sacked from government jobs. A wealthy Iraqi Jewish businessman
was hanged publicly for allegedly selling British army scrap to Israel.
Iraqi Zionists were arrested. The Anti-Zionist League, led by Jewish
communists, with *al-Usba*, its daily newspaper, very effective in
marginalising Zionist influence in the Jewish community, was
closed down and its leaders arrested, accused of both communism
and Zionism! Israel's expulsion of the Palestinian Arabs was used to
justify threats to expel Iraq's Jews.

Inevitably, the Israeli government and their friends in the West
had a field-day denouncing the posthumous victory of the shadow
of Hitler now said to be stalking the Iraqi nation. And Iraqi Zionists,
determined to destroy the traditional leadership of the Iraqi Jews,
got the scalp of the Iraqi Jewish community's Chief Rabbi, Sassoon
Khedouri, by forcing his resignation.

Khedouri was a key figure, confident that whatever the machina-
tions of the Iraqi government, the deep historical ties between Iraq's
Jews and the rest of the Iraqi people would withstand the present
crisis. As an outstanding comment in the UK-based *Jewish Chronicle*
noted:

Sassoon and those Baghdadi Jews with anything to lose dislike Zionism
because it has brought them misery. They know that there were anti-
Jewish outbreaks in Baghdad before Zionism, but on the whole, Islamic
tolerance has enabled Baghdadi Jews to flourish as a centre of learning
and commerce. They and their kind would like to stay. They are
attached to their homes, traditions and the shrines of the prophets,
and would not like to leave them in order to begin life once more in
an immigrants' camp in Israel, where they believe people are not particularly friendly to oriental Jews. (30 December 1949; cited Shiblak
1986: 77)

These prescient remarks accurately captured the pivotal moment in
the fate of Iraq's 2,500-year-old Jewish community. The Chief Rabbi
had complained bitterly about the denigration of Iraq in the
Western press, which exaggerated out of all proportion the level of
anti-Semitism in the country. He later recalled sardonically how
'American dollars were going to save Iraqi Jews – whether Iraqi Jews
needed saving or not. There were daily pogroms in the *New York
Times* under datelines which few noticed were from Tel-Aviv'
(Shiblak 1986: 76).

The former Chief Rabbi's contempt for the claims of the Zionists reflected his confidence that the wave of anti-Jewish feeling would fade. However, this was an unprecedented crisis, intensified to breaking-point by the outside interference of the British, Americans and Zionists. It also just happens to be a crisis about which there is no satisfactory historical account, despite it effectively destroying the Iraqi Jewish community. What follows are just a few of the basic, albeit quite mind-boggling, facts.

THE FESTIVAL OF REACTION: HOW BRITAIN, THE US AND ISRAEL HELPED THE IRAQI GOVERNMENT DESTROY IRAQ'S JEWISH COMMUNITY

First, we had British government officials whipping up the anti-Jewish attitudes of the Iraqi government, in order to promote their brilliant new plan to help Israel 'solve' the problem of the Palestinian refugees which Israel itself had created. Iraqi Jews could be 'swapped' for Palestinian Arabs expelled from Israel! – a plan, of course, that never materialised. They spiced their proposals with home-grown, anti-Semitic 'insight' of their own. Here are just two samples from Abbas Shiblak's scrupulous perusal of British Foreign Office documents from the period:

> If this threat [to expel Iraqi Jews] could be transmuted into an arrange-ment whereby Iraqi Jews moved into Israel, received compensation for their property from the Israeli government, while the Arab refugees were installed with the property in Iraq, there would seem to be some-thing to commend it ... Iraq would be relieved of a minority whose position is always liable to add to the difficulties of maintaining public order in time of tension ... (Foreign Office to British Embassy, Baghdad, 5 September 1949; cited Shiblak 1986: 83)

That the British government was using diplomatic channels to spread the word to trusted Arab friends seems clear from this letter to the Foreign Office from the British Consulate in Jerusalem:

> It may be of at least academic interest if I now place on record, a remark made to me by Viscount Samuel [the first UK High Commissioner of Palestine after the Balfour Declaration], when he was in Palestine in 1949. He ... had tea with my wife and after having

lunched with King Abdullah [of Jordan]. While discussing the seizure of Arab property by the Jews, Lord Samuel said that the obvious way to settle this question was for the Iraqis to turn out their Jews and seize their property ... (British Consulate, Jerusalem to Foreign Office, 24 March 1951; cited Shiblak 1986: 84n.20)

Second, we had the appearance of Zionist agents from Israel making very dubious secret financial deals with Iraqi politicians, at the highest levels of government, in order to plan the 'evacuation' of Iraqi Jews by air. No one though had bothered to consult the Iraqi Jewish community. A US air transport company was involved in the deal, with the backing of the US government. Some Iraqi politicians stood to gain financially, including the prime minister, al-Suwaidi (Shiblak 1986: 115–19). The account by the veteran conservative Iraqi Jewish scholar at the London School of Economics, Professor Elie Kedourie, confirms the main thrust of Shiblak's description here. Kedourie is venomous about the behaviour of some of the Zionist agents, accusing them of taking 'uncontrolled and usurped power' in the Iraqi Jewish community. He quotes Meer Basri, one of the traditional leaders of the Jewish community, who, whilst not opposed to Iraqi Jews going to Israel, expressed concern about the treatment of poor Jewish emigrants. They never again saw their savings and other valuables which they had put in the trust of the self-appointed Zionist officials (Kedourie 1989: 53–4).

Third was the spectacle of the Iraqi government readying itself to seize the businesses and other properties of the more prosperous Jews. Humphrey Trevelyan, Britain's acting representative in Iraq, was on hand to offer helpful advice. Trevelyan told al-Suwaidi that he should 'study the action taken by the Israeli government in respect of the property left behind by Arab refugees' (Kedourie 1989: 50).

Finally, there were a series of bomb explosions, between April 1950 and June 1951, in areas where Jews gathered, after it became clear that most Iraqi Jews had no intention of leaving the country – despite all the pressures on them to do so.

The Iraqi authorities then announced that they had broken up a spy ring and arrested its ring leaders. Evidence offered in court accused Israeli military personnel of being behind the bombing campaign as well as the involvement of an underground Iraqi Zionist network.

During the 14-month period when no one was arrested for the bombings, panic really did begin to grip the Jewish community in Iraq. Tens of thousands of Iraqi Jews registered for emigration.

Although the Israeli government has always denied responsibility, and the Iraqi government had a cynical self-interest in 'persuading' its former Jewish citizens to leave the country, there have been constant accusations pointing the finger at the Israeli authorities. *Black Panther*, a magazine of disaffected Israeli Jews from Arab countries, provided a detailed account of the Zionist activists in the early 1970s. This is also the view of David Hirst, the *Guardian's* distinguished Middle East correspondent.[3]

Ropes of Sand (1980), the memoir of Wilbur Grane Eveland, a former adviser to the CIA in Baghdad at the time, even hints at US government involvement. He writes that the CIA view was that the situation in Iraq was 'exaggerated and artificially inflamed from without', yet 'the State department urged us to intervene with the government to facilitate an air-lift the Zionists were organising to "rescue" Iraqi Jews' (Shiblak 1986: 121–2).

Jewish historical scholarship tiptoes round these events, even over half a century later. Stillman shunts the whole episode into a convoluted footnote but, to his credit, feels obliged to quote a real pearl of wisdom from Kedourie, who observed simply that 'the Zionists were capable of using such tactics' (Stillman 1991: 162n.49).

In 1958, the corrupt Iraqi monarchy, invented, and then propped up, by British Imperialism, was finally overthrown by the Free Officers coup, led by General Qassem. It was the unfinished business of *Al-Wathbah*, and it sparked massive popular demonstrations in its support.

General Qassem's regime lasted just five years. But even in that short time, it proved, beyond a shadow of a doubt, that Arab nationalist leaders, given the opportunity to govern without outside interference, were capable of honouring their responsibilities to their Jewish citizens.

'It was a golden period for the remnant of Iraqi Jewry,' Meer Basri, the Iraqi Jewish community leader, recalled, on behalf of the approximately 13,000 Jews who had stayed behind (*The Scribe*, June 1988).[4]

The former prime minister, al-Suwaidi was one of a number of former Iraqi politicians put on trial for treason by the new regime. One of the clauses in the indictment read that he had aided Israel 'by allowing one hundred thousand Iraqis to become Israeli citizens' (Woolfson 1980: 196).

COULD A PROGRESSIVE ARAB NATIONALISM HAVE LIBERATED ARABS *AND* JEWS? NASSER'S EGYPT

The military coup of the 'Free Officers' in Egypt in 1952, the model for the revolutionary Iraqi army officers[5] and the subsequent emergence of Colonel Abdul Nasser as Egypt's president, remains probably the most important single event in Arab national history. It came after years of insurrectionary unrest in Egypt and amid widespread demoralisation, throughout the Arab world, following the defeat in the Israeli–Arab war over Palestine in 1948. It signalled a much stronger and dynamic Arab assertiveness after over 100 years of humiliation at the hands of Western Imperialism, especially Britain and France. Nasser would become the focal point for Arab nationalist aspirations across the Middle East.

What was the attitude of the Free Officers to Egypt's Jews? Stillman has given us a fascinating account:

> The new revolutionary regime in Egypt ... went out of its way to reassure Jews and other minorities that had been badly shaken by the events of the late 1940s and early 1950s (when anti-Jewish feeling was running high at the time of Palestine war and the formation of the Israeli state). General Najib, the popular figure head of the ruling Revolutionary Command Council, made public visits to Jewish communal institutions in Cairo and Alexandria, including an unprecedented appearance for an Egyptian head of state at Cairo's Great Synagogue on Yom Kippur, just two months after coming to power. The new government pointedly refused to identify the local Jewish community with the Zionist enemy and vigorously rejected calls within the Arab League for freezing Jewish property in all the member states ...
>
> This brief halcyon period began to end in 1954 when ... Nasser, the real force behind the revolution, deposed General Najib. During the same year, an espionage and sabotage ring composed of young Egyptian Jews working for Israel was uncovered ... This fiasco could not help but undermine efforts to stabilise the position of the Jewish community in Egypt. (Stillman 1991: 168–9)

* * *

Alas, Stillman leaves it there, leaving vital questions begging for answers. Was there a connection between the espionage and sabotage ring, sometimes called *Operation Susannah*, linked to the scandal known as the 'Lavon Affair', and Nasser coming to power? What was Nasser's attitude to the Jewish community or, for that matter, his attitude to the Zionist enemy?

And was there a connection with the sabotage ring in Iraq? At face value, there seems to be an uncanny overlap. However, no connection has been conclusively proved. And there are decisive differences. In Iraq the primary aim was to destabilise the Jewish community. In Egypt, this was certainly a consequence but it was not the main aim. In Iraq, a deeply backward monarchical government shared Israel's desire to uproot Iraq's Jews, what Kedourie called a 'monstrous complicity' (Rejwan 1997: 45). At first, Nasser had no such desire. In Iraq, Israel had no problem with the reactionary government. But from the moment Nasser took power, he was the target of a sustained Israeli campaign to destroy him.

This was in spite of his perhaps surprising, and little known, willingness to explore prospects for a genuine and honourable peace with Israel. Indeed, there is a plausible view that *Operation Susannah* was aimed at these secret peace discussions. Certainly, with the benefit of hindsight, it seems to have initiated the long countdown to Nasser's destruction at the hands of Israel and its Western allies.

What was particularly exercising Israel were the discussions between Nasser and the British government over the withdrawal of the British garrison from the Suez Canal Zone. Israel opposed a genuinely independent Egypt. *Operation Susannah* was a plot to create an impression of anarchy in the new nationalist state in order to persuade the British that their military presence was still necessary (Shlaim 2000: 112).

It was Nasser himself who also privately raised questions about the intention of the plotters to disrupt the secret discussions between his representatives and those of Israeli premier, Moshe Sharett (Shlaim 2000: 119).[6] The memoir of one of the plotters hints at a similar conclusion (Beinin 1998: 278n.32).

Successive Israeli governments have always tried to keep the lid tightly closed on what really happened. The long-term repercussions of *Operation Susannah* or the 'Lavon Affair', it may be recalled from Chapter 1, erupted in Ben-Gurion's face in the early 1960s, seriously damaging his credibility. The basic facts are as follows.

Lavon was Defence Minister in Sharett's government. Sharett was widely regarded as weak and ineffectual. Moreover he was suspected as being soft on Arabs. He even had Arab friends, rare indeed amongst Zionist leaders (Shlaim 2000: 97). Lavon was an extreme hardliner, an appointment encouraged by Ben-Gurion, who, whilst temporarily retired, was still active behind the scenes. *Operation Susannah* was organised without Sharett's knowledge by elements in military intelligence. Lavon always denied giving the orders; nevertheless, he was blamed. Lavon's later insistence that he could prove his innocence precipitated Ben-Gurion's final demise. Although the plot turned out to be a fiasco, and the bombers were caught before any serious damage was done, Nasser and the Egyptian authorities were understandably shaken by it. It was, after all, what today would be called a terrorist threat. One part of the plan would have detonated bombs in cinemas showing British and American films, to coincide with the anniversary of the Free Officers Revolution, with an incalculable potential for loss of life.

Remarkably, Nasser kept lines of communication with Sharett open, accepting Sharett's word that he was not involved. It was Sharett who closed the talks when the Cairo trial of the bomb plotters ended with a death sentence imposed on two of the accused. Sharett had been pressing Nasser to avoid a death sentence. But, as Shlaim points out, Nasser could hardly have commuted it when the death sentence had recently been passed on members of the Muslim Brotherhood convicted of similar terrorist acts. It was untenable that Jewish terrorists should receive more sympathetic treatment (2000: 121).

Meanwhile Sharett had presented a very different version of events to the Israeli parliament and the wider public. He had accused the Egyptian government of a show trial of innocent Egyptian Jews. Now two would be killed. A mood of hysteria was whipped up in Israel against Nasser's Egypt.

Lavon resigned and Ben-Gurion succeeded him as Defence Minister. Ben-Gurion was determined to assert his authority over Sharett *and Nasser*. Within just a week of his appointment he had organised *Operation Black Arrow*, a secret military raid into Gaza (Shlaim 2000: 123–9).

Gaza was under Egyptian jurisdiction following the armistice between Israel and Egypt at the end of the Israeli-Arab War in 1948. *Operation Black Arrow* was designed to combine maximum provocation with maximum humiliation of Nasser. Thirty-seven Egyptian soldiers were killed and 31 wounded, compared to eight Israeli soldiers killed and nine wounded. It was the most serious clash between Israel and Egypt since the armistice, and it destroyed once and for all any illusions that Nasser entertained about a peaceful resolution of the Arab–Israeli conflict. From that point Nasser would regard Israel as a tool of Western Imperialism and an implacable foe.

The road to the Suez Crisis of 1956, and Nasser's defeat in the 1967 war, starts here. Egyptian guns for Palestinians in the refugee camps of Gaza also start here. Ariel Sharon's career built on killing Arabs had started earlier at the massacre in the Jordanian village of Kibya in 1953 (Shlaim 2000: 90), but it was given a tremendous fillip by the Gaza raid. Sharon was its military commander. *Operation Black Arrow* more than made up for the failure of *Operation Susannah*.

But it was Egypt's Jews who paid the ultimate price: after Suez, many were compelled to leave the country (Beinin 1998: 86–7). We have no way of knowing whether Nasser's revolution could have accommodated its Jewish minority, but Israel had sabotaged Nasser's peace efforts as well as the position of Egypt's Jews. Avi Shlaim puts it with uncharacteristic bitterness:

> These attacks seemed to confirm the worst Egyptian stereotypes about Jewish duplicity and double-dealing and the worst fears of devilish plots being hatched by Israel to undermine their national unity and independence. (2000: 118)

Operation Susannah had destroyed confidence about the loyalty and patriotism of Egypt's Jews. An important, and certainly surprising, Israeli witness supports this conclusion. In the early 1990s, the anthropologist Emanuel Marx served as the director of the Israeli Academic Centre in Cairo, an institution commonly vilified by Egyptian nationalists as a centre for espionage and subversion. After leaving Cairo and returning to his teaching post at the University of Haifa, Marx proposed that if it were not for *Operation Susannah*, the Jewish community in Cairo would not have been destroyed: 'Those responsible for the dirty business [*'esek ha-bish*] exploited Jews in Egypt ... This caused the rupture' (Beinin 1998: 239).

JEWS IN THE ARAB WORLD: VICTIMS OF THE POLITICS OF FAILURE IN THE TWENTIETH CENTURY

Alfred Dreyfus, the French Jewish army officer caught in one of the nineteenth century's most infamous anti-Semitic scandals, dismissed Zionism as an *anachronism* (even though Zionism happily traded on his name; see Chapter 6). It was a highly pertinent remark. He meant that it flew in the face of the ideals of the French Revolution of 1789. The revolution had demanded the separation of politics from religion in Europe's newly emerging democratic nation-states.

Zionism, whilst paying lip-service to this ideal, practised the opposite. It strapped the Jewish religion to its nationalist band-wagon, appeared alongside the European nations, in the Middle East, as part of the conquering imperial ensemble, and then demanded Arab land in the name of the Jews of the Old Testament. Why Islam and the Arab nations should have been expected to make the concession to the modern world of separating politics from religion when the West's most provocative representative refused to do so is further proof of Western arrogance and its enduring *Orientalism*.

We have here a grave default in the politics of modernity. The anachronistic, yet deliberately cultivated, fusing of religion with nationality, allowed a time-bomb to tick in the Middle East. The leaders of the British Empire should have foreseen it, but, on the contrary, it suited them to play along with the Zionists as they engineered – fabricated would be a better word – the transformation of the Jewish religion into a nationalist ideology (see Chapter 7). This was the precondition and rationale for the artificial implant of a European Jewish settler population in Palestine. The first victims were the Arabs of Palestine. The second were the Jews in Arab countries.

Zionism succeeded in creating a crisis of political loyalty for these Jews. It made them, quite unnecessarily, foreigners in a culture which, for many of them, had been their own for more than a millennium. Worse, it meant that they could appear as traitors in newly developing countries struggling to throw off foreign domination. Zionism had already won the ideological war and sealed the fate of these Jews, when the United Nations General Assembly, in November 1947, voted to partition Arab Palestine into an Arab state and a Jewish state. The day before, Mohammed Haykal, one of the leaders of the Egyptian Liberal Constitutional Party, a secular nationalist party with a fine record of defending Egypt's Jews, which took for granted that they should be full citizens in an independent Egypt, had warned the UN, 'If Arab blood is shed in Palestine, Jewish blood will necessarily be shed elsewhere, despite all the sincere efforts of governments concerned to prevent such reprisals' (Beinin 1998: 60).[7]

The warning concealed an admission of surrender. The West had succeeded in imposing a distorted and heavily politicised Judaism as a nationality to serve its interests in the Arab world. The predicted reprisals would be the desperate, and quite futile and counter-productive tactics, of the humiliated Arab nation. The violence in the short term would give way to the longer-term isolation of the Jews in the Arab world.

LAYLA MURAD, MOVIE STAR OF THE ARAB WORLD ... AND TRAITOR?

The fate of Layla Murad, one of the Arab world's leading perform-ance artists in the twentieth century, the 'Cinderella of the Egyptian screen ... second diva after the inimitable Umm Kulthum' (Beinin 1998: 83–5), is apposite.[8] After appearing in 28 films over a 20-year period, and recording hundreds of songs, the daughter of a rabbi and cantor (Alcalay 1993: 254) abruptly retired in 1955. In 1952 Egyptian and Arab press reports had accused her of donating a large sum of money to Israel. She strenuously denied the accusations. She was particularly distressed because she had publicly announced her voluntary conversion to Islam when she married the actor-director-producer Anwar Wagdi, in 1946. 'I am an Egyptian Muslim,' she declared.

Despite all this, she remained very popular in Egypt, her mixed Muslim–Jewish identity a source of controversy, certainly, courting intense curiosity and sympathy as well as hostility.

After investigating the charges against her, the Egyptian authori-ties found her innocent. The Syrian government, however, was not convinced and persisted with a total ban on her films and songs. During the negotiations for a United Arab Republic in 1958 between Egypt and Syria, Nasser insisted that the Syrian ban on her work be lifted. The Syrian government complied (Beinin 1998: 84–5).

This story of Layla Murad is a live production, a real Arab–Jewish drama, as well as part of Arab–Jewish history in the twentieth cen-tury. But it is not recognised as such. Here the failure of politics screams at us. The very phrase *Arab–Jewish history* jars. A history lost, it measures Zionism's success at disconnecting Arab from Jew. At the beginning of our new century, the cowed and wizened conservative nationalisms of the repressive Arab states concur with the Zionist view. The growth of militant political Islam has been the inevitable consequence. The communist alternative has discredited itself. The new communists of the anti-globalisation movements, and the handful of progressive Arab nationalists, struggling against the demoralisation and the repression, ready to put their head above the parapet, offer hope but are still far too weak to break the mould. No wonder al-Qaida burst onto the scene – the perfect symbol for political failure.

'FANNING THE SPARK OF *HOPE* IN THE PAST'

We have to get at that lost history. By recovering this past, we can, as Walter Benjamin has put it, discover that

> gift of fanning the spark of *hope* in the past, (which exerts), a retroactive force that will constantly call in question every victory, past and present, of the rulers. (Alcalay 1993: 215)

Ammiel Alcalay, who quotes this gem, has written probably the best book about Jews from the Arab world in the twentieth century. It isn't history, not quite. Rather, it is a bold but highly tentative poetic prophecy. It unwittingly takes its cue from the fable of Layla Murad. There are tantalising hints of a way out, but the future remains shrouded in gloom and uncertainty. Where politics fails, poetry must take over.

Alcalay has assembled a cast of dissidents: Jewish, and some Palestinian, artists, mainly novelists and poets, who grew up in Arab lands. They want an alternative to seeing Jews only 'through the dull and often bloody film called Zionism' (1993: 57). He, and the writers he cites, break the mould of the immediate past by showing how it shrivels when cast in the light of the old past of high Islamic culture. Such an approach also throws light on to the future.

But we begin by looking at that immediate past, through the eyes of these writers, as they examine it with brutal honesty. Did the Jewish communities simply not get too close to the Western European Imperial rulers of Arab countries in the twentieth century? Here is a climactic passage from Yitshaq Gormezano Goren in the second novel of his *Alexandria Summer* trilogy, set in Egypt just before the 1952 Revolution. He is describing a near-riot at the races when the jockey son of a Jewish convert to Islam beats a

Bedouin jockey:

> A hair-raising cry broke out from the bloodthirsty Bedouin's black throat. Even though it had all the signs of second-rate theatre, it succeeded in shocking the crowd for an instant. Of course there were those who found this kind of vulgar behaviour repulsive, seeing in it only an inability to lose with dignity, but the majority heard entirely different echoes in that cry. Later, in court, someone said that in that scream he heard the agony of Egypt, trampled on by foreigners. (cited Alcalay 1993: 259)

The poetry of Amira Hess 'also peers into the past's forbidden box' (Alcalay 1993: 260). In her *And the Moon Dips Madness*, she tells us:

> I am Baghdad's daughter
> Yet could swear
> I were native to London
> Recall those gates of iron
> All that golden glitter
> Horse guards and cavalry
> What a wind nipped my feet
> To remind me I belonged in spirit
> But take not the body
> So weak and trembling

When Hess appeared on a literary chat-show in Israel, the host was completely bewildered by the reference to London in the poem. It took another guest, Sami Mikhael, former Iraqi Jew, to explain that the square in question was a copy of a London square constructed by the British colonial authorities. Alcalay comments, 'Baghdad's colonial architecture, the changing of its guards, is at once the deepest recess of childhood sight, and an imposition, chilling to the bone' (1993: 261).

Sometime around 1160, the Jewish traveller Benjamin of Tudela stopped and stared in amazement at the Great Mosque of Damascus. He wrote:

> Here is a wall of crystal glass of magic workmanship, with apertures according to the days of the year, and as the suns rays enter each of them in daily succession the hours of the days can be told by a graduated dial. In the palace of chambers built of gold and glass, and if

people walk around the wall they are able to see one another, although the wall is between them. (cited Alcalay 1993: 119)

Alcalay compares Benjamin's observations to Jacqueline Kahanoff's, a writer born and brought up in twentieth century Cairo, who sees the region, the Levant, as

> not exclusively western or eastern, Christian, Jewish or Muslim. Because of its diversity, the Levant has been compared to a mosaic – bits of stone of different colours assembled into a flat picture. To me it is more like a prism whose various facets are joined by the sharp edge of differences, but each of which ... reflects or refracts light ... perhaps the time has come for the Levant to re-evaluate itself by its own lights, rather than see itself through Europe's lights, as something quaintly exotic, tired, sick and almost lifeless. (cited Alcalay 1993: 72)

Differences, even sharp differences, need not betray the essential unity of the region. In any case we can see, understand and respect each other through the glass separating us. Eliyahu Eliachar, deeply unhappy with his new homeland, Israel, takes the argument further. The land of Israel notion has betrayed the unity. It flies in the face of the real meaning of the past as well as the solution to the future:

> The Land of Israel is a small portion of the region in which many peoples dwell, most of them having one faith, and a strong desire to be united. Our land has never been a limited geographical unit: it was and still is at the crossroads of East and West, between Egypt, Assyria and Babylonia in the past. Today, our country is the one entity restricting the will towards unity held as an ideal by other Arab configurations. (cited Alcalay 1993: 24)

Did the marketplace exaggerate or minimise difference? Over a thousand years Muslims and Jews proved themselves to be brilliant traders. The great Islamic Arabic trading arc, uniting the Mediterranean with the Indian Ocean, anticipated the revolutionary breakthrough of Western European capitalism by over 500 years (see Chapter 4). And yet it cannot be denied that twentieth-century European anti-Semitism found an audience when it targeted its slogans of murderous hatred at Jews profiting from trade. Yet Islam traditionally held another view. According to Abraham Udovitch and

Lucette Valensi:

> *Haqq al-yahud* – literally translated *the law, the justice, the honesty of the Jews* ... invoked by Muslims as a password to cut short bargaining. Concluding a discussion with the invocation of *haqq al-yahud* is equivalent to giving an oath ... since the people of the book are the people of the law you can deal with them. (cited Alcalay 1993: 21)

Such a discussion inevitably brings us back to Goitein, the towering figure of Arab–Jewish history. Let us remind ourselves (Chapter 4) that Goitein pulled no punches about the greatness of the Islamic Arab empire. He was fascinated by its transformational impact on the Jews of ancient Babylonia in Mesopotamia and their co-religionists everywhere else. It may well be that Goitein has inadvertently filled in one of the gaps left by Abram Leon's pioneering study of how medieval Europe's Jewish communities came to be led by a highly mobile merchant class (see Chapter 3). Introducing the *Geniza* documents, Goitein wrote:

> With the great Arab conquests following the rise of Islam ... thus began *the long and great period of Jewish Arab symbiosis* ... At the time of the Muslim Arab conquest, the majority of Jews were still engaged in agriculture and manual labour ... The Jewish people more or less disappeared as an agricultural people during the seventh and eighth centuries, but, unlike other ancient populations, returned to life as a nation of merchants and artisans ... (cited Alcalay 1993: 36)

The economic transformation coincided with the consolidation of the role of the religious and spiritual guide to Jewish communities everywhere, the Babylonian Talmud, at its proud new centre in the newly built city of Baghdad.

In his history of the *Jews of Iraq*, Baghdadi-born Nissim Rejwan, journalist, literary critic and historian, admirer of Joyce, Kafka, Mann, Orwell (Alcalay 1993: 45), discusses this matter at length. In doing so he gives us, perhaps unintentionally, what might be called a *Reverse Zionism*.

Biblical myths of *Exile*, vital to the Zionist enterprise, are turned inside out. The very early exile myths, the deportations of Jews by the Assyrians 2,700 years ago, and by the Babylonians 2,600 years ago, are turned into celebrations of Jewish life in Babylonia in ancient Mesopotamia.

Most Jews did not 'return' when the Persians occupied Babylonia 2,500 years ago, and the Persian king Cyrus is said to have let the Jews rebuild the Temple at Jerusalem. This in spite of all that 'weeping by the rivers of Babylon' (Rejwan 1989: 24). There is some real history here. There is evidence for and an explanation of continuous Jewish settlement in Babylonia at this time, lasting 1,000 years until the conquest of Islam; Persian rule being generally favoured over Roman rule. Rejwan (1989: 9) summons the great twentieth-century Jewish historian, Salo Baron, as witness.

Rejwan probes more deeply at the Mesopotamian connection. Did the Jewish idea not originate here, in Mesopotamia, home to the region's earliest records of civilisation, as well as to the biblical Abraham, the spiritual founder of the three great monotheistic religions, Judaism, Christianity and Islam? It is almost certain that some of the Bible stories were written in Babylonia. The Creation story, the Flood and the Tower of Babel have 'striking parallels' with Babylonian literature (Rejwan 1989: 5).

Rejwan finds universalism too in the Babylonian Talmud, which is far more authoritative than its Palestinian equivalent (see Chapter 2 n.15), developed centuries later in the aftermath of Rome's victory at Jerusalem. He discovers impressive homilies on the principles of human equality, binding on Jews in their relations with non-Jews (1989: 64–5), amid contradictory messages and despite its mysticism and obscurantism. The Islamic conquest then boosted the Jewish presence in Mesopotamia. A Jewish community grew 'by leaps and bounds' at the Islamic Arab military encampment in Kufa in southern Mesopotamia. A large Jewish community at Basra trained scholars and medical specialists, who went to officiate in Palestine and Egypt (Rejwan 1989: 83–4). The Babylon Talmud is now Baghdad-based. The Islamic revolution prises open Jewish learning to influences it had previously sought to avoid. Rejwan cites Abraham Halkin, who wrote:

> The vocabulary of the Islamic faith finds its way into Jewish books: the Koran becomes a proof-text. The Arabs' practice of citing poetry in their works is taken over by Jews. Jewish writings teem with sentences from the works of scientists, philosophers and theologians ... [there is] no hostility towards foreign learning ... no awareness that it is the same 'Greek wisdom' which Talmudic sources warned Jews to study only when it is neither day nor night. (Rejwan 1985: 148)

There is more, much more, to be said about all of this. Is Benjamin of Tudela to be trusted with the following observation, written in twelfth-century Baghdad, about a visit of the Geonim, who headed the two great academies of Jewish learning in the city?

> Horsemen, Jewish and non-Jewish escort him every Thursday when he goes to visit the great Khalif. Heralds go before him proclaiming, 'Make way for our lord, son of David, as his due' ... He is dressed in robes of embroidered silk ... the Khalif rises and places him on a throne ... and all the Muslim princes rise up before him.

Sunlight and Shadow's author, Lucien Gubbay, cites the passage uncritically (1999: 52). Maybe he is right to do so. Or is it a Josephus motif? (Chapter 2), a poetic crest symbolising the unity of the two religions? To be sure, it speaks to us of *centuries* of *Jewish–Arab symbiosis*.

Let's fast-forward to Jerusalem at the beginning of the twentieth century. Lo and behold, that old symbiosis resurfaces. Here is Ya'aquob Yehoshua's *Childhood in Old Jerusalem* at the beginning of the twentieth century, an old Jerusalem, remember, that had been Arabic and Islamic for the better part of 1,000 years. He is describing the Sephardic Jews, with deep roots in the region that trace back to Islamic Spain:

> The sons and daughters of Sephardic families, in Jerusalem were avid followers of Arabic music. With great vigilance, they kept track of the latest songs composed in Jerusalem or brought in from Egypt. Everyone enjoyed the works of the Arab poet Salama Jijazi Muhammed al-'Ashaq as well as [that of] others who visited Jerusalem and led poetry and music get-togethers in the Arab coffee houses, back when the audience used to sit on low cane stools and smoke *narghilleh*. Everyone went to hear George al-Abyad's Egyptian group when they came to Jerusalem before the first world war. The coffeehouses of the Old City and Damascus Gate served as cultural and entertainment centres for Arabs and Jews alike. There is no doubt too that various melodies from Arabic poetry and music found their way into the *piyyutim*, the religious lyrics and hymns that rabbis and cantors sang on Friday nights, at home and in the synagogue. (Alcalay 1993: 109)

Many Jews from Arab countries ended up in Israel. On their arrival some were sprayed with the insecticide DDT, to rid them of their

'Arabness' (Alcalay 1993: 37). This is no exaggeration, and Alcalay has many pages describing what happened. Though a little dated, Swirski's *Israel The Oriental Majority* is still the best introduction to this rather less well-publicised side of Zionism's in-gathering of the Jewish people. The Jews from Yemen, one of the poorest and most ancient Jewish communities, were 'wild and barbaric', but at least they worked 'naturally and without shame ... and without Mr Marx in their brain', as one Zionist paper put it (Alcalay 1993: 43).

Abba Eban (see Chapter 1), the Israeli 'liberal', popular Western diplomat and Cambridge Persian Studies scholar, once gave an explanation of the Jews from Arab countries. There was a real danger, he said, that the 'immigrants of Oriental origin would force Israel to equalize its cultural level with that of the neighboring world' (Alcalay 1993: 31). No wonder Sami Shalom Chetrit, an Israeli Arab Jew, penned the lament 'Prisoner of Zion' (Alacaly 1993: 29).

Occasionally, too occasionally, an Israeli Jew with a European background tells the truth. Here is Lova Eliav:

> we snatched from them the valuable treasure that they brought with them – Arabic ... we have made Arabic and Arabic culture something hateful and despicable. (cited Alcalay 1993: 24–5)

Over the years, Israeli leaders, backed by billions of American dollars, have been able to privilege the living conditions of the Jews from Arab countries, just sufficiently, for most of them to take out their resentment on the Palestinians at the bottom of the pack. Alcalay writes:

> One can hum the tunes [of well-known Arab artists] Farid al-Atrache, Umm Kulthum, Mohammed Abdel Wahab one minute, and serve as interrogator in which the Palestinian subject becomes an object of misplaced rage the next.
> Such is the nature of Israeli working class dislocation and each turn of the screw in both the hegemonic cultural structure and the continuing occupation, always amply abetted by the industry of official imagery, only serves to further mutilate memory itself ... (1993: 254)

And what do we do about Ya'aquob Yehoshua, whose *Childhood in Old Jerusalem*, part of a six-volume work, was cited earlier? Yehoshua, who became a senior Zionist official, 'could silently fulfil the role of director of the Muslim division in the Israeli Ministry of

Religious Affairs during a period when Islamic institutions and monuments, and landmarks were being systematically neglected, desecrated or seized' (Alcalay 1993: 233).

What is so shocking about this schizophrenic treachery is that for most part it goes unchallenged. But Alcalay remains unshaken by the gloom. The treachery cannot take away the meaning of the childhood memory. Despite its owner, it remains one of the 'testimonial voices, in the wilderness' (Alcalay 1993: 233).

Alcalay is firm in his rebellion against the mutilation of memory. He never claimed anything more than that he was assembling a cast of Arab–Jewish dissidents, a tiny minority. But Alcalay is on a revolutionary mission to 'fan that spark of hope'. He is an inspiring believer that in telling the truth we can at least begin to change the world. He finds inspiration in people like Shime'on Ballas, an Iraqi Jew, who became a novelist in Israel, who tells the truth. And it needed real courage to say what he did.

> I have never denied my Arab origins or the Arabic language, despite also having a French education. The Arab identity has always been part of me … I am an Arab who has taken up an Israeli identity, but I am no less an Arab than any other Arab …

During the first Gulf War when Saddam Hussein fired Scud missiles at Israel, Ballas refused to condemn those Palestinians who supported the Iraqi attack. It meant breaking ranks with the Israeli 'peace' movement: 'I can understand the Palestinians. Those who were clapping when missiles fell on the Israelis, they did so after decades of repression …' (Alcalay 1993: 243–4).

Clearly, the ultimate test is this crossover to the Palestinian side. Who will identify with Mahmoud Darwish, Palestine's greatest poet? His poem in solidarity with the first *intifada* of 1987 caused uproar in the Israeli press and parliament. Many so-called 'left' Israeli artists ran for cover. But a few, like the actor Yossi Shiloah, supported him. He said he went to 'Palestinian Arabic literature in search of my culture' (Alcalay 1993: 231).

Darwish is perhaps *the* pivotal figure where poetry has to fill the political chasm. He can identify with the teenage suicide bomber. In his poem *State of Siege*, a 'martyr' says:

> I love life
> On earth, among the pines and the fig trees

> But I can't reach it, so I took aim
> With the last thing that belonged to me

But Darwish also sees human beings in Israeli soldier uniforms. His 'humanism' is sometimes seen as a lack of vigilance (Mahmoud Darwish, Maya Jaggi's 'Profile', *Guardian*, 6 June 2002).

My guess is that Darwish would agree with the way Joseph Semprun, a former communist fighter in the French Resistance to the Nazi occupation and one of the Holocaust's greatest writers, resolved this dilemma. In his novel *The Cattle Truck*, Semprun's narrator, a prisoner on his way to Buchenwald, humanises his military guard, recognising the way Imperialism and militarism had put the man in uniform.

Semprun revisited the dilemma in his autobiography, *Literature or Life*. He describes a true story from the Resistance movement when he and his comrade came across a young German soldier sitting by a riverbank enjoying the French countryside. The German had a motorbike and a machine-gun. Semprun had no doubt what had to be done. But he was momentarily thrown when the soldier suddenly started singing 'in a lovely blond voice', *La Paloma*. This was a favourite song from Semprun's childhood. It somehow made the soldier innocent: 'Innocent not only of being born a German under Hitler ... of involuntarily embodying the brute force of Fascism. But fundamentally innocent in the fullness of his existence ... It was absurd and I knew it ...' (Semprun 1997: 33, 34). Yet, despite the anxiety of his comrade, he had to wait for the song to end before he shot him dead.

Conclusion: Out of the Ashes

Zionism is the problem; its removal is the precondition for peace in the Middle East. It is the precondition for Arab–Jewish reconciliation in Palestine. That is the only possible conclusion to this book. I do not need to convince an Arab readership of this. For the vast majority of Arabs, this is a self-evident truth.

Most people in Europe and North America are not convinced. Although the case for justice for the Palestinians is heard more loudly than ever, there remains a lingering belief that a Jewish State in Palestine is also justified, and that somehow the two positions can be reconciled.

They cannot. And though there are far too few *Jewish* voices prepared to say so, when they do speak out, they become a uniquely powerful ally of the Palestinians in Europe and America.

Out of the Ashes, by an American Jewish theologian, Marc Ellis, is remarkable in that Ellis too concludes that the problem is Zionism. But his starting point is not the arguments grounded in the logic of the secular Left. His starting point is the Jewish religion itself. And Marc Ellis cannot be dismissed as a fringe character. An earlier book on the need for a Jewish 'liberation' theology received an unsolicited letter of thanks from Dr Jonathan Sacks, then principal of Jews' College, and today Britain's Chief Rabbi (*Jewish Chronicle*, 7 February 2003).

When Sacks himself spoke out against Israel, and even proposed an equality of faiths between Islam, Christianity and Judaism, he was silenced by the heavy hand of Britain's Jewish religious orthodoxy. For Ellis this was a symptom of what he calls the Jewish 'civil war of conscience' (2002: 47), a battle simmering underneath the surface in Jewish communities. Ellis himself pulls no punches and sees in Zionism a threat not only to Palestinians but to the very future of Judaism itself.

A flavour of his writings is given on the book's very first page, where he sees the Israeli helicopter gunship today defining

Jewish life:

> I have a vision of replacing the Torah scrolls in the Ark of the Covenant, that focus Jews on God, justice and peace, with a helicopter gunship that speaks of power and might without ethics or morality. What we do, we worship. (2002: 1)

Irena Klepfisz is one of the great Jewish voices speaking out in Ellis's book. Her father was Michal Klepfisz, an activist in the Jewish Socialist Bund and one of the most courageous members of the Jewish Fighters Organisation in the Warsaw Ghetto. In early 1943, Irena and her mother were smuggled out by her father as he also smuggled in the weapons and materials later used in the Ghetto Uprising against the Nazis. On the second morning of the Uprising, Michal was killed, whilst protecting other ghetto fighters.

Irena Klepfisz has made a life's work of keeping alive the memory of her father and the principles he was fighting for. She has had no hesitation in linking that memory to the plight of the Palestinians. Jews, she says, should feel the 'fierce outrage' of the ghetto fighters when they see the disruption of Palestinian life:

> The hysteria of a mother who has been shot; a family stunned in front of a vandalized or demolished home; a family separated, displaced; arbitrary or unjust laws that demand the closing or opening of shops and schools; humiliation of a people whose culture is alien and deemed inferior; a people left homeless, without citizenship; a people living under military rule. (Ellis 2002: 29)

Ellis himself adds that the image of the Warsaw Ghetto Uprising symbolising the dignity and violation of ordinary Jewish life 'is complemented by the Palestinian uprising'.

*   *   *

In Israel too, far too few Israeli Jews have broken cover. But, again, those who have help crystallise a perspective that makes it possible to foresee a genuine alliance with the Palestinians.

In the 1990s a group of Israeli intellectuals became associated with 'post-Zionism'.[1] Although there remains a lack of clarity about this concept, it has encouraged a number of writers to challenge the overarching 'narrative' of Zionism, as well as to begin to imagine a

Jewish life in Palestine without a Zionist state. Small in number, these intellectuals have at times seemed quite threatening, suggesting a base insecurity within Zionism, despite its arrogance and suffocating violence. Hence the Sharon government actually *banned* a ninth grade school history book because it was 'post-Zionist' and insufficiently patriotic (Nimni 2003: 1).

The most powerful voices, either associated with this trend or co-opted by it, are the tiny number of former senior Labour Zionist establishment figures, who are now really frightened by the Frankenstein monster they themselves helped to create. It is their earlier deep roots in the Zionist project that makes their break so sharp. Perhaps not intended, but it may be that their greatest contribution is to help the rest of us intensify the propaganda war on Zionism in Europe and America: our contribution to the liberation of Palestine.

What follows are short extracts from essays, and they are even more stunning in their original, from two senior former Labour Zionist politicians.

Avraham Burg is a long-standing senior Israeli Labour politician. He was Speaker of Israel's Knesset from 1999 to 2003:

> The Israeli nation today rests on a scaffolding of corruption, and on foundations of oppression and injustice. As such, the end of the Zionist enterprise is already on our doorstep ...
>
> Diaspora Jews for whom Israel is a central pillar of their identity must pay heed and speak out ...
>
> We were supposed to be a light unto nations ... we have failed.
>
> It turns out that the 2000-year struggle for Jewish survival comes down to a state of settlements, run by an amoral clique of lawbreakers.
>
> It is very comfortable to be a Zionist in West Bank settlements such as Beit El and Ofra. The biblical landscape is charming. You can gaze through the geraniums and bougainvilleas and not see the occupation. Travelling on the fast highway that skirts barely a half mile west of the Palestinian roadblocks, it's hard to comprehend the humiliating experience of the despised Arab who must creep for hours along the pocked, blockaded roads assigned to him ... Note this moment well: Zionism's superstructure is already collapsing like a cheap Jerusalem wedding hall. Only madmen continue dancing on the top floor while the pillars below are collapsing ...
>
> Israel, having ceased to care about the children of the Palestinians, should not be surprised when they come washed in hatred and blow

themselves up in the centres of Israeli escapism. They consign themselves to Allah in our places of recreation, because their own lives are
torture. They spill their own blood in our restaurants in order to ruin
our appetites, because they have children and parents at home who
are hungry and humiliated. We could kill a thousand ringleaders a
day and nothing will be solved, because the leaders come up from
below – from the wells of hatred and anger, from the 'infra structures'
of injustice and moral corruption. (*Guardian*, 15 September 2003,
originally published in the Israeli newspaper, *Yediot Aharonot*)

Menon Benvenisti is a former deputy mayor of Jerusalem (see
Chapter 5). Here he describes his rejection of the 'Zionist narrative'.
The real story is

the story of natives who feel that people who came from across the sea
infiltrated their natural habitat and dispossessed them.

For me, that was an overwhelming discovery. It came after Camp
David, after the trauma of 2000 ...

Just as the South African rulers understood, at a certain point, that
there was no choice but to dismantle their regime, so the Israeli
establishment has to understand that it is not capable of imposing its
hegemonic conceptions on 3.5 million Palestinians in the West Bank
and Gaza and 1.2 million Palestinians who are citizens of Israel. What
we have to do is try to reach a situation of personal and collective
equality within the framework of one overall regime throughout the
country.

I don't yet have a coherent proposal. I don't have a work plan. But
the direction of thought is clear. The new paradigm is mandated by
reality ... The executive of the federal government will strike some sort
of balance between the two national groups. It wouldn't bother me if
the basis for the balance is equality: one for one.

I admit that there is an emotional layer here: my own identity. I am
70 now, and I have the right to engage in summing up. And I was part
of it all here: the youth movement and the army and the kibbutz and
politics. I am the salt of the earth and I'm not ashamed of it. I am a
proud Israeli Mayflower person. I won't let anyone tell me I am a traitor.
I won't let anyone say I am not from here – including the Palestinians. I
am exactly what my father wanted me to be: a native. He wanted me
to grow like a tree from the soil of the land. He wanted me to be a natural part of the landscape. And he just may have succeeded: I am a
native son. But this is a country in which there were always Arabs. This

is a country in which the Arabs are the landscape, the natives. So I am not afraid of them. I don't see myself living here without them. In my eyes, without Arabs this is a barren land.

This is where I am different from my friends in the left: because I am truly a native son of immigrants, who is drawn to the Arab culture and the Arabic language because it is here. It is the land ... I love everything that springs from this soil. Whereas the right, certainly, but the left, too, hates Arabs. The Arabs bother them – they complicate things. The subject generates moral questions and that generates cultural unease.

That's why the left wants this terrible wall, which in my view is anti-geography, anti-history and anti-human. That's why the left wants to hide behind this wall, which in my view is the rape of the land.

So I think the time has come to declare that the Zionist revolution is over. Maybe it should even be done officially, along with setting a date for the repeal of the Law of Return. We should start to think differently, talk differently ... Because in the end we are going to be a Jewish minority here ... (*Ha'aretz*, 8 August 2003)

The repeal of the Law of Return, which Benvenisti here calls for, would indeed knock away an important prop of Zionism, which historically claimed this right for any Jew in any part of the world. Elsewhere (Chapter 5) he has accurately described as 'ethnic cleansing' the expulsion of Palestinian Arabs refugees in 1948. *Their* right of return is also a precondition for a just settlement.

Benvenisti's comparison with the apartheid state in South Africa is highly apposite. An important truth was recognised, just in time. The oppressive structure of the racist state was dismantled before it was swept away by bloody revolution.

Notes

1 'THE BIBLE IS OUR MANDATE'

1 1936 was the beginning of the Palestinian Arab uprising against British rule and the Zionist colonial settlements. An increasingly desperate British government had sent Lord Peel at the head of a Royal Commission to Palestine in search of ways of resolving the conflict. The 1936 uprising is discussed in Chapter 7.

2 Lavon had been an Israeli minister in the 1950s, who may or may not have been responsible for a scandal involving young Egyptian Jews, recruited by Israeli intelligence, who planted bombs in Egypt. Three of the Egyptians were hanged and Lavon, protesting his innocence, was forced to resign in disgrace. In 1960 Lavon appealed to premier Ben-Gurion with 'new evidence' demanding the case be reopened. In the proceedings that followed Lavon hinted at a cover-up in the defence establishment involving supporters of Ben-Gurion. However, there was never a satisfactory outcome and the Lavon Affair virtually destroyed Ben-Gurion's political career.

    Michael Keren, who obtained access to Ben-Gurion's private documents, charted the row in fine detail. In the fallout, Keren shows how Ben-Gurion's myth-making abilities began to unravel.

3 Martin Gilbert is actually quoting Shabati Teveth, Ben-Gurion's very sympathetic biographer, here.

4 Yigael Yadin, former Chief of Staff of the Israeli Defence Forces and the country's most famous archaeologist, once explained that for young Israelis a 'belief in history' had become a substitute for 'religious belief'. But this distinction collapses if you interpret the Old Testament literally or even just take selected passages literally. Yadin is discussed by Nadia Abu-Haj, one of the very few Palestinians to write about the misuse of archaeology by Zionism (Abu El-Haj 2001: 1). Unfortunately, Abu El-Haj published just before Israeli archaeology itself began to implode.

5 In defence of a scientific approach to history, see Evans (1997).

6 This argument hinges on the role of Nathan, David's court prophet. David confessed his sin to Nathan. But was Nathan a 'Hebrew prophet' or adviser to another local king, upholding higher standards of morality and justice than David? (Armstrong 1996: 40).

    The point here is that 'pagan' (polytheistic) standards of justice varied from one local tribal chieftain to another. 'David' was simply just another tribal king and not a very attractive one, even by the standards of his day.

7 You can obtain videos as well as the book based on the TV series, see Sturgis (2001). The television series, introduced by John McCarthy, can be obtained from CTVC, email: library@CTVC.co.uk.

8 Finkelstein and Silberman's book provides the most recent account to date.

9 There is also fierce anti-royalist propaganda – the books of Samuel.
   I would like to thank Moshé Machover for the following insight: 'These
   are possibly the most interesting and beautiful prose books of the Old
   Testament. Written no doubt by anti-monarchist priests, they are full of
   sharp denunciation of monarchic practices and do not miss a single
   chance to bad mouth David, who is depicted as a right villain.'

2 'THE DISTINGUISHING CHARACTERISTIC OF THE JEWS HAS BEEN THEIR EXILE'

1 Zerubavel's book is beautifully written, sensitive, yet mercilessly debunks
   several major Zionist distortions of ancient Jewish history. See, for example, her critical analysis of the way Zionism has mythologised the mass
   suicide at Masada after the fall of the Second Temple at Jerusalem or the
   later Jewish revolt against Roman rule by the legendary rebel leader, Bar
   Kokhba. In 1996, the book won the highly prestigious Salo Baron Prize
   presented by the American Academy for Jewish research. I would like to
   thank Professor David Cesarani at Southampton University for drawing
   my attention to this book.
2 Unfortunately, it is not possible in this chapter to give the extraordinary
   phenomenon that was Josephus the attention it deserves. The best study
   is by Tessa Rajak (1983). Because Josephus is so unreliable, my use of him
   in this chapter depends exclusively on well-established modern scholarly
   interpretations.
3 The rulers of the Persian Empire restored a Jewish religious leadership to
   Jerusalem after they had captured Babylon. Nebuchadnezzar, Babylon's
   (biblically infamous) earlier ruler, had destroyed an earlier Jewish spiritual centre at Jerusalem. He had then deported the Jews, or at least their
   religious leaders, to Babylon. There is some 'real' history in this famous
   Bible story. For an introduction to a secular analysis, see the Prologue to
   the book by the progressive, non-Zionist, Israeli writer, Boaz Evron (1995:
   15–16). See also n.15 below. For a part-scholarly, part-iconoclastic history
   of the Jewish religion, see *Jewish History, Jewish Religion* by the late Israel
   Shahak, an anti-Zionist, Israeli human rights campaigner.
4 Tcherikover and Fuks jointly edited an astonishing collection of papyri
   discovered in the Egyptian desert known as the *Corpus Papyrorum
   Judaicarum* (CPJ). These are the remains of official and semi-official legal
   documents which reflect the regulations of social life in Egypt under
   Ptolemaic Greek, and later Roman rule.
5 This is extraordinarily similar to the argument about *homeland* and the
   Jews in Egypt, 1,000 years later. See Chapter 4.
6 Ben-Gurion complained to Deutscher about rootless Jewish cosmopoli-
   tans (Deutscher 1968: 92).
7 For a brief but brilliantly lucid analysis of how Judaism was on its way to
   becoming a religion of the masses of the Roman Empire, with a description of Paul's intervention, see Harman (1999: Chapter 6).
8 This wonderful inscription recalls the point made at the end of Chapter 1
   that Samaria considered itself the 'true' Israel!

9   According to Shaye Cohen, 'Josephus wanted Eleazar to ... publicly confess that he and his followers, those who had fomented the war, had erred, and were now receiving punishment from God for their sins' (Cohen 1983: 396). This is an essay by Cohen in Vermes and Neusner (1983). Cohen argues that Josephus uses the speech to signal to Rome that the Jewish rebels were wrong to have instigated the revolt, a position that suited Josephus, as he settled down to write his histories, and as he sought to ingratiate himself with Rome after the revolt had been crushed. As Rajak puts it, with rather too much delicacy, 'The very act of redressing with a sequel of praise for his compatriots [at Masada], the pro-Flavian [pro-Roman] balance ... brings with it its own inconsistencies' (Rajak 1983: 221). For a recent, very readable, exciting, though somewhat misleading, account of the Jewish revolt against Rome, see Faulkner (2002) and my friendly criticism of it in the journal *International Socialism* 98. (Faulkner replied to me in *International Socialism* 101.)

10 One of the Dead Sea Scrolls discovered at the Qumran site, in the twentieth century. The Dead Sea Scrolls are one of our most important historical sources for ancient Judaism.

11 The Diaspora revolt of 117 CE destroyed the Jewish communities in Egypt and Cyrenaica (today's Libya). There are several references in Barclay (1996).

12 Unfortunately, space prevents any discussion of this little-understood revolt. For a satire on modern Zionism's efforts to incorporate Bar Kokhba, see Zerubavel (1995: Chapters 4, 7 and 10).

13 'It is remarkable ... that the Jewish intelligentsia were manual labourers' (Goodman 1983: 93).

14 The evidence seems to come mainly from the border areas with the Galilee (Goodman 1983: 41–53).

15 The Jewish seat of learning in Babylonia at this time, under the auspices of renewed Persian dynasties, though we know much less about it, is actually more important for the evolution of Judaism in the common era. The Babylonian Talmud is regarded as far superior to the Palestinian Talmud. In no sense can these Jewish communities, living under Persian rule, be described as being in 'Exile'. It is true that they date a religious 'Exile' from the time of Nebuchadnezzar (see n.3 above). But most of these Jews did not move to Jerusalem after the Persians restored its spiritual significance. Abba Eban, the Zionist politician referred to in Chapter 1, was also a Persian Studies scholar. Even he concedes Jews had lived in the region of Babylonia 'continuously' (Eban 1984: 101), for over 500 years *before* the 'Exile'! Chapter 10 takes up the story of the Jews of Babylonia.

3 '... EIGHTEEN CENTURIES OF JEWISH SUFFERING'

1   Carlebach (1978), for example, devoted his book trying to show a link between Martin Luther, Karl Marx, the 'self-hating Jew', and Adolf Hitler.

2   Professor Maxime Rodinson published Leon's manuscript on the Jewish Question at the University of Sorbonne in 1968.

3 For an interesting account of the Khazari conversions and comment on Arthur Koestler's wilder claims of much more widespread Jewish conversions at this time see Halevi (1987: 93–102).
4 See the annual *Studies in Polish Jewry*, edited by Antony Polonsky. According to one Jewish sage, 'This is why it is called Poland (Polin), from the Hebrew poh lin, which means "here shalt thou lodge" '.
5 Who shocked his followers by converting to Islam!

4 'US' JEWS, 'THEM' ARABS I: A MESSAGE FROM A CAIRO SYNAGOGUE, A THOUSAND YEARS AGO

1 Understandably, Goitein is preoccupied with a detailed exploration of the internal dynamics of Jewish religious and community life as well as Jewish relations in the wider Islamic economic, political and cultural context. The focus here is almost exclusively on the latter.
2 See Said's (1995) comments on Lewis.
3 *Legal religious community* may be a better definition, given the idea of 'nation' that is so fixed in the modern mind. I am grateful to Phil Marfleet for this observation.

5 'A LAND WITHOUT PEOPLE ...'

1 *The Israel/Palestine Question* (1999), edited by İlan Pappe, has helped to break the mould here.
2 Providing accurate histories of peasants who leave no written evidence of their own is notoriously difficult. Doumani's pathbreaking investigation compensates with great ingenuity from local sources: Islamic court records and Nablus advisory council records, which include peasant petitions, and merchant family private papers.
3 This does not mean that the Palestinian peasants of Nablus were the descendants of the Samaritans. Some may well have been. But we should remember, as Chapter 1 made clear, just how robust Canaanite culture was. It meant that many peasants will have resisted Judaism's overtures in whatever guise.
4 The formal position was that the Ottoman Empire owned most of the land and peasants paid tax for land use. But they exercised what are called usufruct rights, which meant that as long as the land did not lie fallow for more than three years, they could consider the land their own: indeed they could, and did, buy and sell land – though with mounting debt it was usually the latter.
5 Lack of space prevents any discussion of the fate of the 1,000-year-old Palestinian cotton industry which boomed and then slumped in the middle of the nineteenth century. For details, see Doumani's (1995) chapter 'Cotton Textiles and Trade'.
6 Rashid Khalidi is a member of a famous family of Jerusalem notables. Jerusalem's first mayor was a member of the same family. Rashid was an adviser to the Palestinian delegation at the Madrid peace conference in 1991.

This generation of intellectuals were educated in the secondary schools that were established throughout the Ottoman Empire in the early part of the twentieth century. The Ottoman authorities could not keep up with the demand for secondary education and so a number of private schools flourished. They were modernist in outlook, teaching mathematics, sciences and foreign languages as well as a love of the Arabic language and Arab history. One of the most famous in Jerusalem deliberately brought the sons of different faiths into the same school. Another particularly impressed the Palestinian editor of a Cairo newspaper with its willingness to warn against the dangers of Zionism. He wrote that the school was a 'foundation stone to build the future of Palestine'. These schools acted as crucibles forging Palestinian national identity (Khalidi 1997: 46–53).

6 '... FOR A PEOPLE WITHOUT LAND'

1 'People without roots in the social structure ... without any occupation ... hawkers, rag and bone men, people who made a living as match makers – they did not make matches but marriages and weddings, and haggled over the percentage of the dowry' (Deutscher 1968: 62).
2 Jonathan Frankel's widely acknowledged scholarship provides the balance missing in Zionist historiography.
3 Workers from ethnic minority backgrounds in marginal industries, fighting for their rights, have often played a disproportionate role in dramatically raising the political stakes in a progressive direction. In 1977, I had the good fortune to be the *Socialist Worker's* reporter at the mass strike for trade union recognition by poorly paid Asian women at the tiny Grunwick factory in north London. The strike captured the imagination of the entire trade union and labour movement in the UK, with Arthur Scargill's Yorkshire miners and Labour cabinet ministers, including Shirley Williams, visiting the pickets. The strike symbolised both the defence of trade union rights and solidarity between Asian and white workers at a time when the racist National Front was making significant electoral gains in white working-class areas.
4 Trotsky, of course, was a Jew. This did not stop him being elected as leader of the workers' soviet in St. Petersburg.
5 The Bund never fully recovered after 1905, certainly not to anything like its former strength. Though the slow reconstruction of the party had begun by 1910, 'it was no longer the same. The Bund now faced competition from the RWSDP – Mensheviks and Bolsheviks – which developed their activities among Jewish workers. All in all, the Russian socialist parties had resisted the crisis better than the Bund' (Weinstock 1984: 223).
   For a history of the Jewish workers' movement in the twentieth century, see Nathan Weinstock's *Le Pain de misère, histoire du mouvement ouvrier juif en Europe* (1984) (available in French only). I am grateful to Sabby Sagall for translating the passage from Weinstock for me.
6 Weinstock (1979), now unfortunately out of print, remains one of the best Marxist histories of the Zionist settlement in Palestine.
7 Tony Cliff recalled a Jewish café in Tel Aviv attacked and almost broken up just because of a *rumour* that there was an Arab worker in the kitchen (Cliff 2000: 8).

8   These are the words of Karl Kautsky, who carried the tradition of Marx's thought immediately after the death of Friedrich Engels, Marx's life-long collaborator.

9   Beit Hallahmi (1992) is particularly good on the Jewish success story in America.

7   PLUCKY LITTLE ISRAEL OR GREAT POWER PROTÉGÉ? I: BRITAIN AND THE ZIONIST COLONY IN PALESTINE

1   Adapted from Foot (1980: 18). Robert Stewart, Viscount Castlereagh, was War Minister in 1806–7 and 1807–9, and Foreign Secretary in 1812. John Scoff, first Viscount Eldon, was Lord Chancellor. Henry Addington, first Viscount Sidmouth, was Prime Minister in 1801–4, and Home Secretary in 1812–21.

2   'Hypocrisy on a crocodile rode by', and what a long pedigree, as it stretched into the future. Recall David Blunkett, Home Secretary, borrowing Thatcher's charm-word 'swamping', in 2003, to complain about asylum-seekers and in the same breath insisting that Britain would stand by its commitments to asylum-seekers.

3   The dire behaviour of the Zionists as they struggled to put themselves at the head of the Jewish community in Britain is captured in Levene (1992a), a thoughtful study of one of the leading non-Zionists of the period, now more or less forgotten, Lucien Wolf.

4   Zionism is without doubt the main cause of the 'anti-Semitism' in the Arab and wider Islamic world. I return to this theme in the last chapter.

5   In Chapter 5, I was highly critical of Vital's *The Origins of Zionism*, the first of his three-volume history of Zionism. However, volume III, *Zionism, The Critical Phase*, is essential reading to begin to understand the peculiar processes which resulted in the Balfour Declaration.

6   Churchill exaggerated the importance of the *American* Jews believing that Britain's support for Zionism would consolidate *their* support for America in the war (Cohen 1985: 74). Vital has offered a possible explanation for the wartime obsession with Jewish power. He writes that the balance of power in the war between the antagonists was 'so even and precarious, the fear or hope that the smallest increment might tip it one way or the other had solid origins' (Vital 1987: 191).

7   The revolt began as a general strike – a campaign of non-cooperation economically with the British and the Zionists and which lasted six months. It then became a prolonged guerrilla war in the countryside. There is no satisfactory history of it.

8   'THE NAZI HOLOCAUST PROVED THE URGENCY FOR A JEWISH STATE'

1   Although Primo Levi denies that he was a true witness: see his reasons cited in Hobsbawm (1994: 1). Holocaust testimony and art also explore the theme, for which words seem inadequate, of Jews surviving at the expense of dead Jews. See the 'barber' scene in Landzmann's *Shoah*, the

text of the film (1985: 114–16) and several examples in the extraordinary cartoon books, *Maus I & II* (Spiegelman 1987 and 1992).

2   I would like to thank Moshé Machover for drawing my attention to this privately published book.

3   The extract from the letter is quoted by 'N. Israeli' in Bober (1972). 'N. Israeli' was a pseudonym used by Moshé Machover and Akiva Orr, radical Israelis who mounted a major challenge to Zionist influence in the world-wide radical student movement in 1968 and its aftermath.

4   Some of the documents relating to the 'Transfer' agreement are reprinted in Brenner (2002). I offer a critical comment on Brenner's approach in n.5 below.

5   The problem with Brenner's approach is summed up in the subtitle of his *51 Documents* book. His earlier book, *Zionism in the Age of the Dictators* (1983), was a genuine innovation highlighting some appalling cases of Zionists collaborating with the Nazis at particular periods. It showed the capacity for Zionism sometimes to mimic its tormentor. But it is very foolish to draw the conclusion that 'Zionist collaboration with the Nazis' was typical or somehow automatically built into the Zionist project, an interpretation which could be put on the subtitle of Brenner's *51 Documents* book. Zionism was perfectly capable of inspiring resistance to the Nazis, as 'Antek' Zuckerman, a leader of the Warsaw Ghetto Uprising, makes clear in his massive autobiography, *A Surplus of Memory*. (It is true that Antek is himself critical of the inertia of the Zionist leaders when it came to rescue and resistance, but this never made him question assumptions about Zionism itself.) See also Levi's superb, and partly autobiographical, novel, *If Not Now, When?* (1987) about the Jewish partisans fighting the Nazis in the forests. That Zionism later misused its genuinely heroic anti-Nazi resistance fighters for cynical ideological ends in Palestine is another matter.

6   *Exodus* became just such a legend in my own home.

7   For the problematic Arab response, see Pappe's first chapter, 'The Diplomatic Battle'.

8   Ghada Karmi's *In Search of Fatima*.

9   But we know that it is not confined to the Nazi era. In 1994 nearly one million people were slaughtered in just 100 days in Rwanda, a rate of killing far faster than during the Holocaust. The United Nations, for the first time since the Holocaust, used the word genocide. This was a systematic attempt to exterminate an ethnic group, the Tutsis; the Hutu-power government in Rwanda (Hutus are a majority in the country) organised the killings. They called it the Final Solution; The *Interahamwe*, the Hutu killing squads, were recruited directly out of the economic collapse in the late 1980s; An Englishman had brought 'race science' to Rwanda in the nineteenth century. After a careful study, he concluded that the Tutsis were a superior race, possibly of European origin; Belgium, later the colonial power, made Hutu/Tutsi differences the defining feature of Rwanda existence; During the genocide, Hutu propaganda relentlessly promoted these 'differences'. All these facts are taken from Phillip Gourevitch's (1999) award-winning book.

10 Even though there is no serious international authority with the power or the will to enforce it.
11 Machover has drawn my attention to what he calls the 'missing chapter' in my book, which, chronologically, should come next. This concerns all the Zionist myths surrounding the 1948/9 war. As he says, fortunately, not only a chapter but a book exists demolishing these myths, one by one. The book is *The Birth of Israel: Myths and Realities* (1987) by Simha Flapan, a lifelong Zionist who had a change of heart at the end of his life. The myths demolished are: (1) 'Zionists accepted the UN partition and planned the peace'; (2) 'Arabs rejected the partition and launched the war'; (3) 'Palestinians fled voluntarily, intending reconquest'; (4) 'All Arab states united to expel the Jews from Palestine' (see also my Chapter 10); (5) 'The Arab invasion made war inevitable'; (6) 'Defenceless Israel faced destruction by the Arab Goliath'; and (7) 'Israel has always sought peace, but no Arab leader has responded.'

9   PLUCKY LITTLE ISRAEL OR GREAT POWER PROTÉGÉ? II: HOW ISRAEL BECAME THE *STRATEGIC ASSET* FOR THE UNITED STATES

1 As I was completing this chapter, in the summer of 2003, the Palestinian scholar Professor Naseer Aruri published his *Dishonest Broker: The US Role in the Middle East and Palestine*. This is an excellent book and should be read alongside Chomsky.
2 For a comprehensive analysis of US military aid to Israel, visit the websites of the *Washington Report on Middle East Affairs*. U.S. Financial Aid to Israel: Figures, Facts, and Impact: http://www.wrmea.com/html/us_aid_to_israel.htm. See the results of this financial aid: http://www.adc.org/index.php?id=1240.
3 Middle East Research and Information Project: www.merip.org.
4 I discuss 'Arab anti-Semitism' in Chapter 10.
5 An account of this particularly sordid episode of the Bush presidency is given by Aruri (2003: 205–9).
6 This is discussed in much more detail in Alex Callinicos, 'The Grand Strategy of the American Empire', in *International Socialism Journal* 97 (London: Socialist Workers Party, 2002).
7 See M.T. Klare, 'Bush's Master Oil Plan', 23 April 2002, www.alternet.org; also discussed by Callinicos (see n.4 above).
8 See also Jason Vest, 'The Men from JINSA and JSP', in the US magazine, *The Nation*, 2 September 2002 (available online).
9 At the time of the final editing of this book in April 2004, the fate of the Road Map looked very clear. Bush had just endorsed Sharon's unilateral plan for a pull-out of Gaza and his consolidation of most of the Jewish settlements on the West Bank. The US had refused to criticise Israel's assassinations of Hamas leaders Sheikh Yassin and Abdel Rantisi, in stark contrast to Bush's earlier criticism of the botched assassination of

Rantisi. In addition, the US was allowing Israel to complete the building of its so-called 'security fence' – dubbed the Apartheid Wall by commentators across the world. Bush and Sharon appeared to have dispensed with even the most moderate Arab leaders as they tore up the Road Map.

Now, surely, the neo-conservatives were in full control of the Bush White House. Perhaps. But wasn't the Bush White House also signalling its desperation, hanging on to its only friend in the Middle East, as its entire policy in the region was literally going up in (bomb) smoke? The Bush policy in Iraq was mired in chaos, with Bush pleading with the United Nations to help him out of the mess. Exactly the policy the neo-conservatives detested. Bush even publicly praised Lakhdar Brahimi, the UN special envoy to Iraq, at the same White House Rose Garden press conference, on 16 April 2004, when he announced his backing for Sharon. (British readers may recall a forlorn-looking British prime minister, Tony Blair, in his shadow.) Yet Brahimi loathed Bush's Israel policy and wasn't afraid to shout about it. Immediately after Bush's capitulation to Sharon, Brahimi several times repeated his sensational attack on Israel, describing its policies as nothing less than 'poison in the region' (*Ha'aretz*, 24 April 2004).

10 'US' JEWS, 'THEM' ARABS II: THE LOST JEWISH–ARAB SYMBIOSIS – IN SEARCH OF THE 'SPARK OF HOPE IN THE PAST'

1 Kramer discusses the extremely diverse ethnic background of Egypt's Jews in *The Jews of Modern Egypt 1914–1952*. The oldest Jewish community in Egypt, at the beginning of the twentieth century, was probably the Karaites (Kramer 1989: 22–6). There were between 6,000 and 7,000 indigenous Jews, out of an expanding migrant total of about 25,000, in Egypt in 1897 (Kramer 1989: 9).
2 Abbas Shiblak is one of very few Palestinians to have written about the Jews in Arab countries.
3 Read Naiem Giladi, of the Black Panthers, at http://www.inminds.co.uk/jews-of-iraq.html. You can also read the relevant chapter in David Hirst's *The Gun and the Olive Branch* at http://www.mideastfacts.com/iraqi_jews_hirst.html. I am grateful to Roland Rance for drawing my attention to these web-sites.
4 *The Scribe* is an English language journal for former Iraqi Jews. On line at scribe@dangoor.com.
5 That military coups, by low- and middle-ranking Arab army officers, were necessary finally to shake off Imperial rule represented the failure to do so both by liberal democratic and communist political movements.
6 See Shlaim (2000: 117–23) for details about this ignored aspect of Middle East history. Nasser's openness and almost naive reasonableness in this early period of his rule flies in the face of all the Zionist and Western stereotypes of the former Egyptian leader.
7 Joel Beinin's research (1998) is outstanding, but I part company with him on his interpretation. He tends to see Arab nationalism and Zionism as *equally* responsible for the demise of Egypt's Jews.

8   So is the fate of Youssef Darwish. I had the good fortune to meet this former Egyptian communist leader in Cairo in 2002. Aged 91, and in aston-
ishingly good health, he talked freely and widely about his Jewish
background, his hostility to Zionism and the damage done to the communist cause by Stalin's recognition of Israel. Darwish had had every reason to break with his Egyptian background. He was tortured, along with
dozens of other communists, in one of Nasser's prisons. The Egyptian
communists themselves operated a ban preventing its Jewish members
from being elected to the their central committee. This was despite the
fact the three potential candidates, including Darwish, had all converted
to Islam. It was a crude but accurate measure of the inability of even the
left-wing variant of Egypt's political culture to withstand the dominant
political discourse, driven by Zionism, but adhered to by Arab nationalism, especially in the aftermath of Suez. Every Jew, even a Jewish convert
to Islam, was a potential traitor to the Arab nation. Of course, this can be
interpreted as Arab anti-Semitism. But, much more importantly, it meas-
ured Zionism's victory in determining the definition of 'Jew' in the
Middle East as a potential and rightful citizen of the Jewish state on
stolen Arab land. None of this dimmed Darwish's enthusiasm for his left-
wing beliefs, or, for that matter, for his love of Egypt and his confidence
in the potential of its people.
   For a recent profile of Darwish, see the English language *Cairo Times*
(November 2000). Joel Beinin also discusses Darwish and other Jewish
communists in *The Dispersion of Egyptian Jewry* and *Was the Red Flag Flying
There? Marxist Politics and the Arab-Israeli Conflict in Egypt and Israel,
1948–1965.*

CONCLUSION: OUT OF THE ASHES

1   See Silberstein (1999) and Nimni (2003).

Bibliography

Abramsky, C. et al. (eds). *The Jews in Poland* (Oxford: Blackwell, 1986).

Abu El-Haj, N. *Facts on the Ground, Archaeological Practice and Territorial Self-fashioning in Israeli Society* (London: University of Chicago, 2001).

Abu-Lughod, J. *Before European Hegemony* (Oxford: Oxford University Press, 1989).

Alcalay, A. *After Jews and Arabs, Remaking Levantine Culture* (Minneapolis: University of Minnesota Press, 1993).

Anderson, P. 'Scurrying towards Bethlehem', *New Left Review* (London: New Left Review, 2001).

Arendt, H. *Eichmann in Jerusalem* (New York: Viking Press, 1963).

Armstrong, K. *A History of Jerusalem* (London: HarperCollins, 1996).

Aruri, Naseer H. *Dishonest Broker: The US Role in Israel and Palestine* (Cambridge, MA: South End Press, 2003).

Barclay, J.M.G. *Jews in the Mediterranean Diaspora* (Edinburgh: T. and T. Clark, 1996).

Baron, S. et al. *Economic History of the Jews* (Jerusalem: Keter Publishing House, 1975).

Batatu, H. *The Old Social Classes and the Revolutionary Movements of Iraq* (Princeton, NJ: Princeton University Press, 1978).

Beinin J. *Was the Red Flag Flying There? Marxist Politics and the Arab–Israeli Conflict in Egypt and Israel, 1948–1965* (London: I.B. Tauris, 1990).

Beinin, J. *The Dispersion of Egyptian Jewry: Culture, Politics, and the Formation of a Modern Diaspora* (Berkeley: University of California Press, 1998).

Beit Hallahmi, B. *Original Sins, Reflections on the History of Zionism and Israel* (London: Pluto Press, 1992).

Beit Zvi, S.B. *Post-Ugandan Zionism on Trial*, Volume I (Tel Aviv: Beit Zvi, 1991).

Ben-Gurion, D. *Recollections* (London: Macdonald Unit Seventy-Five, 1970).

Benvenisti, M. *Sacred Landscape: The Buried History of the Holy Land since 1948* (London: University of California Press, 2000).

Biale, D. *Power and Powerlessness in Jewish History* (New York: Schocken Books, 1986).

Bober, A, *The Other Israel* (New York: Anchor Books, 1972).

Bonds, J. et al. *Our Roots Are Still Alive* (San Francisco: Peoples Press, 1977).

Brenner, L. *Zionism in the Age of the Dictators* (London: Croom Helm, 1983).

Brenner, L. *51 Documents, Zionist Collaboration with the Nazis* (New Jersey: Barricade, 2002).

Burns, M. *Dreyfus: A Family Affair 1789–1945* (London: Chatto and Windus, 1992).

Callinicos, A. 'Plumbing the Depths: Marxism and the Holocaust', in *The Yale Journal of Criticism*, volume 14, number 2: 385–414 (New Haven, CT: Yale University and The Johns Hopkins University Press, 2001).

Callinicos, A. 'The Grand Strategy of the American Empire', in *International Socialism 97* (London: Socialist Workers Party, 2002).

Carlebach, J. *Karl Marx and the Radical Critique of Judaism* (London: The Littman Library of Jewish Civilization, 1978).

Cesarani, D. *The Final Solution, Origins and Implementation* (London: Routledge, 1994).

Chomsky, N. *World Orders Old and New* (New York: Columbia University Press, 1996).

Chomsky, N. *The Fateful Triangle, The United States, Israel and the Palestinians*, updated edition (London: Pluto Press, 1999).

Cliff, T. *A World to Win, Life of a Revolutionary* (London: Bookmarks, 2000).

Coggins, R. 'Jewish Local Patriotism: The Samaritan Problem', *Jewish Local Patriotism and Self-Identification in the Graeco-Roman Period*, ed. S. Jones and S. Pearce (Sheffield: Sheffield Academic Press, 1998): 66–79.

Cohen, M.J. *Churchill and the Jews* (London: Frank Cass, 1985).

Cohen, S.D. 'Masada: Literary Tradition, Archaeological Remains, and the Credibility of Josephus', in G. Vermes and J. Neusner, *Essays in Honour of Yigael Yadin* (Oxford: Oxford Centre for Postgraduate Studies, 1983).

Davidson, N. 'The Trouble with Ethnicity', in *International Socialism 84* (London: Socialist Workers Party, 1999).

Davies, N. *History of Europe* (Oxford: Oxford University Press, 1996).

de Ste Croix, G.E.M. *The Class Struggle in the Ancient Greek World* (London: Duckworth, 1983).

Deutscher, I. *The Non-Jewish Jew* (Oxford: Oxford University Press, 1968).

Doumani, B. *Rediscovering Palestine: The Merchants and Peasants of Jabal Nablus 1700–1990* (Berkeley: University of California Press, 1995).

Draper, H. *Karl Marx's Theory of Revolution*. Volume 1 (New York: Monthly Review Press, 1977).

Eban, A. *Heritage, Civilisation and the Jews* (London: Channel 4 Book/Weidenfeld and Nicolson, 1984).

Ellis, M. *Out of the Ashes* (London: Pluto Press, 2002).

Evans, R. *In Defence of History* (London: Granta, 1997).

Evron, B. *Jewish State or Israeli Nation* (Bloomington: Indiana University Press, 1995).

Faulkner, N. *Apocalypse* (Stroud: Tempus, 2002).

Finkelstein, I. and Silberman, N.A. *The Bible Unearthed, Archaeology's New Vision of Ancient Israel and the Origin of its Sacred Texts* (New York: Touchstone, 2002).

Finkelstein, N. *The Holocaust Industry* (London: Verso, 2000).

Flapan, S. *The Birth of Israel: Myths and Realities* (London: Croom Helm, 1987).

Foot, P. *Red Shelley* (London: Sidgwick & Jackson, 1980).

Frankel, J. *Prophecy and Politics, Socialism, Nationalism and the Russian Jews 1862–1917* (Cambridge: Cambridge University Press, 1981).

Fromkin, D. *A Peace to End All Peace, Creating the Modern Middle East, 1914–1922* (London: André Deutsch, 1989).

Geras, N. *The Contract of Mutual Indifference* (London: Verso, 1998).

Ghosh, A. *In an Antique Land* (London: Granta, 1992).

Gilbert, M. *Israel, A History* (London: Doubleday, Transworld, 1998).

Goitein, S.D. *A Mediterranean Society* 5 vols (London: University of California Press, 1999).

Goodman, M. *State and Society in Roman Galilee, AD 132–212* (Oxford: Oxford Centre for Postgraduate Hebrew Studies, 1983).

Goodman, M. *The Ruling Class of Judaea* (Cambridge: Cambridge University Press, 1987).

Gourevitch, P. *We Wish to Inform You that Tomorrow We Will be Killed with Our Families* (London: Picador, 1999).

Gubbay, L. *Sunlight and Shadow, The Jewish Experience of Islam* (London: The Sephardi Centre, 1999).

Halevi, I. *A History of the Jews* (London: Zed, 1987).

Harman, C. *A People's History of the World* (London: Bookmarks, 1999).

Hirst, D. *The Gun and the Olive Branch* (London: Futura, 1977).

Hitler's Table Talk 1941–1944 (London: Phoenix Press, 2000).

Hobsbawm, E. *Nations and Nationalism since 1780* (Cambridge: Cambridge University Press, 1990).

Hobsbawm, E. *Age of Extremes: The Short Twentieth Century 1914–1991* (London: Michael Joseph, 1994).

Hobsbawm, E. and Ranger, T. (eds). *The Invention of Tradition* (Cambridge: Cambridge University Press, 1983).

Holt, J.C. *Magna Carta* (Cambridge: Cambridge University Press, 1992).

Hourani, A. *A History of the Arab Peoples* (London: Faber and Faber, 1991).

Hundert, G. *The Jews in a Polish Private Town* (London: The Johns Hopkins University Press, 1992).

Israel, J. *European Jewry in the Age of Mercantilism 1550–1750* (Oxford: Oxford University Press, 1985).

Jacobs, J. *On Socialists and 'The Jewish Question' after Marx* (New York: New York University Press, 1992).

Johnson, P. *A History of the Jews* (London: Phoenix, 1993).

Jones, S. and Pearce, S. (eds). *Jewish Local Patriotism and Self-Identification in the Graeco-Roman Period* (Sheffield: Sheffield Academic Press, 1998).

Josephus. *Against Apion* (London: Loeb Classic Library Edition, 1996)

Kahan, A. *Essays in Jewish Social and Economic History* (Chicago: University of Chicago Press, 1986).

Karmi, G. *In Search of Fatima* (London: Verso, 2002).

Kedourie, E. 'The Break between Muslims and Jews in Iraq' in M.R. Cohen and A.L. Udovitch (eds). *Jews among Arabs* (New Jersey: The Darwin Press, 1989).

Keren, M. *Ben-Gurion and the Intellectuals* (Northern Illinois: Northern Illinois University Press, 1983).

Kershaw, I. *Hitler 1889–1936 Hubris* (London: Allen Lane/The Penguin Press, 1998).

Kershaw, I. *Hitler 1936–1945 Nemesis* (London: Allen Lane/The Penguin Press, 2000).

Khalidi, R. *Palestinian Identity: The Construction of Modern National Consciousness* (New York: Columbia University Press, 1997).

Kimmerling, B. *Zionism and Territory: The Socio-Territorial Dimension of Zionist Politics* (Berkeley: University of California, 1983).

Kimmerling, B. *Politicide: Ariel Sharon's War against Palestinians* (London: Verso, 2003).

Kramer, G. *The Jews of Modern Egypt* (London: I.B. Tauris, 1989).

Landzmann, C. *Shoal* (the text) (London: Pantheon, 1985).

Langer, L. *Preempting the Holocaust* (London: Yale University Press, 1998).

Lenin, V.I. *Collected Works* 20 (London: Lawrence and Wishart, 1972).

Leon, A. *The Jewish Question* (New York: Pathfinder, 1970).

Levene, M. *War, Jews and the New Europe* (Oxford: Oxford University Press, 1992a).

Levene, M. 'The Balfour Declaration: A Case of Mistaken Identity', in *English Historical Review* (London: Longman Group UK, 1992b).

Levi, P. *If Not Now, When?* (London, Abacus Sphere Books, 1987).

Levine, H. *Economic Origins of AntiSemitism* (London: Yale University Press, 1991).

Lewis, B. *The Jews of Islam* (Princeton, NJ: Princeton University Press, 1984).

Marshall, P. *Intifada* (London: Bookmarks, 1989).

Medem, V. *The Memoirs of Vladimir Medem, the Life and Soul of a Legendary Jewish Socialist* (New York: Ktav Publishing House, 1979).

Mendelsohn, E. *Class Struggle in the Pale, The Formative Years of the Jewish Workers Movement in Tsarist Russia* (Cambridge: Cambridge University Press, 1970).

Mendes-Flohr, P. and Reinharz, J. (eds). *The Jew in the Modern World* (Oxford: Oxford University Press, 1995).

Meyer, M. *The Origins of the Modern Jew* (Detroit: Wayne State University Press, 1967).

Millar, F. *The Roman Near East, 31 BC–AD 337* (London: Harvard University Press, 1993).

Modrzejewski, J.M. *The Jews of Egypt* (Chichester: Princeton University Press, 1995).

Molyneux, J. *Rembrandt and Revolution* (London: Redwords, 2001).

Nimni, E. (ed.). *The Challenge of Post-Zionism* (London: Zed Books, 2003).

Nimtz, A.H. Jr. *Marx and Engels, Their Contribution to the Democratic Breakthrough* (New York: State University of New York Press, 2000).

Novick, P. *The Holocaust and Collective Memory* (London: Bloomsbury, 1999).

Organski, A.F.K. *The 36 Billion Dollar Bargain* (New York: Columbia University Press, 1990).

Pappe, I. *The Israel/Palestine Question, Rewriting Histories* (London: Routledge, 1999).

Pappe, I. *The Making of the Arab-Israeli Conflict 1947–1951* (London: I.B. Tauris, 2001).

Pearce, S. 'Belonging and Not Belonging: Local Perspectives in Philo of Alexandria', in S. Jones and S. Pearce (eds). *Jewish Local Patriotism and Self-Identification in the Graeco-Roman Period* (Sheffield: Sheffield Academic Press, 1998): 79–106.

Pearlman, M. *Ben-Gurion Looks Back* (London: Weidenfeld and Nicolson, 1965).

Penslar, D. 'The Origins of Political Economy', *Jewish Social Studies* 3:3 (1977).

Poliakov, L. *The History of Anti-Semitism.* Volume IV, *Suicidal Europe, 1870–1933.* (Oxford: Published for the Littman Library by Oxford University Press, 1985).

Polonsky, A. (editorial chair). *Polin, Studies in Polish Jewry* (London: The Littman Library of Jewish Civilisation, annual volumes from 1986).

Rajak, T. *Josephus* (London: Duckworth, 1983).

Rees, J. *The Algebra of Revolution: The Dialectic and the Classical Marxist Tradition* (London: Routledge, 1998).

Rejwan, N. *The Jews of Iraq* (London: Weidenfeld and Nicolson, 1989).

Rejwan, N. *Elie Kedourie and His Work: An Interim Appraisal* (Jerusalem: The Leonard Davis Institute/The Hebrew University, 1997).

Reynolds, H. *An Indelible Stain? The Question of Genocide in Australia's History* (London: Penguin, 2001).

Rodinson, M. *Israel and the Arabs* (London: Penguin, 1970).

Roth, C. *History of the Jews in England* (Oxford: Clarendon Press, 1949).

Said, E. 'Introduction' in E. Said and C. Hitchens (eds). *Blaming the Victims* (London: Verso, 1988).

Said, E. *Orientalism* (London: Penguin, 1995).

Said, E. *The End of the Peace Process* (London: Granta, 2000).

Scholch, A. 'European Penetration and Economic Development of Palestine, 1856–82', in R. Owen (ed.). *Studies in the Economic and Social History of Palestine in the Nineteenth and Twentieth Centuries* (Carbondale and Edwardsville: Southern Illinois University Press, 1982).

Segev, T. *The Seventh Million, The Israelis and the Holocaust* (New York: Hill & Wang, 1993).

Segev, T. *One Palestine Complete* (London: Little, Brown, 2000).

Semprun, J. *The Cattle Truck* (London: Serif, 1993).

Semprun, J. *Literature or Life* (London: Penguin Books, 1997).

Shahak, I. *Jewish History, Jewish Religion* (London: Pluto Press, 1994).

Shakespeare, W. *The Merchant of Venice*, The Arden Shakespeare (Walton-on-Thames, Surrey: Thomas Nelson and Sons, 1955).

Shapira, A. *Land and Power* (Oxford: Oxford University Press, 1992).

Shapiro, J. *Shakespeare and the Jews* (New York: Columbia University Press, 1996).

Shiblak, A. *The Lure of Zion* (London: Al Saqi Books, 1986).

Shlaim, A. *The Iron Wall* (London: Penguin, 2000).

Silberstein, L.J. *The Postzionism Debates, Knowledge and Power in Israeli Culture* (London: Routledge, 1999).

Somekh, S. 'Lost Voices', in M.R. Cohen and A.L. Udovitch (eds). *Jews among Arabs* (New Jersey: The Darwin Press, 1989).

Spiegelman, A. *Maus I. A Survivor's Tale: My Father Bleeds History* (London: Penguin Books, 1987).

Spiegelman, A. *Maus II. A Survivor's Tale: And Here My Troubles Began* (London: Penguin Books, 1992).

Stein, L. *The Balfour Declaration* (London: Valentine, Mitchell, 1961).

Stillman, N. *The Jews of Arab Lands in Modern Times* (New York: The Jewish Publication Society, 1991).

Storrs, Sir R. *Orientations* (Bristol: Purnell and Sons, 1939).

Sturgis, M. *It Ain't Necessarily So, Investigating the Truth of the Biblical Past* (London: Headline, 2001).

Swedenburg, T. *Memories of Revolt, The 1936–1939 Rebellion and the Palestinian National Past* (London: University of Minnesota Press, 1995).

Tcherikover, V.A. and Fuks, A. *Corpus Papyrorum Judaicarum* (Cambridge, MA: Harvard University Press, 1957).

Teveth, S. *Ben-Gurion, The Burning Ground 1886–1948* (Boston: Houghton Mifflin, 1987).

Traverso, E. *The Marxists and the Jewish Question* (New Jersey: Humanities Press, 1994).

Traverso, E. *Understanding the Nazi Genocide* (London: Pluto Press, 1999).

Trotsky, L. *1905* (New York: Vintage Books, 1972).

Vermes, G. *Jesus the Jew* (London: SCM Press Press, 1983).

Vermes, G. and Neusner, J. (eds). *Essays in Honour of Yigael Yadin* (Oxford: Oxford Centre for Postgraduate Hebrew Studies, 1983).

Vital, D. *The Origins of Zionism* (Oxford: Oxford University Press, 1975).

Vital D. *Zionism, The Crucial Phase* (Oxford: Oxford University Press, 1987).

Wasserstein, B. *Britain and the Jews of Europe, 1939–1945* (Oxford: Oxford University Press, 1988).

Weinstock, N. *Zionism: False Messiah* (London: Ink Links, 1979).

Weinstock, N. *Le Pain de misère, histoire du mouvement ouvrier juif en Europe*, 1. *l'empire russe jusqu'en 1914*, three volumes (Paris: Editions La Découverte, 1984).

Wistrich R. and Ohana D. (eds). *The Shaping of Israeli Identity: Myth, Memory and Trauma* (London: Frank Cass, 1995).

Woolfson, M. *Prophets in Babylon, Jews in the Arab World* (London: Faber and Faber, 1980).

Zell, M. *Reframing Rembrandt: Jews in the Christian Image in 17th-Century Amsterdam* (London: University of California Press, 2002).

Zerubavel, Y. *Recovered Roots, Collective Memory and the Making of Israeli National Tradition* (London: University of Chicago, 1995).

Zuckerman, Y.Z. ('Antek'). *A Surplus of Memory: Chronicle of the Warsaw Ghetto Uprising* (Berkeley and Oxford: University of California Press, 1993).

Index

Printed and bound by CPI Group (UK) Ltd, Croydon, CR0 4YY

09/06/2025

14685864-0001